For Mischa and Max

Contents

List of Figures

Preface

Games can be used as a tool to convey and experience profound aspects of what it means to be human. *Making Deep Games* combines theoretical discussions about the expressive nature of games, the case studies of existing games, and hands-on design exercises. Grounded in cognitive linguistics, game studies, and a deep appreciation for metaphor, this book explores systematic approaches on how to tackle complex concepts, inner processes, emotions, and the human condition through game design. This book offers insight into how to make games that teach us something about ourselves, enable thought-provoking, emotionally rich experiences and promote personal and social change.

Author

Doris C. Rusch, PhD, is a game designer, a researcher, and a play aficionado and holds a position as a game design faculty member at DePaul University. Before that, she did postdoctoral work at GAMBIT Game Lab, the Massachusetts Institute of Technology, and the Vienna University of Technology (Austria). Rusch's work is focused on the theory and practice of game design, particularly in regard to games that model the *human experience*. She has won numerous awards for experimental, metaphorical games, many of which contribute to mental health awareness and activism, such as *Akrasia* (a game about substance abuse), *Elude* (a game about depression), *Zombie Yoga—Recovering the Inner Child* (a Kinect game in which the player does yoga poses to fight inner fears, represented by zombies), and *Soteria—Dreams as Currency* (a game for teens to learn how to overcome anxiety disorder). Having completed studies in literature, philosophy, comparative media studies, and English at the Vienna University of Technology, she earned her PhD in applied linguistics and interactive systems in 2004.

Introduction

Making Deep Games: Designing Games with Meaning and Purpose

Wherein:

- *A definition of the term "deep games" is attempted.*
- *The background of the book is explained.*
- *A case is made on why we should care about deep games.*
- *A chapter overview is provided.*

To explain what *Making Deep Games: Designing Games with Meaning and Purpose* is all about, it is useful to start with a bit of personal history. This is fitting, since much of the notion of making *deep games*, as interpreted in this book, has to do with creating games about the whole spectrum of the human experience and making it tangible through gameplay. I am not going to attempt a comprehensive, unambiguous definition of what I mean by *human experience* or *human condition*. (And, yes, I will use both terms in all their glorious fuzziness interchangeably!) It is one of these concepts that everyone understands somehow, but, as soon as you try to pin it down, the quibbling begins. Here is as far as I will go: by human experience or human condition, I mean the intricate web of thoughts and feelings we find ourselves entangled in and are trying to navigate and make sense of. It's the stuff of philosophy, TV series, movies, books, comics, poetry, art, and music, which all, in one way or another, explore what it means to be human—to love, to lose, to persevere, to grow, to die, to overcome, to avenge, to flourish, to dream, to hope, to have faith, to disappoint and be disappointed, and to deal with adversity. There. You will find more elaborations sprinkled throughout the following, and I trust that your understanding of the human condition is as good as mine, being a fellow human after all, so you may just as well run with what makes sense to you. I suppose we will not be too far off.

When I was a researcher at the Massachusetts Institute of Technology (MIT), designing and studying games at the Singapore–MIT GAMBIT Game Lab in Cambridge, Massachusetts, I underwent a crisis that forced me to ask some crucial questions about myself, my personal and professional life. I faced the end of a 12-year relationship; I dreaded my return to Austria, my home country; and I wasn't sure I wanted to be in academia anymore. To sort through that mess, I read a ton of self-help books, philosophy (a less-frowned-upon form of self-help literature), and poetry. I went to museums, flea markets, and concerts. I ran every morning along the Charles River. I tried everything in the book to regain direction. Most of all, I tried to *make sense*, to *find meaning* in what was happening. One useful tool in that regard, which I learned from Julia Cameron's fabulous book *The Artist's Way* (2002) and which I encourage all my students to use as well, were morning pages: writing three pages of stream of consciousness in longhand every day right after waking up. The other tool was game design. Every dilemma I faced and every underexplored feeling became the subject of a design exercise. It helped me structure the sense-making process by offering guiding questions: What is the goal here? What are the elements at play? What are their variables? What if I take this out/add this/tweak this? What exactly is the conflict? What is the lose state? Is there a win state? How can I fix this broken system so that there *is* a win state? It further taught me to go beyond commonsense understandings of abstract ideas such as *loyalty*, *faith*, and *love* and to really dig deep to figure out what they meant: e.g., what constitutes the feeling of sadness? There needs to be something you treasure and that you either had or hoped to obtain. This something becomes unobtainable. Sadness sets in once you explored every option to get it (back), and the realization has sunk in that there is nothing left that you can do. Sadness presupposes the death of hope. If you already find yourself arguing with this, that is a very good sign—it means you are thinking about the mechanics of the *inner life*, how things work, and how we humans *tick*. There is not one right answer, but some answers are more plausible and relatable than others.

Apart from Cameron's *The Artist's Way*, the other books that hugely influenced me at the time were Stuart Brown's work on *Play* (2009) and Joseph Meeker's *The Comedy of Survival* (1997). They opened my eyes to the healing qualities of play as a state of mind that enables you to get your back off the wall and see new solutions to intricate problems. This was exactly what I was trying to do with game design: playing through issues, finding solutions, and getting unstuck.

In this approach—using game design as a vehicle for personal inquiry—the designer gets to have all the *fun*, and, while the process of design can be insightful to the creator, the product may be meaningless to the player. A lot of the little design experiments I did to map out my inner swampland did not translate to others (and neither was it their purpose). There is something to be said about making radically personal games whose sole intent is self-exploration and self-expression, but, most of us, most of the time, want to make games for players, including me. Over the past seven years, I thus experimented with and researched systematic approaches to create games that make salient aspects of the human experience tangible to players; that enable insightful aha moments and make players see themselves, others, and life with fresh eyes; and that have transformative potential—deep games, if you so will. These experiments resulted in a bunch of award-winning projects, journal articles, conference presentations, workshops, and a course called *Making Deep Games*, which I have been teaching since 2009 at the MIT, the Vienna University of Technology (Austria), and DePaul University in Chicago and which is the basis of this book.

Making Deep Games aims to tie all of that previous piecework together into a coherent approach—a guide to designing games with meaning and purpose. It looks carefully at both sides of the process: (1) how to dig deep and analyze in a structured and systematic way the aspects of the human experience and (2) how to translate these experiences into a design that becomes comprehensible and emotionally intelligible to others, potentially increasing their understanding of the human experience as well. A profound self-knowledge (or the knowledge of complex, abstract ideas such as emotional concepts) needs to be complemented by a solid grasp of how games work as communicative medium capable of conveying ideas, messages, and experiences. This book presents tools and techniques for self-exploration, as well as the notion of *experiential gestalts* and ways to identify them systematically. It further discusses the process of turning experiences, personal themes, and complex abstract concepts into games by taking games' medium-specific characteristics into account and leveraging their unique strengths. It is complemented by hands-on exercises for instructors or (aspiring) game designers to use as starting points for deep games; in-depth analyses of existing games with profound messages; and postmortems of the games I have made, their iterative design evolutions, and the lessons learned from that.

Before we jump right in, maybe a case needs to be made on why anyone should make deep games. The simple answer is because we can! Games can communicate deep messages; they can make us think and feel deeply; and they can move us in a way no other medium can because games enable embodied experiences—meaning that, in a game, we learn by doing and by acting upon the gameworld and seeing the consequences of our actions just like in real life (see Gee 2003). They are thus particularly well suited to evoke empathy, and to engage in perspective taking, because they do not just *show* aspects of someone else's life; they also allow the player to walk in someone else's shoes, *experiencing* life from their perspective. Games can tackle the human experience in their own way, and make it tangible through gameplay, and it would be a waste to not tap this potential. We long for media that helps us make sense of that funny, old thing called life, our role within it, and what it all means. From the dawn of time, our favorite tool to do so has been narrative. The worth and social acceptability of each new storytelling medium have been measured by its capability to provide insights into how humans tick, why we do the things we do, what we fear and desire, and how we deal with adversity and relate to each other. Over the centuries, a canon of forms has been developed that is broadly recognized as having the potential to capture and illuminate the human experience. We love this canon. Each of its members had to learn its unique language and has fought hard for acceptance. Now, there is a new kid in the hood. It has been lurking around for a good while now, but nobody noticed it. It looked and behaved so differently from traditional media that only very few people paid any attention to it or considered it a serious candidate for the canon of media that could move us profoundly, make us think, and provide meaningful insights into ourselves. I am, of course, talking about video games. In the early 1980s, US courts decided that video games were insufficiently expressive to even qualify for First Amendment protection (i.e., freedom of speech):

> [The plaintiff] has failed to demonstrate that video games import sufficient communicative, expressive or informative elements to constitute expression protected under the First Amendment… [I]t appears that any communication or expression of ideas that occurs during the playing of a video game is purely inconsequential. [The plaintiff] has succeeded in establishing only that video games are more technologically advanced games than pinball or chess. That technological advancement alone, however, does not impart First Amendment status to what is an otherwise unprotected game. *Caswell v. Licensing Commission for Brockton*, 444 N.E.2d 922, 926-927. (Mass 1982)

Video games continued to stick around. They continued to be seen largely as the leering, rowdy, smelly neighbors who may be fun to hang out with at a barbecue but no one would invite over for a serious, heart-to-heart conversation. And yet, video games were here to stay. To stretch the metaphor further, they made themselves at home, wore shorter skirts, carried heavier weapons, bought bigger, flashier cars, and became harder and harder to ignore—but not necessarily for reasons that endeared them to a philosophical audience. Over the following 20 years, their technological progress was enormous. A video game's fictional worlds and characters have become more and more elaborate and gained previously unimaginable graphical richness and detail. None of this brought them any closer to acceptance into the canon reserved for media that successfully tackled the human experience.

In the Foreword to Eric Zimmerman's and Katie Salen's seminal book *Rules of Play* (2004), Frank Lanz addresses the authors' impatience with the reality of the game store, "the endless racks of adolescent power fantasies, witless cartoon characters, and literal minded sports simulations" (p. x). While games' fictional components have evolved, their continuing lack of thematic and experiential range can still not be denied. In the same year, however, Steven Spielberg made a legendary declaration: "I think the real indicator that games have become a storytelling art form will be when somebody confesses that they cried at level 17." Spielberg did not say this with skepticism. He said it with confidence that this would happen. Someone, a famous, well-accepted member of the community, had stretched out a hand to the unshaven, unrefined, unwanted neighbor. While it is arguable whether video games should become a *storytelling* art form or an art form all of their own, Spielberg's statement contributed greatly to changing the public discourse around the interactive medium forever. While respectable citizens still might have loathed the very idea of video games in the hood (and many still do), there was now a debate on whether they could maybe be *educated* and *integrated* into the finer society. Only one year after Spielberg wondered whether games could make us cry, legendary game developer Raph Koster (2005) calls for games that capture and illuminate the human condition.

> Games thus far have not really worked to extend our understanding of ourselves. Instead, games have primarily been an arena where human behavior – often in its crudest, most primitive form – is put on display. There is a crucial difference between games portraying the human condition and the human condition merely existing within games. The latter is interesting in an academic sense, but it is unsurprising. The human condition manifests anywhere. We may come to [sic!] better understanding of ourselves by examining our *relationship* to games, as this book attempts to do, but for games to truly step up to the plate, they need to provide us with insights into ourselves. (p. 174)

In his brilliant rant at the Game Developers Conference in 2008, Clint Hocking, at that time, still the creative director of Ubisoft, draws attention to games' bias toward physical concepts (weapons, running, jumping) and wonders passionately why they are not about "things that real human beings give a shit about. (...) Why don't we make games that challenge people? We make all kinds of movies and books and paintings and songs that challenge people. Why can't we make a game that means something? A game that matters. We wonder all the time if games are art, if computers can make you cry. Well, stop wondering. The answer is 'yes' to both." To support his point, he brings examples from two small indie games—Rod Humble's *The Marriage* and Jason Rohrer's *Passage*. Both games tackle aspects of human relationships in deeply personal ways. He goes on to ask, "Why isn't *Call of Duty* actually about duty? Or why isn't *Medal of Honor* actually about honor?"

Citing *The Lord of the Rings*, Hocking points out that what touched the readers and moviegoers were the relationship between Sam and Frodo, their mutual trust, and Gollum's redemption. Yet the games focus on glowing swords, armor, and ropes that give you a +5 power up. He ends his rant by claiming that it is not the lack of creativity that stops the games industry from reaching the next level and helping games take their place as the dominant cultural medium of the twenty-first century:

> What we lack is the **courage** to back up all of our creativity by making games that challenge something in us besides our reflexes. We lack the courage to show that we care about real things. We lack the courage to be seen crying in the movie theatre when **Frodo says thank-you to Sam**. We lack the courage to risk ourselves for our art and the reality is that is the ONLY difference between being the basically juvenile medium we are, and the mature medium we will inevitably become.
>
> Every time any one of us makes a game that fails to be about something that people give a shit about, we're letting ourselves down and dragging out the inevitable. We have the fucking pieces of the puzzle in our hands. We have the creativity. We have the money. The demand is there.
>
> And fuck – **it's code** – **we can do anything**.

For games to mature as an art form, and to reach a broader audience and fulfill their potential as communicative and expressive media, they need to tackle more personal themes and to model salient aspects of the human experience. Does that mean all games need to be deep in that sense? Not at all. In literature, *Remembrance of Things Past* can coexist with *Fifty Shades of Grey*. Games like Minority Media's *Papo & Yo*, which deals with a little boy's struggle with an alcoholic father, will not eliminate titles like *Candy Crush* or *League of Legends*, which are worthy in their own right and will continue to be highly popular. What I am arguing for is to expand the repertoire of games to include profound, thought-provoking, and emotionally diverse experiences, not to extinguish or ban existing gameplay pleasures.

Luckily, I am not alone in this plight. Over the past few years, what I call deep games have become *a thing*, as demonstrated by the works of Brenda Romero (*Train, Siochan Leat*), Jason Rohrer (*Passage, Creativity*), Anna Anthropy (*Dys4ia*), Zoe Quinn (*Depression Quest*), Mattie Brice (*Mainichi*), Ed McMillan (*Binding of Isaac, Super Meat Boy*), Jonathan Blow (*Braid*), Team Ico (*Ico, Shadow of the Colossus*), thatgamecompany (*Journey*), and Minority Media (*Papo & Yo, Spirits of Spring*) to name just a few that come to mind. These games have also illustrated how the design of illuminating and potentially transformative gameplay is not only relevant for entertainment games. It also has its place in the design of games with a purpose beyond fun. The Games 4 Change and Games 4 Health movements are growing steadily. Both put considerable emphasis on the creation of empathy games to raise awareness for social and personal issues such as mental illness (e.g., depression), Alzheimer's disease, bullying, genocide, immigration laws and political conflicts, etc. Modeling *inner worlds* and making them tangible through rules and mechanics are powerful tools to increase the understanding of the whole spectrum of the human experience. Being able to use these tools systematically, intentionally, and purposefully is relevant for every game designer who wants to use his or her medium as a vehicle for expression, insight, activism, and learning.

The following eight chapters unpack the idea of deep games through theoretical explorations, case studies, design exercises, and application areas. They deal with how to find inspiration for deep game ideas, and dissect and analyze experiences as the basis of the design process, understanding and purposefully using a video game's expressive means to translate experiences into gameplay, and the role of metaphor as a core constituent of games about the human condition. Parts of these chapters have been published elsewhere and have been elaborated upon for the purposes of this book. Chapter 3—"Modeling the Human Experience—Or the Art of Nailing a Pudding to the Wall"—has been coauthored with Matthew Weise and published under the title "Games about LOVE and TRUST—Harnessing the Power of Metaphors for Experience Design" in the conference proceedings of SIGGRAPH in 2008. Parts of Chapter 4—"Experiential Metaphors— Or What Breaking Up, Getting a Tattoo, and Playing *God of War* Have

in Common"—have appeared in the paper "Mechanisms of the Soul—
Tackling the Human Condition in Videogames" in the conference proceedings of DiGRA in 2009.

Some thoughts from Chapter 5, "Allegorical Games—Or the Monster
Isn't a Monster Isn't a Monster," have appeared in an article published in the
ETC Press's *Well Played* series as "Staring into the Abyss—A Close Reading
of Silent Hill 2."

Chapter Overview

Chapter 1, "Diving for Deep Game Ideas," talks about how to become more
aware of the aspects of the human experience in order to identify deep game
ideas. It discusses Julia Cameron's *morning pages* and *the artist date*, as well as
conversations with the inner game designer (*IGD*), as the main tools to tune in
to and make sense of one's own inner life. What the artist date and morning
pages bring to light is the raw material that is then interrogated by the IGD
in regard to its systemic qualities, the goals, the conflicts, and the win-and-
lose state of the human experience themes at play. The IGD asks *the next
question*, constantly probing deeper, about why something is important, what
is at stake, how it works, why it makes us feel a certain way, etc. How the
technique works is illustrated by way of a case study, the design evolution
of the personal game project *The Bridge*, which tackles the mechanisms of
possessive love and letting go. The chapter then proposes tracing the human
experience in other media, finding the theme in various artistic expressions
such as songs, books, movies, graphic novels, fine art, and performances.
Themes are powerful waypoints toward our dreams, desires, and struggles
and can be decoupled from the actual plot or artwork to serve as inspiration
for a deep game without being an adaptation. Finally, Chapter 1 suggests
we pay attention to our fellow humans, to become excellent listeners and
overcome our shyness to really engage and take an interest in what moves
them and how they tick. Empathy, in the sense of *seeing things from another's
perspective* and *walking in their shoes*, is a hallmark of good game designers.
We need to put ourselves in our players' shoes to create worthwhile experiences for them. It is also the precondition for making deep games that *ring
true* and go beyond our limited, experiential horizons. The best authors are
usually also excellent observers. The same is true for deep game designers. To
make deep games, we cannot be satisfied with scratching the surface of the
human condition.

Chapter 2, "Games as an Expressive Medium," looks at how inspirations for deep games can be turned into design. What are the specific affordances of the medium to make meaning and to communicate ideas and provide thought-provoking, insightful aha moments that make us see life and ourselves with fresh eyes? This rather-grandiose discussion is kicked off with a brief definition of *game,* followed by an exploration of how games can be *about something* and what constitutes their ability to *represent.* A case is made that rules and mechanics are the main vehicle for meaning in games rather than fiction. It is explained how games that are about something are simulations of *source systems* and that modeling a source system is a kind of authorship that includes making subjective choices about what we want to say about these source systems. We make statements with our rules and convey ideas through how things work, what is possible in our simulations, what is prohibited, what is incentivized, and what is punished. The difference between procedural expression and procedural rhetoric is elaborated in order to understand games as media of persuasion and the responsibility we carry as authors of such media.

Chapter 3, "Modeling the Human Experience—Or the Art of Nailing a Pudding to the Wall," explores how to use simulation deliberately and purposefully to make deep games.

It argues that the salient aspects of what it means to be human reside in the realm of abstract concepts (rather than what is physically tangible) and that, in order to make the abstract concrete—to nail the pudding to the wall—we need metaphors. This chapter provides a relevant theoretical foundation to understand the nature of structural metaphors, their importance to make sense of intangible ideas, and how to use them systematically and sensibly for the purpose of designing coherent, insightful gameplay experiences that make salient aspects of the human experience tangible through rules, mechanics, and moment-to-moment gameplay.

Drawing on cognitive linguistics as developed by Mark Johnson and George Lakoff, it starts with an exploration of how we understand and structure our experiences in real life through multidimensional gestalts or image schemata. These gestalt structures are unified wholes that organize our experiences and cognition and constrain meaning. Our whole conceptual system (including abstract ideas) is based on them. Multidimensional gestalts are derived from our physical being in the world as humans. Our bodies and how they interact with a tangible environment are the basis of all our abstract thinking and the basis of metaphorical mappings that help us understand the intangible by way of what's tangible, e.g., verticality or the compulsive force schema. Peer pressure is an abstract concept, which we can understand by way of the physical idea *pressure*—a force imposed on us by others that makes us do things we might not want to do or that we have to resist. Much emphasis is put on how structural metaphors *make sense* and how the mappings between the dimensions of the abstract experience they are trying to grasp and the dimensions of the physical concept that facilitates that need to be completely consistent. Multidimensional gestalts and structural metaphors are thus presented as a main method of pinning down the source systems that constitute the human experience and translating them dimension for dimension into a game's rule structure. It suggests that our experiences are subjective and individual but (unless we suffer from some severe mental illness) not idiosyncratic. We can express ourselves in ways that make sense and are relatable to others when we tap into the multidimensional gestalts that organize all of our conceptual systems.

Chapter 4 is "Experiential Metaphors—What Breaking Up, Getting a Tattoo, and Playing *God of War* Have in Common." Building on Chapter 3, which focused on grasping the source system of complex, abstract concepts by way of structural metaphors and modeling them through rules and mechanics, and conveying *how it works*, Chapter 4 investigates how games can enable meaning through *what it feels like* to play them. The metaphors at play here are *experiential*, providing parallels between gameplay experience and real-life experience on the level of bodily enactment. Through their rules and mechanics, games can replicate the physical grounding with which we make sense of abstract experiences and allow us to feel it directly. Moments of transition—e.g., a breakup, job hunting, relocating, getting a tattoo or a haircut—all more or less share the same experiential gestalt: a dissatisfying status quo A and an as-of-yet-unknown status B. (Will there be new love, a new, better job, a new, better life in the new city, or a better look?) There is the fear of letting go of A, the thrill of the free fall as you are transitioning to B, the temptation to go back to A if B seems too daunting, the moment of realization one made a mistake (e.g., B turns out to be unachievable), or the moment of triumph after the transition is successfully completed and one has left A behind and landed safely on B. The experience of *life transitions* is rarely physical. It is constituted of emotions—our fears, dreams, and desires related to the salient parts of the transition gestalt—and, as such, abstract. A game can allow us an embodied experience of this gestalt (e.g., through swinging from pillar to pillar in a sequence of *God of War*), grounding it in its physicality and allowing us to explore the feelings associated with transition in a tangible, immediate way. The chapter then goes on to explore how experiential metaphors—what game structures *feel like* and what they can remind us of in the realm of abstract concepts—can undermine or support a game's stated theme or create subtexts relevant for the interpretation of a game's ideology. Examples are *Angry Birds* (the mechanics of vengeance), *American McGee's Grimm: Little Red Riding Hood* (the game's cleaning gestalt undermines its theme of anarchy and chaos), and *Left Behind: Eternal Forces* (the cleaning gestalt being contextualized as religious purge).

Chapter 5, "Allegorical Games—Or the Monster Isn't a Monster Isn't a Monster," looks at a metaphorical narrative—allegory—rather than individual structural metaphors, to illuminate salient aspects of the human condition. By way of a comparative analysis of *Journey, Silent Hill—Restless Dreams, Papo & Yo*, and *Spirits of Spring*, it examines how allegory can promote deep gameplay experiences by way of making inner processes tangible, creating a *magic door* to a difficult idea, reinforcing a theme across all levels of meaning generation, engaging curiosity, and making players think. The chapter explores the different expressive and communicative goals of allegorical games depending on how they go about revealing their true theme, presenting the notion of *metaphor as mystery, message*, and *muse*. When metaphor is used to create mystery (e.g., *Silent Hill*), it acts as the *dangling carrot*—the vehicle to keep people guessing and playing. The mystery is revealed in the end, and everyone can go home satisfied. Players who dig deeper, though, will be rewarded with additional insight. Since these games are mainly for entertainment, it doesn't matter whether all aspects of their meaning are uncovered. Not so in games that use metaphor to convey a message. In *Papo & Yo* and *Spirits of Spring*, metaphor is employed to lure the player in to explore a difficult idea (alcoholism, bullying). For the game to fulfill its communicative agenda—to deliver the designer's message or personal statement—players need to *get it*. The metaphor must be dismantled and its underlying meaning made apparent for the message to be conveyed. Metaphor as muse is yet a different case, leveraging allegory as a projection screen for players. Metaphor as muse shifts the emphasis from imposing a prepackaged meaning onto the player to providing evocative settings, characters, and events that promote self-exploration and the question "What does it mean to me?" The chapter then proposes the transformative story structure of the hero's journey as a potential way to chart the narrative progression when designing allegorical games.

Chapter 6, "Designing with Purpose and Meaning—Nine Questions to Define Where You're Going and Make Sure You Get There," serves as an overview of the key points that are helpful to consider to define a vision for a project and stay on track throughout the development process. From asking what the game is about to its purpose/communicative goal, to whether it should take a literal or metaphorical approach, to identifying the right metaphor for an experiential gestalt, to deciding whether the game should model *how it works versus what it feels like*, to identifying how much of the source system shall be modeled, to considering from which perspective the player will interact with the system, to finding suitable core mechanics to reinforce the game's meaning, to contemplating how to create strong alignment between a player and an avatar—all this is discussed to make the many decisions that go into the design process apparent and facilitate making these decisions intentionally and purposefully rather than *letting them happen*.

Chapters 7 and 8 provide an outlook and new areas of exploration for deep games.

Chapter 7, "It's Not Always about You!—Lessons Learned from Participatory Deep Game Design," discusses the tricky issue of making games about aspects of the human experience the designers do not have firsthand knowledge of. The focus is particularly on nonfiction games and how their obligation toward authenticity requires the active participation of people with lived experience of the modeled issue into the design process. Traditionally, participatory design focuses on the inclusion of end users/players because they are the ones most affected by the product to be created and thus most need to be empowered through cocreation. The higher the stakes for a specific group, the more important it is to get their input so that the project most effectively addresses their needs. In regard to games that tackle a lack of awareness, understanding, or empathy for a salient aspect of the human experience, the people for whom most is at stake are those with lived experience of this aspect. An argument is made that they are the ones who first and foremost need to be included in a participatory design process. Participatory design, while well intended and *the right thing to do*, is nevertheless extremely challenging. How do you cocreate with people who may or may not have any gaming or game design experience whatsoever? How do you leverage their personal experiences to inform design? How are design decisions made? What role does playtesting play?

To provide tentative, exploratory answers to these questions, the chapter presents a case study of *For the Records*, an interactive documentary project including four experiential games on young adults and mental illness. All the media pieces (short films, games, animation, photo essays) of *For the Records* were made in strong collaboration with people with lived experience of the portrayed mental illnesses. The case study features a comparative analysis of the design and development of the four games on obsessive–compulsive disorder, attention deficit disorder, bipolar disorder, and eating disorder. It discusses how including subject-matter experts with different levels of gaming/game design experience and different degrees of integration into the development teams impacted the identification of the games' communicative goals, finding the games' core metaphors, balancing the desire for authenticity with the desire for engaging and relatable gameplay, negotiating responsibilities and the decision-making power, and ensuring the overall quality of the final product. The lessons learned from this project inform a list of takeaways at the end of the chapter that—while not comprehensive—can provide valuable guidance for other participatory deep game design undertakings.

Chapter 8, "The Same New Kid in Yet Another Hood—Deep Game Design as Creative Arts Therapy?" brings us back to the origin of deep games—personal crisis—and investigates the path not yet taken: using the power of design not to make games about the human experience for others, but rather for oneself. How can we use game design to increase our understanding of ourselves and transform through the creative exploration and creative modification of our emotional landscapes and inner worlds? This chapter is coauthored with Susan Imus, chair of the creative arts therapies department at Columbia College Chicago. Susan provided the theoretical background to this chapter: an introduction to the basic concepts and criteria of creative arts therapies. This includes a differentiation between art as therapy and art in therapy, an overview of the education of creative arts therapists, the criteria for purposeful interventions, an exploration of the therapeutic relationship in creative arts therapy, and an investigation of the transformative power of the creative process. The focus is then directed toward fundamental mechanisms used across creative arts therapies such as safety, cocreation, dynamism, risk taking, witnessing and reflection, meaning making, empowerment, varied approaches, informed decision making, coherence and integration, the use of symbols and metaphors, improvisation, and play, a relational aspect, as well as concretization and distancing, to make inner processes tangible and enable new perspectives.

To apply theory to practice and illustrate how game design fits in as one possible mode of creative arts therapy, we conducted an experiment at Columbia College, including a volunteer *patient* and five faculty members (including Susan Imus) from Columbia's creative arts therapies department, all practicing creative arts therapists, and me as the game designer. The experimental therapy session took two hours. It started off with an introductory phase that explained deep game design and the impetus behind making games about the human experience to the observing therapists and the patient. This was followed by the game design therapy part itself and concluded with a debriefing where present therapists shared their observations and helped orient the practice of game design within the existing canon of creative arts therapies, identifying parallels, as well as unique aspects. The chapter closes with an experience report from our volunteer patient written a day after the session, describing the impact designing a game about a personal issue (in this case, social anxiety) had on her.

References

Brown, S. 2009. *Play: How It Shapes the Brain, Opens the Imagination, and Invigorates the Soul.* New York: Penguin.

Cameron, J. 2002. *The Artist's Way: A Spiritual Path to Higher Creativity.* New York: Tarcher/Putnam.

Gee, J. 2003. *What Video Games Have to Teach Us About Learning and Literacy.* New York: Palgrave Macmillan.

Grossman, L. 2004. The art of the virtual: Are videogames starting to—Gasp!—Mean something? Available at http://www.time.com/time/magazine/article /0,9171,995582,00.html.

Hocking, C. 2008. GDC 2008 Game Designer's rant. Available at http://www.click nothing.typepad.com/click_nothing/.

Koster, R. 2005. *A Theory of Fun for Game Design.* Scottsdale, AZ: Paraglyph Press.

Meeker, J. 1997. *The Comedy of Survival: Literary Ecology and a Play Ethic.* Tucson, AZ: The University of Arizona Press.

Rusch, D. 2009a. Mechanisms of the soul—Tackling the human condition in videogames. In DiGRA '09 Proceedings of the 2009 DiGRA International Conference: *Breaking New Ground: Innovation in Games, Play, Practice and Theory, Vol. 5,* Brunel University.

Rusch, D. 2009b. Staring into the Abyss—A Close Reading of Silent Hill 2. In Davidson, D. (Ed.), *Well Played 1.0: Video Games, Value and Meaning* (pp. 235–255). Pittsburgh, PA: ETC Press. Available at http://press.etc.cmu .edu/content/silent-hill-2-doris-c-rusch.

Rusch, D. and Weise, M. 2008. Games about LOVE and TRUST?—Harnessing the power of metaphors for experience design. In Sandbox '08 Proceedings of the 2008 ACM SIGGRAPH Symposium on Video Games (pp. 89–97). New York: ACM.

Zimmerman, E. and Salen, K. 2004. *Rules of Play: Game Design Fundamentals.* Cambridge, MA: The MIT Press.

1

Diving for Deep Game Ideas

Wherein the means and methods of finding and fleshing out deep game ideas are discussed:

- *The importance of self-awareness as a source for deep game ideas*
  - *Julia Cameron's self-awareness tools: "morning pages" and "artist date"*
  - *The "inner game designer" as a method to systematically unpack deep game ideas*
    - *Case study: "The Bridge"—the inner game designer in action*
- *Finding the themes of art and media that reveal the human condition*
- *Trying to understand other people and their experiences*

1.1 Becoming a Mind Reader

In order to make games that enable insightful, thought-provoking, and emotionally rich experiences, it is helpful to become a mind reader—not necessarily of other people's but at least one's own mind. So often, we live our lives barely aware of what is going on with us. We might wake up cranky and not know why, but unable to shake the feeling, or somehow anxious for no apparent reason. We have a conversation with a friend and suddenly find ourselves seething or resentful. Some buttons must have been pushed, but what they are remains mysterious. We watch a sunrise and are filled with an overwhelming sense of hope and optimism, a feeling that might dissipate as suddenly as it has set upon us. To create deep games, we need to study ourselves and pay attention to how we see the world, what drives us, what holds us back, how we relate to others, and why. We need to become attuned to and aware of our experiences, and learn to study and analyze them systematically and conscientiously, because, as game designers, creating experiences is our job, our purpose, and maybe even our calling. We cannot model something we do not understand ourselves.

Granted, every game evokes an experience when played. But is it the experience that we *intended* to convey, that we *wanted* players to have? Admittedly, there is no way to predict with certainty what players will feel when playing a game, but neither should it be completely arbitrary, if you know what you're doing. Before we can worry about how an experience translates into rules, mechanics, and other game aspects, though, we need to be able to define the experience we want to model—to identify its quality or, as Jesse Schell (2008) calls it, its essential elements. This is much easier said than done. As Schell puts it, experiences are hard to describe. They are all we know, but we cannot see them, touch them, or hold them. They are inner processes, and, as such, they are abstract. (In Chapter 3, we will talk more about the nature of abstract concepts, the challenge of modeling them in games, and the strategies to approach this challenge systematically.) Schell continues:

> But as tricky as experiences can be, creating them is all a game designer really cares about. We cannot shy away from them, retreating into the concreteness of our material game. We must use every means we can muster to comprehend, understand, and master the nature of human experience. (p. 10)

What strikes me as particularly relevant in Schell's quote is the insight that if we want to design experiences with deliberation and intent, we cannot fast-forward to creating rules and mechanics (the concreteness of our material game). We need to know first what we want to model. Otherwise, it's like blindly pounding the keyboard in the hopes that the next great American novel will unfold. It is very tempting to start thinking about rules and mechanics or the story, characters, and the environment before we are ready. These things are concrete, but, if they are not informed by a vision for the experience they should enable, or the message they are meant to convey, they lack substance. They can only be deep or meaningful by accident. Exploring the source system—the experience the game aims to capture—is a crucial part of the design process and deserves careful consideration. I spent more than 6 months designing *Elude* (a short game about the experience of depression), yet it took only 9 weeks to develop it. It took so long to get a grip on what being depressed felt like, what the core of the experience was, and how this could be turned into something *playable*.

When modeling the aspects of the human experience and making statements about *how things work* or *what they feel like*, every rule needs to make sense in regard to the source system (Chapter 2). No game element is allowed to be in the game that does not support the message lest it dilutes or even undermines it. Exploring the experience thoroughly before starting the design process will also help solve design problems. You can always refer back to your insights about how it works or what it feels like to identify or tweak a rule or mechanic. When you get stuck, always go back to the source. That's why creating a strong vision for the game—knowing what it should model and for what purpose—is so important and will contribute to the game's depth and inner coherence.

1.1.1 Morning Pages

The realization that self-awareness is conducive to creativity and expressive depth is not new. Two very effective tools in that regard have been introduced by Julia Cameron (2002): (1) the *morning pages* and (2) the *artist date*. They are best used in conjunction with each other. Morning pages foster *mind-reading skills*, while the artist date provides the *reading material*. Cameron (2002) describes morning pages as follows:

> Morning pages are three pages of longhand writing, strictly stream-of-consciousness: "Oh, god, another morning. I have NOTHING to say. I need to wash the curtains. Did I get my laundry yesterday? Blah, blah, blah…" They might also, more ingloriously, be called *brain drain*, since that is one of their main functions. *There is no wrong way to do morning pages.* These daily morning meanderings are not meant to be *art*. Or even *writing*. (…) Writing is simply one of the tools. Pages are meant to be, simply, the act of moving the hand across the page and writing down *whatever* comes to mind. Nothing is too petty, too silly, too stupid, or too weird to be included. The morning pages are not supposed to sound smart – although sometimes they might. Most times they won't, and nobody will ever know except you. Nobody is allowed to read your morning pages except you. And you shouldn't even read them yourself for the first eight weeks or so. Just write three pages, and stick them into an envelope. Or write three pages in a spiral notebook and don't leaf back through. *Just write three pages…*and write three more pages the next day. (pp. 9–10)

Cameron uses the morning pages as a way to outwit and silence the *inner critic* or *censor* that blocks creativity, but, apart from that, they are also very effective to point toward one's personal themes and issues. Whatever is there, buried in the subconscious or preconscious, slowly bubbles to the surface and makes itself known through the morning pages. Suddenly, that unspecified, uneasy feeling or nondescript restlessness has a name, and you can put your finger on it: e.g., I've been missing my grandparents. I need to go visit them, to get in touch with my roots. I never liked those curtains; why don't I get new ones? I need to show myself that I care about myself. I used to love playing music but haven't in ages. I need to find a piano somewhere that I can use. Why do I always think work is so much more important than play?

Sometimes, morning pages directly lead to game ideas, and, the more you do them, the more often this will happen. However, that is not their primary purpose. Their primary purpose is to pay attention to your inner chatter. You're tuning in to your very own frequency and listening to what you have to tell yourself. When personal themes start to crystallize, morning pages help you explore them and make sense of them. They help you ask questions to understand yourself better. It is a skill that also translates to understanding others better. You stop just assuming things or blindly projecting (e.g., what's true for me must be true for others). A critical analysis of thoughts and feelings becomes second nature. This is a precondition for grasping the elements at play in the human experience, for getting beyond a superficial, shallow, commonsense understanding of emotional concepts and dynamics.

1.1.2 Artist Date

Morning pages get you in touch with your personal themes, dreams, and desires and help you make sense of your experiences. This presupposes, though, that there is something to make sense of. You can't read without reading material. If you sit in your room all day, staring at the wallpaper, your realm of experiences is quite limited. The artist date takes care of that. It is a commitment to yourself to expand your horizons, to play, and to fill the well. What is it?

> An artist date is a block of time, perhaps two hours weekly, especially set aside and committed to nurturing your creative consciousness, your inner artist. In its most primary form, the artist date is an excursion, a play date that you preplan and defend against all interlopers. You do not take anyone on this artist date but you and your inner artist, a.k.a. your creative child. That means no lovers, friends, spouses, children, no taggers-on of any stripe. If you think this sounds stupid or that you will never be able to afford the time, identify that reaction as resistance. You cannot afford *not* to find time for artist dates. (…) Spending time

in solitude with your artist child is essential to self-nurturing. A long country walk, a solitary expedition to the beach for a sunrise or sunset, a sortie out to a strange church to hear gospel music, to an ethnic neighborhood to taste foreign sights and sounds – your artist might enjoy any of these. Or your artist might like bowling. (...)

Above all, learn to listen to what your artist child has to say on, and about these joint expeditions. For example, "Oh, I hate this serious stuff," your artist may exclaim if you persist in taking it only to grown-up places that are culturally edifying and good for it. Listen to that! It is telling you your art needs more playful inflow. A little fun can go a long way toward making your work feel more like play. We forget that the imagination at play is at the heart of all good work. (Cameron 2002, pp. 18–20)

Artist dates are invaluable to identify your *true north*. They point you toward the themes that resonate with you at a given point in life, and morning pages help you figure out why. There was a time when my artist dates frequently led me to flea markets. I was both fascinated and appalled by them. There is the thrill of finding a gem among all the junk, but there is also the sadness that very personal items, such as reading glasses, that once were almost a part of someone are now being discarded. Flea markets provided a tangible meditation on the fleetingness of life, on how our belongings—maybe once coveted and treasured—will inevitably end up as garbage. It made me realize that *now* is the only time to be happy and that moments we have with our loved ones are precious. It made me think about culture and civilization and what it all means and who we are without all of our *stuff*. There is a game in there somewhere about love and loss and the meaning of objects.

Morning pages and artist dates promote authentic creativity. If we do them regularly, we start to feel more strongly about things; we know better what we like and what we don't like, and what is important to us and why. This fosters the development of authentic projects—projects that are informed by a certain inner clarity, that have a point of view, that want to express something, and that mean something. Maybe not everyone will get their meaning, and much depends on the actual implementation of the experience into the game, but, nevertheless, this is the seed of conceptual depth and coherence, of thought-provoking and insightful gameplay.

1.1.3 Conversing with the Inner Game Designer

As your connection to yourself gets stronger, and you become more attuned to your inner life through morning pages and artist dates, ideas will start to bubble to the surface. While they very rarely arrive as fully fleshed-out game designs, they tend to have a special quality that marks them as *personally meaningful* and worthy of further exploration. You will know when an idea has such a quality. It might be an image, a sentence, a quote, or just a very strong feeling you cannot shake. This could very well be the seed for a deep game. The nature of a seed, however, is that it needs to undergo a transformation to fulfill its potential. It is still a mere promise of a plant, and what it will turn into has yet to be discovered. With the right nourishment and care, though, it will grow and bloom. The following case study of *The Bridge*—a short, personal game I worked on with a small team of students during the Spring semester of 2009 at the Massachusetts Institute of Technology (MIT)—describes a technique to cultivate idea seeds by using the most basic structural elements of games as guides: (a) goal, (b) conflict, and (c) win-and-lose condition. This technique is only a precursor to game design. It is still part of the toolbox that helps investigate salient concepts of the human experience. Using structural game elements to systematize the inquiry of ideas and personal themes facilitates the transition to the actual design. This is comparable to approaches in screenwriting, where the author asks about the main protagonist's needs and wants, his or her strengths and shortcomings, and how all of this defines his or her journey of transformation. It is a good way of getting a clearer vision of the theme, but the actual design work/writing is yet to come. *The Bridge* is a good example of a game prototype that remained in the service of exploring the theme. It helped my team and me to think through the concept of love, loss, and the art of letting go, and, at the end of that Spring semester, we would have been ready to start over and make the actual game, but, as students graduated, the team dissolved, and it never happened. Yet, we learnt a lot about the process of methodically questioning big, diffuse, abstract ideas to prepare for their transformation into a deep game.

1.1.3.1 Case Study: The Bridge It started with an image: an empty tire swing in an empty field. This image didn't come with an explanation, only with an emotional overtone of loss, and hoping against hope. A bit like a cone without ice cream, a tire swing is a sad affair when it just hangs there without a child on it. Of course, one can take either image both ways: as a promise for future fun or as the memory of past pleasures. To me, it meant the latter. But why a tire swing? No idea, but there it was, and it would not go away. Instead, the tire-swing image evolved into this interactive scene: you enter an empty space with nothing but a swing in it and nothing to do but to push it. Pushing the swing produces faint laughter. The transparent outline of a child becomes visible on the swing. Since the child appears a bit more *solid* with every push, the implied goal is that you keep attending to the tire swing until the child is fully *materialized*. Stop pushing, and the child grows fainter; the laughter fades and is replaced by sobbing and whimpering. After a while, you realize that no amount of pushing allows the child to manifest fully. The only way to *win* is to accept that and *let go*.

To me, this scene perfectly captured an emotional state I'd been wrestling with at the time—being stuck in unproductive behavior (i.e., pushing the metaphorical swing), unwilling to accept loss. I wanted to build a game based on this because externalizing inner conflicts through design helps to gain distance to them and promotes clarity. By manifesting the issue outside of oneself and making it manipulable (through design or gameplay), one can further regain a sense of agency and perspective. Making *The Bridge* was a form of self-exploration through design, but it was also my hope that the end product would be meaningful to players in a similar situation. Before that could happen, I needed to get a better sense of what that situation actually was, what it all meant. The initial scene was not rich enough. The rules described a *state* rather than a complex system of interconnected elements, and not much meaning or insight could be derived from that. By using the most basic structural elements of games as guidelines—goal, conflict, win-and-lose condition—I started to dig deeper to uncover the emotional conflict the game should investigate and illuminate. The conversation with my inner game designer (IGD) went like this:

> *IGD:* What exactly is the goal?
>
> *Me:* To let go, to move on, to be happy again.
>
> *IGD:* What makes *letting go* hard? What is the conflict?
>
> *Me:* Attachment makes it difficult.
>
> *IDG:* What creates attachment?
>
> *Me:* Love, I guess…?
>
> *IGD:* So the way to overcome attachment is to overcome love?
>
> *Me:* Now that you put it this way, it doesn't sound right. Love is important. If you had to overcome love to win, that would send the wrong message.
>
> *IGD:* Are you sure it is love, then, that keeps you stuck? Maybe it is fear?

>   *Me:* Fear of what? Fear of losing love…you cling because you are afraid.
>
>   *IGD:* What exactly are you afraid of?
>
>   *Me:* I just said that: fear of losing love!
>
>   *IGD:* What happens when you lose love? Sounds like love serves a purpose.
>
>   *Me:* It protects…makes you feel good about yourself.
>
>   *IGD:* That is not a healthy kind of love. You realize that, yes?
>
>   *Me:* I guess…sure does not feel healthy…
>
>   *IGD:* Since you don't want to lose what makes you feel good, *love* itself creates fear. It is both a curse and a cure, it seems.
>
>   *Me:* That's right. Fear creates clinging. You're only safe when close to your *love object*.
>
>   *IGD:* Is there no potential for happiness when you're on your own?
>
>   *Me:* There used to be. Doesn't seem like it now.
>
>   *IGD:* Let me ask again: what is the goal?
>
>   *Me:* To let go of the need for someone else.
>
>   *IGD:* To achieve this, you need to regain the ability to take care of yourself. Let's revisit the fears; what are they really?
>
>   *Me:* To not be love-worthy.
>
>   *IGD:* You don't have to internalize love. There is little self-love. This creates the dependency on someone else's appreciation, and being dependent on that fosters the fear of loss. This is not about the other person; it is about you.
>
>   *Me:* Great. How do I get out of this? How do I win?
>
>   *IGD:* Face your fears. Learn to take care of yourself, and make yourself happy. This is the only way to create a path to non-possessive, fearless love.

Obviously, this is a simplified representation of the conversation with the IGD, but it illustrates how asking about the goal, conflict, and win-and-lose condition helped to clarify the theme, the system including its elements at play, and their rules of interaction. Also, these insights did not happen all at once, and it must be acknowledged that my IGD benefitted from many insightful real-life conversations with my amazing teammates Trey and Jamie.

The prototype we ended up building worked like this: the player plays as a little boy who pushes a tire swing. A ghost-like girl appears on it. She is surrounded by a golden glow that acts as a protective shield against the black, inky monsters whose spawning coincides with the girl's manifestation. Once the girl is fully *charged*, she jumps off the swing and follows you around. Her golden glow prevents the monsters—representations of fears—from attaching themselves to you and bogging you down (limiting your movement). The golden glow shrinks over time, and the girl starts to disappear. Once her timer is up, she needs to be reactivated by pushing the tire swing. This creates a clinging behavior: (a) you try to stay close to the girl to remain within her protective sphere, and (b) you hurry back to the tire swing to recharge her once she starts to fade. Her *distancing* herself from you is perceived as a threat that needs to be prevented.

If you only focus on her keeping you safe, you remain stuck in this loop with nowhere to go and nothing to win. There is a way out, though; stop recharging her, and fight the monsters. Shake them off, and stomp on them. When you crush a monster, it releases gold dust—the stuff that will form the path forward, the bridge to the other side, your future (Figure 1.1).

Monsters spawn in three waves, and you need to defeat all three of them, meaning that facing your fears takes patience and practice. It doesn't happen from one day to the next. But, if you persist, you will grow stronger and more autonomous. After the third successfully defeated wave, the gold dust bridge transforms into solid wood, and you can cross it, leaving the semitransparent

FIGURE 1.1
GAMBIT MIT's *The Bridge*—Defeating the Fear Creates a Bridge into a Brighter Future

girl on the tire swing behind. Halfway across the bridge, your avatar is being turned to face her and watch her disappear. You let go. You move on.

1.2 Tracing the Human Experience in Art—Finding the Theme

The human experience is reflected in and shaped by many works of art (*art* being understood very broadly here to avoid fruitless discussions about what art is and isn't): literature, film, comics, music, dance, theater, painting, sculpture, installations, performance, etc. In one way or another, they all try to capture and express what it means to be human, how we tick. In turn, we seek out artworks in order to be moved by them, to reflect on ourselves the meaning of life, and our existence. Even the most abstract pieces, such as Mark Rothko's rectangles, have the potential for profound personal resonance. The Rothko chapel is seeped in tears (see Elkins 2004).

Paying attention to the themes of the whole range of artistic expressions provides excellent inspiration for deep game ideas. What is the theme? The theme is the point, the essence of an artwork, its subject—what it's about beneath the surface. In a narrative medium, theme is not the plot. The plot is only a vehicle for the theme. When a book or film resonates with us, it's because of the theme, not the plot. The details of the plot we will forget, but we will remember the emotional resonance of the theme. Digital media designer Hillman Curtis (2002) speaks insightfully about his experiences with Jack Kerouac's classic *On the Road* (1957) and how it inspired him to hitchhike to New Orleans in his college days:

> *On the Road* is 307 pages long. I can remember parts of it, here and there, but I'll always remember the theme. The theme of the book is reckless discovery. And the book is so effective because it never forgets that theme. Its passages read like a car speeding crazily across a freeway. The prose rambles feverishly, without the restrictions of punctuation. Rather, simple dashes pepper the book with their short pauses, like Charlie Parker taking a breath between phrases. And it's not so much the plot that made me step out in the freeway, cardboard sign in hand… it was the theme. Themes have that power. They can communicate so much deeper than literal messaging. (p. 41)

Identifying the themes of art and media provides great inspiration for deep game ideas. Paying attention to what songs, movies, plays, and pictures are essentially about is a great exercise for tracing the human experience. Admittedly, themes are open for interpretation; they are sometimes elusive and vague—maybe that is part of their appeal. In order to design games based on a theme, though, you need to be able to make the abstract concrete, to pin it down and figure out *how it works*. I claim that, if we want to purposefully and deliberately design deep games, an intuitive, preconscious understanding of the theme is not cutting it. How are you going to create game rules that reflect and convey the theme if you don't know what exactly you are trying to model? The following sketches out the process of identifying the theme of *Billy Elliot* (just because I'm thinking of this movie as I'm writing this), so it could serve as the (rough) basis for a game.

What is *Billy Elliot* about? The story revolves around a young boy who grows up in a rough, English coal-mining town. It is expected of him to behave *manly*, but he performs poorly in boxing class. He is much more drawn to the girls-only ballet school. His love for dancing is only supported by his secretly gay friend and has to survive strong opposition before his friends and family finally accept it, and Billy successfully auditions for the Royal Ballet. What is the theme? It's easy to say the theme is *follow your heart*, but what does that mean? Let's dig deeper; there are social expectations, peer pressure, and stereotypes on the one hand, and there are true passion, authenticity, and hard work on the other. Also, there are allies along the way: the friend who believes in Billy and supports him unconditionally and the ballet instructor, who recognizes Billy's talent, trains him secretly, and encourages him to audition. If you look beyond the actual plot—the specific characters and events—what *Billy Elliot* boils down to is a *power struggle* between the *outwardly expected* and the *inwardly desired*. This power struggle complicates the simplistic idea of following your heart and is essential to a full understanding of the theme. The tension between what others want for you and what you want for yourself is familiar to most people and thus has a huge potential for personal resonance; you are told you should wear dresses as a girl and play with dolls, but you really want to wear pants and play soccer. You are told you should become a dentist like your father, but you really want to be an artist and paint landscapes. You have been brought up to believe that playing is for children and that, as an adult, you have to be serious, responsible, and suppress your goofy side (as if those things were mutually exclusive!). You got the message that your emotional nature is a weakness and that you need to be rational and analytical.

Thinking about the theme in terms of its abstract structure (instead of its concrete manifestation in a specific story) is the first step to designing theme-based games that take the specific characteristics of the medium into account rather than just portraying the theme through story elements and audiovisual design, which may not become tangible in the actual moment-to-moment gameplay. Let's continue to interrogate the *Billy Elliot* theme with the help of the IGD. How could we go about designing a game that captures the theme of *Billy Elliot* without retelling the story? What is the abstract structure of the theme, and what are its essential elements?

We have already determined that there are two sides that are engaged in a power struggle: the outside and the inside, society's expectations, and the individual's desire at odds with these expectations. Why is that a problem, though? Conflict is related to one's goals. There are two goals at work in our theme: self-fulfillment and personal happiness on the one hand and the wish for approval and appreciation through others on the other hand. These two goals are incompatible, which constitutes the conflict. If we just leave it at that, we have a broken system, an impasse; we are stuck. Many people, in fact, do get stuck in the power struggle between outside expectations and inner desire, which might be a reason why books or movies that portray the successful navigation of these issues are so powerful; they show that there is hope and might even provide a model for how to move forward (or, in the case of a bad outcome, they make us aware of how much is at stake when we suppress our desires!). What does it take to positively resolve the conflict? A productive question in that regard is to ask about the win condition. Does the win condition depend on achieving self-fulfillment *and* getting society's approval for it? (This is the best-case scenario and the outcome of *Billy Elliot*.) Or is it enough to leave the concern for society's approval behind and follow one's heart regardless of what others think? In any case, a positive resolution privileges self-fulfillment over external approval. The lose condition by implication is the suppression of personal desires for the sake of acceptance and belonging (or because there is simply no other perceivable choice).

Stories that present this outcome to the power struggle between external expectations and internal desires often end in the main character's suicide (e.g., *Dead Poets' Society*). What can shift the conflict in one direction or another? What is the main resource that can tilt the scales in favor of self-fulfillment or submission? How about *inner drive* or *passion*? Passion is definitely important if we want to go our own way against big odds. How does passion work as a resource? You start out with a certain amount of passion, but passion—like any emotion—needs to be cultivated, or it will fade over time. You cultivate passion by doing what you are passionate about. If you neglect your passion, it does not simply go away, though; that would solve the problem because you would just stop caring. Suppressed passion, however, turns into regret, resentment, self-loathing, or some other negative, poisonous psychic cocktail. It eventually deadens the soul—an internal death that preceded and promoted Neil's suicide in *Dead Poets' Society*. Another important resource that can positively impact the power struggle is *emotional resilience*. Where does resilience come from? A part might be psychological precondition—some people may just happen to be more resilient than others from the get-go. Another part might be access to a support system. Let's assume that very few people are so radically self-reliant and self-sufficient that they do not need a sense of belonging or appreciation from others at all. (For those people, there probably would not have a conflict to begin with.) Most of us need some kind of encouragement to help us through the hard times— someone who believes in us and cheers us on. In *Billy Elliot*, the friend and the ballet teacher were the support system. Also, the antagonistic forces (family, townspeople)—while powerful—were not as overbearing in *Billy Elliot* as Neil's father in *Dead Poets' Society*. Billy Elliot still found ways to cultivate his passion by dancing secretly and working toward his goal of joining the Royal Ballet, whereas Neil's father extinguished Neil's opportunity to act.

Thinking of the theme in terms of the elements that constitute its abstract structure both clarifies it and facilitates the translation of the theme into a game, because games are essentially systems. By interrogating the *Billy Elliot* theme with the help of the IGD, the cornerstones of an abstract game system revealed themselves. This is the skeleton onto which we could put flesh by adding a fictional layer, finding a suitable metaphor, and extending the theme to all levels of game design: core mechanics, the way the player interacts with the game in real life (e.g., mouse control, keyboard, joystick, or even body movement, if we create a Kinect game), and audiovisual design. A game based on the *Billy Elliot* theme would allow players to experiment with the power struggle between internal desire and external expectations and to really ponder all the elements at work, rather than playing through a story with one fixed outcome. This potential of exploration is unique to the interactive medium and will be elaborated on in Chapter 2.

It is important to note that every artwork—narrative or not—can have a theme. Some might be more obvious than others, but few artworks are completely random (and, even then, we could appeal to the power of the subconscious that informed the process of creation and infused the piece with thematic substance). We do not need to rely on a story to help make sense of the theme or identify its abstract structure because identifying the theme is only the starting point. A story might help to pinpoint essential elements, but it is not necessary. By channeling your IGD, asking productive questions, and tapping into your personal life experiences, you will be able to find those elements yourself. Also, using themes found in art and media as an inspiration source for games is really just that: inspiration. You do not need to be true to the original piece! If *Billy Elliot*, for some weird reason, makes you think of your great aunt Bertha, who kept her money in a sock underneath the mattress, and the associative chain leads you to ponder frugality, the fear of poverty, or skepticism toward institutions (such as banks), that's fine, too—you stumbled upon a rich material for a deep game!

1.3 Become a Sucker for Other People's Experiences

"How are you?" is one of the most misused phrases in the English language. We say it as a form of greeting—an extended *hello*—rather than as a sincere inquiry about the other's well-being or state of mind. If we want to create powerful and thought-provoking games, we need to expose ourselves to a broad range of experiences (which we then analyze, reflect upon, and dissect with the help of the IGD). But, no matter how much we try, there will always be limits. Some are good and healthy—games are not worth walking down the freeway naked just to know what it's like—other limits are inevitable because we always remain ourselves. We are wired a certain way, and, unless there is some crisis that requires us to change, we usually don't. That does not mean we can't understand somebody else's perspective and see life through someone else's eyes. A good start is to mean it when we ask "How are you?" and then listen closely to the answer. If you want to make deep games, get beyond small talk whenever possible. Have meaningful, in-depth conversations with people. Don't be too shy to ask personal questions. It is not prying if your interest in the other person is authentic, if you care. More often than not, people *want* to talk about themselves. They long for someone who'll listen and try to understand. We live in a world where we think the only appropriate setting to get truly personal is when we pay for it in a therapist's office. But, sometimes, it is really nice to be able to open up in other contexts, possibly even to strangers. If you listen with real sympathy and without judgment, it is amazing what people will confide. With his easy charm and caring nature, Vander Caballero, a creative director at the Canadian game company *Minority Media*, and a pioneer in the development of empathy games such as

Papo & Yo and *Spirits of Spring*, is a master at establishing trust right off the bat, and it is almost impossible to resist his (sometimes explicit, sometimes unspoken) invitation to talk about private matters.

As part of my *deep games* class, a student team was making a game to raise awareness for the social issue of homelessness. They wanted to portray the perspective of a homeless person. None of the students had personal experience with homelessness, though. As part of their homework, I asked them to go speak to a homeless person. They were hesitant at first and understandably so; it takes courage to approach someone, and more so, the bigger the difference between you and the other person. But how could you model the experience of homelessness if you've never been homeless yourself and don't even want to get a homeless person's perspective on it? In the end, they interviewed two homeless people and came back with an enriched and more nuanced understanding of the situation. More importantly, they have learned that talking to people is much less scary than it appears in the beginning and that their interviewees were glad someone took an interest. Of course, there is always a real possibility that someone does not want to be bothered, and that is his or her good right. I'm not advocating for becoming an obnoxious snoop. I'm advocating for the cultivation of a true interest in our fellow human beings and paying attention to them, their stories, and the ways they behave and speak. The latter is sometimes particularly informative. There is plenty of research, mostly from cognitive science and linguistics, that indicates that language is a window into the soul. The everyday metaphors we use reveal how we perceive life.*

I recently came across a group of young women and overheard one of them saying, "I don't know where the fuck that shit's at!" She did not say it as a joke, but neither did she seem particularly upset, and the *shit* she referred to was nothing unpleasant but some restaurant or coffee shop they were trying to find. I can guarantee you that I have no interest in judging her verbiage. My friends (and unfortunately also my students) know I'm no stranger to the occasional, *passionate* expression. But, to the point, what I'm interested in is to understand what motivates such word choice. What is someone's outlook on life who nonchalantly swears like that? Not that I could tell in regard to the young woman whom I overheard. Neither am I trying to make a comprehensive, generalizable claim about the psychology of swearing. But here are

---

*Steven Pinker even wrote a whole book called *The Stuff of Thought: Language as a Window into Human Nature* (2007), but Lakoff and Johnson (1980) and Johnson (1990) have also published extensively about the topic, mostly from the perspective of the bodily foundation of metaphor and how metaphors reveal our conceptual systems.

some musings about the meaning of swearing derived from self-observation, talking to my friends and colleagues, and doing some Internet research on *why we swear*.

Derogative language is devaluating. By using it, we show our detachment, that we don't care, that we are aloof. Not caring serves a purpose. If we don't care, we can't be disappointed or hurt. It's only necessary to appear invulnerable; if we feel vulnerable, there is a lot of (potential) disappointment in our lives, and we want to protect ourselves from it. Apart from the simple release of negative (or even positive!) emotion, swearing is often a defensive strategy. I know a lot of wonderful and very artistic people who swear all the time. They are all also very sensitive. I remember swearing a lot myself. It was when I felt most vulnerable during a painful breakup. It became part of my everyday language, not just reserved for special occasions when you drop a carton of eggs or step into a dog turd. Swearing is a form of putting up a tough front, of distancing yourself. Sometimes, I'm still tempted to swear in front of people who are very proper and/or in a position of authority. In that case, it's a (childish, ineffective) way of trying to arm myself against their potential judgment of me.

Long story short: listening to others and trying to understand how they tick can be a rich source of inspiration for deep game ideas. What would a game look like in which your environment was a minefield of disappointment and personal attacks, and swearing was a core mechanic that protected you from emotional harm? The goal of the game would be to establish a true and meaningful connection with someone, but, to achieve that, you'd need to find a way to deal with your vulnerability, to open yourself up to it and let go of the swearing defense mechanisms. I believe there is a deep game idea here!

Becoming a sucker for other people's experiences can also manifest in a tendency toward psychologically minded literature. I personally love reading books that illuminate people's inner world, such as Alison Bechdel's graphic novels *Are You My Mother?* (2012) and *Fun Home* (2007). These works explained a lot to me about family dynamics and how they impact psychological development. Julia Kristeva's opus *Black Sun* (1992) and William Styron's *Darkness Visible* (1992) complemented my research on the experience of depression, when I was working on *Elude*—a game that aims to communicate to friends and relatives of people with depression what it is like to struggle with this mood disorder. Gail Hornstein's *Agnes' Jacket* (2009) and Louis Sass' *Madness and Modernism* (1994) are impressive and insightful investigations of the hard-to-grasp and multifaceted phenomenon of psychosis. Every term, I have at least one student who wants to make a game with a schizophrenic antagonist or protagonist. So far, none of these ideas were based on anything but a superficial (or just plain-wrong) understanding of what psychosis is.

Cultivating interest in, respect for, and an understanding of our own and other people's experiences is an essential precondition for the creation of games that tackle a wider range of emotions and provide insights into the human condition. Looking for themes in art and media, paying attention to fellow humans, engaging in deep conversations, and doing research are all helpful tools in making sense of the thoughts and feelings that shape our inner landscapes. Before it makes sense to worry about a single mechanic and how to use games' specific means to convey salient aspects of the human experience to players, we need to have a good grasp on this experience in the first place. The following exercises aim to promote self-knowledge, the knowledge of others, and finding inspiration for deep game ideas. They are classroom tested but can certainly be adjusted as needed.

EXERCISES

The following exercises only differ in regard to their method of finding inspiration for deep game ideas. The process of exploration remains the same.

OPTION 1: SELF-EXPLORATION

Step 1: Tools—For 2 to 3 weeks, use *The Artist's Way* tools described in Sections 1.1.1 and 1.1.2 (morning pages and artist date). It is important to do them regularly and conscientiously. Do not reread anything you wrote for the duration of this time.

Step 2: Personal themes—After 2 to 3 weeks, go back through your notes, and try to identify the personal themes that seem most salient to you. What has been on your mind lately? Write down keywords to capture those themes, e.g., moving houses, visiting relatives, taking more time for myself, feeling adventurous with nowhere to go, relationship ready for next level?, hating my job, and feeling misunderstood all the time.

Step 3: Conversation with IGD—Pick the theme with the strongest personal resonance. Explore it, writing down the dialogue with your IGD. Focus on the goal, conflict, and win-and-lose condition to get a better sense for what that theme is all about. If you do this conscientiously, this dialogue will fill several pages.

Step 4: Report—Write a one-page report on your findings. State the theme you picked in the beginning, and summarize what you have learned about it through the conversation with the IGD.

Step 5: Archive—Keep the written dialogue and the summary page in your game design journal. Repeat this exercise as often as you'd like. This will become a rich source for deep game ideas and a solid starting point for turning personal themes into rules and mechanics.

Step 6: Design—At a later time, revisit these ideas, and turn them into playable game prototypes. Make sure the themes are captured in the game's actual rules and mechanics. The later chapters will provide guidance about this process and provide a series of questions to help you create a vision for the game you want to make and stay on track during development.

OPTION 2: TRACING THE HUMAN EXPERIENCE IN ART AND MEDIA

Step 1: Select—Pick a (children's) book, movie, poem, art piece, song, etc., you feel really passionate about (either love it or hate it).

Step 2: Theme—What is the art or media piece about? Try to find one word to identify the theme.

Repeat steps 3 through 6 from option 1.

OPTION 3: ART-INSPIRED MECHANICS

Step 1: Visit a museum of contemporary art.

Step 2: Be a super-aware visitor. Do the following:

- Read the descriptions that accompany the artworks.
- Ask yourself: what themes can you identify in the exhibit?
- Take notes on anything that seems interesting, curious, and inspiring to you.

Repeat steps 3 through 6 from option 1.

References

Bechdel, A. 2007. *Fun Home: A Family Tragicomic.* Boston and New York: A Mariner Book.

Bechdel, A. 2012. *Are You My Mother? A Comic Drama.* New York: Houghton Mifflin.

Cameron, J. 2002. *The Artist's Way: A Spiritual Path to Higher Creativity.* New York: Tarcher/Putnam.

Curtis, H. 2002. *MTIV (Making the Invisible Visible): Process, Inspiration and Practice for the New Media Designer.* Indianapolis, IN: New Riders Publishing.

Elkins, J. 2004. *Pictures & Tears: A History of People Who Have Cried in Front of Paintings.* New York: Routledge.

Hornstein, G. 2009. *Agnes' Jacket: A Psychologist's Search for the Meaning of Madness.* New York: Rodale Books.

Johnson, M. 1990. *The Body in the Mind. The Bodily Basis of Meaning, Imagination and Reason.* Chicago and London: University of Chicago Press.

Kristeva, J. 1989. *Black Sun: Depression and Melancholia.* New York: Columbia University Press.

Lakoff, G. and Johnson, M. 1980. *Metaphors We Live By.* London and Chicago: University of Chicago Press.

Pinker, S. 2007. *The Stuff of Thought: Language as a Window into Human Nature.* New York: Penguin.

Sass, L. 1994. *Madness and Modernism: Insanity in the Light of Modern Art, Literature, and Thought.* Cambridge, MA: Harvard University Press.

Schell, J. 2008. *The Art of Game Design: A Book of Lenses.* Boca Raton, FL: CRC Press.

Styron, W. 1990. *Darkness Visible: A Memoir of Madness.* New York: Vintage Books.

2

Games as an Expressive Medium

Wherein it is discussed how games convey meaning and make statements in ways specific to the medium:

- *Starting with the definition of a "game,"*
- *Moving on to an in-depth exploration of the role of rules and fiction in the process of meaning generation,*
- *Establishing a representational hierarchy of rules over fiction when it comes to identifying the games' main vehicle for meaning,*
- *Thus suggesting that thinking of games as "simulations" when it comes to meaning generation is more medium specific than thinking of them as "narratives,"*
- *And, finally, identifying the differences between "procedural expression" (communicating ideas through rules) and "procedural rhetoric" (communicating an agenda through rules).*

2.1 Introduction

Now that we have some strategies to identify deep ideas, we can start to explore how to turn them into deep games. As Jesse Schell remarked in *The Art of Game Design* (2008), the experience is not the game yet. There is no way to directly convey an experience to someone else. Whether you use language, visuals, rules, or mechanics, you *mediate* the experience to share it with others. According to the Oxford English Dictionary, the word "medium" is Latin for "middle." In regard to communication, it denotes something that is *in the middle* between a sender and a receiver. "Immediate" means "without a medium" and applies only to what we are able to experience firsthand. As such, we can experience the playing of a game immediately but not the experience that is modeled in the game. To intentionally, deliberately, and effectively turn deep ideas into deep games—insightful, thought-provoking, and emotionally rich experiences—we need to understand games as an expressive and conceptual medium. Let's start by asking, what are games?

2.2 What Are Games?

There are myriads of game definitions. In his article "The Game, the Player, the World: Looking for a Heart of Gameness" (2003), game scholar Jesper Juul provides an overview of the most prominent ones as a starting point to articulate his own. The game definition I gravitate toward is Katie Salen & Eric Zimmerman's (2004): "A game is a system in which players engage in an artificial conflict, defined by rules, that results in a quantifiable outcome" (p. 80). This definition allows games the most breathing room (which is important for a still-evolving medium) but covers the basics of what they all have in common and enables a productive discussion about their medium-specific characteristics: their systemic, rule-based nature and the fact that they have some kind of conflict for the player to overcome and a clear way of assessing whether this has happened successfully or not. Let's explore the main terms of this definition a bit further; Donella Meadows, the author of *Thinking in Systems* (2004), defines systems as

> [A]n interconnected set of elements that is coherently organized in a way that achieves something. If you look at that definition closely for a minute, you can see that a system must consist of three kinds of things: *elements, interconnections* and a *function* or *purpose*. (p. 11)

Conveniently for us, she goes on to explain systems by way of a football team. The elements are players, coach, field, and ball.

> Its interconnections are the rules of the game, the coach's strategy, the communications of the players, the laws of physics that govern the motions of ball and players. The purpose of the team is to win games, or have fun, or get exercise, or make a million dollars, or all of the above. (p. 11)

Artificial conflict, in its most basic sense, means that, when playing a game, we expose ourselves to problems we would not have otherwise, e.g., it is easy to put a billiard ball into the table pocket, but, if we submit to the rules of the game of *Pool*, this task suddenly becomes difficult, creating an artificial conflict for us—a conflict that is created by the rules of the game. I understand *conflict* or *challenge* very broadly, though. *Gone Home* is a game in which you navigate through a house and collect notes and other story pieces that slowly uncover the reason why no one's home to greet you in the middle of the night, when you return after a year abroad. There are no enemies and very few puzzles in the game. However, I argue that there is conflict because the easiest way would be to just find one note in the beginning that explained everything. The conflict lies in finding the information pieces and putting them together to a coherent story in your mind. It's a game of narrative comprehension, and the challenge lies in filling the gaps and making sense of it all.

Lastly, Salen and Zimmerman's game definition mentions a *quantifiable outcome*. *Quantifiable* means that something can be measured or counted. In this case, it refers to how the game interprets the player's interaction with the rule system, which is either clearly successful or clearly not, 0 or 1; there are no gray areas. You either hit the target, or you missed. You either found the object, or you didn't. On the larger scale, it means that the game's conflict is either overcome or not; you win, or you lose. We will come back to this definition of games later and explore how it informs a medium-specific understanding of how games generate meaning and communicate ideas.

2.3 How Can Games Be *about Something*?

The whole notion of a *deep game* (in the way it is defined here) rests on the assumption that games can be about something: that they can have themes and topics and communicate ideas, make statements, and provide insights into matters beyond the game itself. A game that is about something is *representational* in one way or another—it represents the aspects of a real or imagined world. Its various elements have meaning beyond the context of the game. Not every game is about something. Some games are *nonrepresentational*.

To get a better sense of how games can represent and how their representational aspect is related to their about-ness, let's consider a few different games that are representational in different ways and to different degrees: (a) the ancient Chinese board game *Go*, (b) the classic board game *Chess*, (c) the popular casual game *Candy Crush*, (d) Rod Humble's art game *The Marriage* (Figure 2.1), and (e) the horror survival game *Silent Hill—Restless Dreams* (also referred to as *Silent Hill 2*). Which of these games are nonrepresentational?

Which are representational? How do the representational games represent? What is the relationship between their representational aspect and their meaning? And, last but not the least, how *do* we determine what games *really* are about, and how do we *design for meaning*?

By answering these questions, we will get a better sense for games as expressive and conceptual tools, their medium-specific characteristics, and how we can use them deliberately to tackle the human experience.

2.3.1 *Representation, Abstraction, Fiction, and Rules*

In the interest of building a common vocabulary that helps us talk about games and their characteristics, it is helpful to define essential terms in the discussion about how games generate meaning: representation, abstraction, fiction, and rules.

A game's representational quality is most obvious (although, as we will see later, not exclusive) on its (audio-) visual level, or what is commonly called

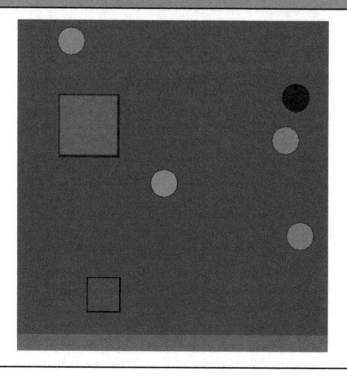

FIGURE 2.1
Rod Humble's *The Marriage*

the game's *fiction*. According to the game scholar Jesper Juul (2005), "most video games also project a *fictional world*: the player controls a character; the game takes place in a city, in a jungle, or anywhere else" (p. 121). Juul goes on to state that "[s]uch fictional game worlds, obviously, do not actually exist; they are worlds that the game presents and the player imagines" (p. 121). I would like to note that the term *fiction in games* is used not just for nonexistent, imagined worlds but also to describe the representation of real places. The depiction of various locations in a documentary game about World War II would still be referred to as the game's fiction, even though those places truly exist, and the playable scenarios actually took place. Generally, we can say that games that feature (audio-) visual representations of environments, characters, and/or items of real or imagined worlds have a fictional layer. Juul (2005) further distinguishes between fiction and storytelling:

> *Fiction* is commonly confused with *storytelling*. I am using fiction to mean any kind of imagined world, whereas, briefly stated, a story is a fixed sequence of events that is presented (enacted or narrated) to a user. Herman Melville's *Moby Dick* is a story and a fiction, whereas a painting such as Georges Suerat's *La Grande Jatte* is a fiction but not a story since it only presents one moment in time. (p. 12)

Games whose game objects—i.e., any isolatable entity that can interact with other entities in the game (see Begy 2013)—depict aspects of real or imagined worlds thus have a fictional layer and are representational, at least on this visual level. Of the five example games in Section 2.3, *Chess*, *Candy Crush*, and *Silent Hill 2* have a fictional component and qualify as representational. *Chess*' game objects, while stylized, represent existing things. As Bogost (2009) describes in his Gamasutra article "Persuasive Games: Puzzling the Sublime,"

> *Chess*, for example, clearly draws inspiration form military conflict, not only because of its historical lineage and mechanics of capture, but also thanks to its named, carved pieces. When a knight takes a pawn, it's easy to relate the gesture to combat.

Silent Hill 2 has a strong fictional component and very clearly depicts an imagined world with its environments (the little town Silent Hill), characters (the player character James Sunderland, his dead wife Mary, the mysterious Maria, and enemies such as Pyramid Head, mannequin dolls, etc.), and various items (e.g., radio, crowbar, gun, flashlight). The game objects in *Candy Crush*, as the name indicates, are different kinds of candy. Although the game's fictional aspect is deemphasized—there is no sense of place, and, apart from candies, no other aspects of a gameworld are represented—candies as game objects are representational. What about *Go* and *The Marriage*? Bogost (2009) writes about *Go* in comparison to *Chess:*

> *Go* is somewhat harder to characterize. As philosophers Gilles Deleuze and FÃ©lix [sic!] Guattari wrote of the game, "Go pieces, in contrast [to chess], are pellets, disks, simple arithmetic units, and have only an anonymous, collective, or third-person function: 'It' makes a move. 'It' could be a man, a woman, a louse, an elephant.

It is safe to say that *Go* does not have a fictional level, and *Go* pieces do not represent aspects of a real or imagined world. The same is true for *The Marriage's* game objects. Like in *Go*, where the pellets could just as well be "a man, a woman, a louse, an elephant," there is no compelling reason for the use of circles and squares in *The Marriage*. According to Jason Begy (2013), both *Go* and *The Marriage* are *abstract* games: "Abstract games are those in which the game objects are not signs in the game's fiction, or, if they are, they operate primarily in the symbolic mode." Does that mean that neither *Go* nor *The Marriage*—despite its title that indicates that the game is about a marriage—are representational games?

To disentangle the relationship between representation and abstraction in games, which is important for our further discussion on how games generate meaning and communicate ideas, we need to have a look at Peirce's sign modalities. Charles Sanders Peirce, a semiotician—i.e., someone who studies signs and how they convey meaning—mentions three sign modalities: (1) iconic, (2) indexical, and (3) symbolic. Each sign is constituted of three elements: (1) the *representamen* (the form the sign takes, e.g., the word *table*, or a traffic light), (2) the *interpretant* (how the sign is interpreted), and (3) the *object* (that which the sign refers to). The sign's modality—what kind of sign it is—is defined by the relationship between these three sign aspects. In symbolic mode, the relation between the representamen and the object is arbitrary. According to Peirce (1998), symbols "have become associated with their meaning by usage" (p. 5). Music notes are symbolic. There is no intrinsic connection whatsoever between the sign of the note *c* and the piano key it refers to or the sound it makes. Most words are symbolic. There is no reason why the object *table* should be referred to as table, and we only know what table means because the word is used, by the agreement of a language community, to refer to the object.

In iconic mode, the representamen resembles the object. Iconic signs "serve to convey ideas of the things they represent simply by imitating them" (Peirce 1998, p. 5). A picture of a table is an icon, and so are imitative gestures, such as making a punching motion to support a story about a boxing match. Words that sound like the thing they represent (onomatopoeia) are icons, too. *Sizzle* is such a word. It imitates the sound the contents of a hot frying pan make.

Lastly, we have indexical signs in which the relation between the representamen and the object is neither arbitrary nor imitative, but they "show something about things on account of their being physically connected with them" (Peirce 1998, p. 5). Smoke is an index for fire; sweat is an index for heat; footprints are indexical signs; and so are measuring devices that indicate temperature (thermometer) or time (clocks). Lastly, it needs to be noted that we can understand signs only if we are familiar with the code within which they function—"the framework within which signs make sense" (Chandler 2007, p. 147). For example, we only know that the word table refers to the object table if we have access to the code, which is the English language. According to Begy (2013), "game objects can operate as signs that signify through both the game fiction and the rules." Like him, I will use the term *fiction-sign* when considering how the game object operates as a sign in the game's fiction and *rule-sign* when considering how it operates as a sign in the rule system.

Let's take another look at *Go* and *The Marriage:* if we consider *Go*'s stones as rule-signs, the stone is the representamen, and the object is the set of rules that govern its behavior. The relationship between the stone and behavior in the game is arbitrary; the stones are symbolic rule-signs. Begy (2013) states, "But if the stones are taken as fiction-signs, it becomes apparent that they are not signs at all: they are simply stones that do not represent anything. Thus, Go is an abstract game because its objects do *not* function as fiction-signs." Begy (2013) writes about *The Marriage:*

> [T]he objects here operate as symbolic rules-signs: there is no relation between their form and their function. However, these objects do function as fiction-signs as well. According to Rod Humble, the pink square represents the female in the marriage, and the blue square, the male. What differentiates these signs from chess pieces is that they are *symbolic* fiction-signs: the relationship between their form and what they represent is arbitrary. (...) As such, *The Marriage* is an abstract game.

What is noteworthy about this discussion of *Go* and *The Marriage* is how the existence or absence of a fictional layer is determined. *Go* is simply claimed to have none, and, in regard to *The Marriage*, we are supposed to take Rod Humble's word for it. Couldn't we just as well claim that the *Go* stones also represent male and female characters, or good and evil? Possibly, but can we make a convincing argument for it? In the case of *The Marriage*, the rules themselves back up the existence of a fiction. While the visual surface is abstract, the game really is *about* something. The rules are only symbolic in regard to the game objects—the circles and squares—but they are *iconic* in regard to that which the game objects represent! According to Rod Humble (2007), "The game is my expression of how a marriage feels," and the rules imitate the dynamics between him and his wife. His Website features a detailed breakdown of the rules and an interpretation of their meaning: http://www.rodvik.com/rodgames/marriage.html.

If the definition of an abstract game is that its game objects are either not signs in the game's fiction at all or only have a symbolic connection to the fiction, then the definition of a representational game is that there is an iconic relationship either between the game objects and the game's fiction or between the game rules and that which the game objects (iconic or symbolic) represent. As such, out of our five example games, only *Go* is truly nonrepresentational. *Chess, Silent Hill*, and *Candy Crush* are representational on the fictional level. *Silent Hill 2* is representational on the fictional and rules level because the relation between the game objects and their in-game behavior is iconic, and *The Marriage* is only representational on the rules level. Table 2.1 shows the relationships between abstraction and representation in games by taking into account whether the game is representational on the rules level, the fictional level, or neither. By sorting our five example games into these categories, we can see whether and, if so, how they are representational, e.g., *Silent Hill 2* is representational on the fictional and rules level. *Go* is neither representational on the fictional nor the rules level.

TABLE 2.1
Representational versus Nonrepresentational

	Representational		Nonrepresentational
	Fictional Level	*Rules Level*	
Abstract	–	The Marriage	Go
Fiction	Silent Hill 2	Silent Hill 2	–
	Candy Crush		
	Chess		

2.3.2 Representational Hierarchy in Games: Rules before Fiction

As argued in Section 2.3.1, games can be representational on the fictional and rules level. The following explores how both levels relate to each other and the role they play for a game's meaning, its *about*-ness. When asked how games communicate ideas and convey thought-provoking, insightful, and emotionally rich experiences, many people think about the fictional level first: the look and feel of the game, the story, the characters, the animations, music, sound effects, and cut scenes. This is no surprise because, as stated in Section 2.3.1, the fictional level is the most obvious and easily accessible, and, traditionally, it has indeed been the sole source for riveting media experiences. When Steven Spielberg made his famous claim that games would have reached maturity as storytelling media when "somebody confesses that they cried at level 17," his claim implied that the way to make more emotionally compelling games was by way of their fictional component: the story and characters. After all, empathy for the hero or heroine has been cinema's main way of enhancing our understanding of ourselves, the human condition. But what has worked in traditional media simply does not work the same way in games (Grodal 2000).

If we compare *The Marriage* and *Candy Crush* one more time, it becomes obvious that the dominant way in which games generate meaning is not through fiction but rather through the rules. The lack of a fiction does not render *The Marriage* meaningless, and the existence of one does not turn *Candy Crush* into a game about candy. *Candy Crush*—despite depicting candy on the fictional level—isn't really about candy, is it? If it were, wouldn't you expect the game to somehow capture salient aspects of candy, e.g., its sweetness, stickiness, how it can give you energy but also challenge your pancreas and cause cavities? The relationship between *Candy Crush*'s game objects (the candies) and their rules, however, is arbitrary. The game objects might be iconic fiction-signs, but they are symbolic rule-signs. In no way do the rules model the behavioral aspects of real candy. During gameplay, it is thus easy to forget that *Candy Crush*'s game objects are candies at all because the rules are so disconnected from the fiction. What this game really is about is pattern matching. You can match candies, but you could just as well be matching buttons, beetles, pebbles, or…jewels.

Admittedly, the fiction in *Candy Crush* couldn't be flimsier, and it seems unfair to use this example to discuss the importance of fiction in games in general. The point, however, is not that fiction in games is unimportant. The point is that it is not the primary vehicle for meaning generation and that, when the rules and fiction are in conflict with each other, or at least the fiction is not supported by the rules, it will recede into the background. Psychology helps us understand why. Bear with me as I am building up my argument for why the rules level trumps the fictional level. According to Jesper Juul (2005), video games are *half-real:*

> Video games are *real* in that they consist of real rules with which players actually interact, and in that winning or losing a game is a real event. However, when winning a game by slaying a dragon, the dragon is not a real dragon, but a fictional one. To play a video game is therefore to interact with real rules while imagining a fictional world, and a video game is a set of rules as well as a fictional world. (p. 1)

Jonathan Frome (2006) calls the emotions evoked by a game's fiction *represented-world emotions* and the emotions evoked by the engagement with the rule system *game emotions:*

> Represented-world emotions are simply those that are generated by the world represented in the artwork, including the characters, situations and narrative events. This category includes most ordinary responses to popular films and books, such as happiness that Rocky Balboa wins the heavyweight title in *Rocky II* (1979), frustration with Rorschach's unyielding Manichaean morality in the graphic novel *Watchmen* (DC Comics, 1987), or concern for the minimum-wage workers profiled in *Nickel and Dimed* (Enrenreich, 2001). (…) Game emotions are emotions of competition; the emotions generated due to winning, losing, accomplishment, and frustration. (p. 18)

According to Frijda's law of apparent reality, "emotions are evoked exclusively by events that are appraised as real and their intensity corresponds to the degree to which this is the case" (Tan 1996, p. 67). Now, let's put these three observations together: since the rules level of games has a higher reality status than the fictional level (*winning and losing are real events*), game emotions are stronger than fictional-world emotions. A game's fiction becomes a powerful emotion machine if it piggybacks on the more immediate game emotions during moment-to-moment gameplay. The fiction then serves to contextualize the mechanics, adding another compatible layer of meaning to the rules. This is the case in games that we commonly perceive as powerful because of its fiction, like *The Last of Us*. This game most definitely benefits enormously from awesome graphics, a compelling storyline, and brilliant characters. I claim, though, that the game's emotional impact is not due to the fiction alone. It is also due to the successful integration of rules and fiction so that both levels of meaning generation leverage each other instead of getting into each other's way. In games, the fiction alone cannot effectively communicate ideas, but the rules can. As Soren Johnson (2013) states,

> Ultimately, designers need to recognize that a game's [fictional] theme does not determine its meaning. Instead, meaning emerges from the game's mechanics – the set of decisions and consequences unique to each one. What does a game ask of the player? What does it punish and what does it reward? What strategies and styles does the game encourage? Answering these questions reveals what a game is actually about. Furthermore, while people buy games for the promise of the theme ("I want to be a space marine!"), the fun comes from the mechanics themselves. When there is a severe dissonance between the two, players can feel cheated, as if the designers executed a bait-and-switch.

Even games with amazing fictional worlds and great storylines can fall flat in regard to integrating rules and fiction and delivering on their main themes, as Clint Hocking (2009) laments in his insightful article on the "Ludonarrative Dissonance in Bioshock: The Problem of What the Game Is About."

2.3.3 Games as Simulations

From Section 2.2, we know that games are defined as rule-based systems in which players engage in artificial conflict with quantifiable outcome. "From Sections 2.3.1 and 2.3.2 we know that games can be representational—about something—on the rules and fictional level, and that the primary vehicle for meaning in games is the rules level. This suggests that the most productive way to approach games as expressive and conceptual media—media that can communicate ideas; make statements; and convey thought-provoking, insightful, and emotionally rich experiences—is to think of them as *simulations* (rather than narratives). Gonzalo Frasca (2001, 2003), a game researcher, designer, and ludologist, has written extensively about the subject of games as simulations and presented the simulationist approach as an alternative to the narrative approach that viewed games as an extension of storytelling media. He defines simulation as follows:

> To simulate is to model a (source) system through a different system which maintains (for somebody) some of the behaviors of the original system. (Frasca 2003, p. 223)

Nonrepresentational games (as defined in Section 2.3.1) are systems, but not simulations. For games to qualify as a simulation, they need to model aspects of a real or imagined world (what he calls the *source* system). They do not need to be representational on the fiction level. As long as the game's rules are derived from a source system, the graphics can be abstract. *The Marriage* counts as a simulation game because the rules model the dynamics of a marriage (= source system). *Go* is not a simulation game because the rules do not model a source system. Games can be perceived as simulations by their players without the designer's intent to model a source system. (When that happens, it is due to a process of metaphorical projection.) This is quite interesting and shall be discussed in Chapter 4. To further clarify the definition of simulation, Begy adds the notion of communication: "the simulation must communicate to the player that it is based on another system in some manner" (2013). I agree with this addendum. For example, while abstract, *The Marriage* communicates its about-ness through the title. This is an important interpretative clue that prompts a reading of the game rules as iconic rule-signs in regard to the source system that they model. Without this prompt, it would be much harder to connect the game's rules to what they represent.

Deep games, as understood here, are simulations. Their source systems are aspects of the human experience, which they model with rules and mechanics. Some might feature elaborate fictions (e.g., *Spirits of Spring*, a game about bullying; see Figure 2.2); others might be fairly simplistic (e.g., *Passage*, a game about companionship) or even abstract (e.g., *Lim*, a game about the violence of blending in; see Figure 2.3).

I do not claim that the simulationist approach is the only possible approach to making games that effectively tackle the human condition and teach us something about ourselves. I do believe, though, that it taps into the medium-specific strengths of games and allows for unique experiences no other medium could provide. Before we apply the idea of simulation to the design of deep games, I'd like to give a general introduction on how simulation generates meaning, communicates ideas, and even persuades.

2.3.3.1 Simulations Are Not Objective—They Express a Point of View The fact that simulations model source systems might suggest a certain objectivity—that simulation games merely depict *what is there* and *how it works*. This is not true for several reasons. Understanding these reasons will shed some light on a simulation game's expressive potential. First of all, even if the source system exists in the real world, there is a degree of subjectivity in our perception of it. We never see reality *as is*. We always only see *our* reality. Unless we suffer from a severe mental illness, our perceptions are certainly not completely

idiosyncratic—we share large parts of them with others, or we could not coinhabit social spaces and arrive at any kind of agreement about them. Still, everything we experience has been prefiltered by our senses and interpreted by our brain and is not the raw, objective truth anymore. Just think about how many people with cowboy boots you suddenly see when you are looking to buy a pair yourself. Or, when I was pregnant, it seemed like the whole female population of Chicago was pregnant at the same time! Our state of mind shapes what we pay attention to and what stands out to us in our environment. As the Austrian philosopher Ludwig Wittgenstein (1922) observed, "The world of the happy is quite different from the world of the unhappy."

FIGURE 2.3
Merritt Kopas' *Lim*

The subjectivity of experience alone calls into question the possibility of an objective representation of any kind of source system. As Ian Bogost (2007) writes,

> [...] meaning in videogames is constructed not through a re-creation of the world, but through selectively modeling appropriate elements of that world. Procedural representation models only some subset of a source system, in order to draw attention to that portion as the subject of the representation. (p. 46)

Juul (2007) calls the modeling of "some subset of a source system" *abstraction*. This is different from our definition of *abstract games* in Section 2.3.1, which referred to game objects as either not being game-fiction signs at all or only symbolic ones. Juul explains what abstraction means in simulation games. According to him, video games always have "a certain level of abstraction" (2007, p. 510). For one, the designer always has to decide which aspects of the gameworld shall be represented on screen and, further, which aspects of the world shall be implemented into the rule system.

> If we assume the perspective that games have two complementary elements of *rules* and *fiction* all content in the game can either be purely fictional and not implemented in the rules system (such as in the case of a game's back story), purely rules and unexplained by the fiction (such as the multiple lives of a player), or in the zone in between where the rules of the game are motivated by the game's fiction (cars that can drive, birds that can fly, etc.) [...] The combination of rules and fiction is sometimes described as *virtual* or *simulation*. The level of abstraction concerns the border between the content that is purely fictional and the content that is presented in the fiction as well as implemented in the rules of a game. (Juul 2007, p. 510)

The process of abstraction includes highlighting certain aspects of an experience and hiding others. The designer makes a deliberate decision about which elements of the real or imagined world shall be implemented into the rule system and which shall remain purely fictional. She also determines the degree of detail to which actions are available to the player. When abstracting, game designers adopt a certain perspective toward an experience and shape the virtual part of the gameworld (i.e., the part that is implemented into the rule system) according to what they define as crucial to the experience they want to convey and what is neglectable. (Conscious muscle movement might not be essential to the experience of cooking; adding the right ingredients, stirring, and regulating the heat at the right time are. However, if the game should convey the experience of cooking from the perspective of an Alzheimer's patient, then maybe conscious control of body parts becomes an essential element.)

Not only does our state of mind impact which system elements stand out to us in a source system; it also further determines our interpretation of causal relationships between system elements. Especially when we talk about complex socioeconomical, ecological, and psychological systems, people's assumptions about how things are connected can deviate enormously. If we are depressed, we do not just focus on the negative; we furthermore might believe everything is our fault, that our friends don't really want to have anything to do with us because we are not lovable, and that making even the smallest mistake will ruin our reputation forever. If we are very critical of capitalism/communism, we will see money/communism as the source of all evil everywhere. No matter our worldview, it will influence how we perceive source systems, which elements are highlighted for us, and how they are connected by rules.

Simulation games are thus not more objective than any other medium. What they contain within their rules and mechanics, as well as their fictional world, is based on an author's choices, and these choices—willingly or not— reflect an author's point of view on the (real or imagined) source system, his or her values, and beliefs.*

To acknowledge the authorial voice of the designers of simulation games, Frasca (2003) coined the term *simauthor*. The following brief case study aims to illustrate how even very mundane simulation games communicate ideas within their rule systems.

2.3.3.2 Case Studies

2.3.3.2.1 Diner Dash—Flo on the Go by Game Lab   Diner Dash—Flo on the Go (*DD*) is a two-dimensional (2D) strategy/time management game about being a waitress. The source system it models is a restaurant. The main system elements are Flo, the waitress (player character), the customers who need to be seated, the orders that need to be taken, the food that needs to be served, the dirty dishes that need to be cleared off tables, the bill that needs to be brought, and the (better or worse) tip that is received after a job (more or less) well done. For a simulation to also qualify as a game, there needs to be some kind of a goal and a conflict. The goal in *DD* is to get as many tips as possible, which depends on customer satisfaction. Customer satisfaction depends on the following variables: how promptly customers are seated; whether they are seated according to their preferences; and how quickly their orders are taken, their food is being served, their table is cleared, and their check is brought. There are different types of customers—e.g., businesspeople, tourists, families, lovebirds, seniors, bookworms, joggers, young ladies—with different attributes (e.g., varying degrees of patience, noise tolerance, willingness to tip well, the desire for privacy). These elements and their relationships to each other add up to a pretty complex system from which arises the conflict of getting all tasks done as efficiently as possible while accounting for the customer's individual preferences and ensuring their utmost satisfaction.

Everyone who has ever waitressed (or even possesses moderate imagination) will find *DD* to be a pretty accurate representation of what waitressing is like. It hardly feels like anything has been left out because the simauthors did an excellent job at focusing on what was most important about waitressing, translated that into rules, and thus enabled to evoke the essence of the experience.

---

*Mary Flanagan (2009, p. 223), the founder of Tiltfactor Laboratory and the initiator of the *Values at Play* research project, notes, "As a cultural medium, games carry embedded beliefs within their systems of representation and their structures, whether game designers intend these ideologies or not."

What has made its way into the final product looks like an obvious choice, but the game could also have taken quite a different form. The simauthors could have decided to concentrate on modeling hurting feet, increasing exhaustion during a long shift, working for minimal wage, suffering from an abusive boss, and actually dreaming of a different career from waitressing, which, for one reason or another, is not getting off the ground but slowly reduces the player character's ability to put up with customers' crap day in and day out. All of this is a reality for many people in this profession; none of it made it into *DD*. *DD* portrays a hectic yet very satisfying take on waitressing—waitressing is fun, and, if you do everything right, you make good money! Playing the game feels great once you get the hang of seating customers, taking orders, bringing food, clearing tables, and bringing the check in the most efficient way. The rules of the game further make statements about the different types of customers. (That there are types instead of individual people with individual personalities is a necessary abstraction to make the game playable at all. It would be so confusing if you had to figure out each customer's likes/dislikes anew and impossible to get better at satisfying customer's needs if they keep changing on you.) For example, businesswomen are impatient but tip well and hate noise (including crying babies); joggers are moderately patient, and immune to noise due to wearing headphones, but never order dessert. These behavioral traits might seem to make a lot of sense (as most clichés do), but they are not objective truths. It was a simauthor's choice to not define joggers as people who reward themselves with ice cream after a good run, and to not portray businesswomen as patient, family friendly, and music loving.

Admittedly, *DD* does not provide mind-blowing insights or overwhelm us with thought-provoking ideas, but, as stated before, that's exactly why I picked it to start the discussion about a simulation's expressive potential: that, despite the game's mundane topic, it still offers a specific and deliberately chosen point of view on the subject of waitressing and contains claims within its rules. Let's look at another game, one whose primary purpose does not consist of delivering gameplay fun but rather making some meaningful statements about life and the value of companionship: *Passage*.

2.3.3.2.2 Passage by Jason Rohrer   Passage is a simple, single-player 2D game designed by the independent game developer Jason Rohrer (Figure 2.4). It is a game about how life's journey is changed by companionship. It does not take longer than five minutes to play through. It was the first game that touched me deeply and made it irrevocably clear to me how powerful games can be as expressive media that teach us something about the human experience.

FIGURE 2.4
Jason Rohrer's *Passage*

The game space is a rectangular field. You can go up and down, forward and backwards (to an extent), but you only see a small part of your surroundings. The furthest you can see in any direction is forward—like anticipating a linearly progressing future. The more you walk around to see it all and discover the little packages that represent *life experiences*, the more confining the game space starts to feel. Like in life, the realization that you can't see and experience it all is strongest and most painful when you actually try to. The deliberate design of a constrained game space allows this idea to arise dynamically from gameplay (although, admittedly, this depends on the player's perception of this feature. Not all players may find the game space confining, no matter how much they roam around). In the beginning of the game, you can either meet your companion or pass by her and walk through life alone. *Passage* has no predefined win condition, only a suggested goal of collecting as many experience points (the little stars you get from opening the packages) as possible. The conflict is life's literal *deadline*: the game ends after five minutes, regardless of how you decide to spend them. That means the conflict is only a conflict if you actually care about collecting experience points. *Passage* allows you to set your own goal, and, if you decide to just sit there and wait until the game ends, you can do that, too. If you decide to venture out, though, there will be obstacles that interrupt your path (meaning life is rarely a straight line from A to B, and, very often, we have to find an alternative way forward to get where we want to go) and prevent direct access to *experience packages*. Some of these packages become completely inaccessible when you journey with your companion. The pathways leading up to them are simply too narrow to accommodate for two passengers. This represents life experiences that become unavailable once there is someone else, whose dreams and desires need to be accounted for and might not be compatible with one's own. To counterbalance this potential downside, the packages that are opened when you're with your partner give you more experience points than when you are alone. This rule says life is richer when shared with someone. As time passes, the past (the left side of the screen) becomes blurrier and blurrier as memory fades. The future (the space on the right side of the screen) begins to shrink and becomes shrouded in fog. There is not much life left to live. Then, suddenly, your companion, who, like you, has become gray haired and stooped, is suddenly replaced by a small gravestone. You can't turn back. The past is forever gone. You can keep moving up and down, but there is nothing left to discover, and there is no more future, either. No more packages await, meaning life alone is now meaningless and empty. You can also stay right there, next to your companion's gravestone, until you turn into one yourself. That's what I did.

I was and still am incredibly touched by this game, but some people I've seen playing it complain that, once you run into the companion, you're stuck with her. She can't be dumped and prevents you from getting to all the packages. It is noteworthy why people get so annoyed at this because it points toward an important distinction between a simulation game like *DD* that—while containing statements in its rules, is optimized for gameplay and as expressively neutral and uncontroversial as possible—and a game like *Passage*. At first glance, *Passage* might look like an equally neutral simulation of the journey through life because it models some irrefutable truths, such as the past fades, the future dwindles as you get older, and death is inevitable. It offers a possibility space that invites players to explore their own journey through life. It is thus jarring (to some) to realize that the game models the simauthor's subjective experience and that an important choice in real life—ending a relationship one has entered—has been abstracted away. The game does not *belong* to the player in the same way *DD* or other games do, which—while inevitably containing ideas within their rule systems—are not intended to communicate personal messages. Every game constrains the player, but, in *Passage*, the constraints are not primarily to facilitate gameplay fun but to communicate a message. Rohrer uses simulation as a declaration of love for his wife: life is richer and more rewarding with you. Yes, maybe I can't go everywhere with you, but whatever we can do together more than compensates me for that. Once you'll be gone, there will be nothing left to live for. Games that are expressive in that way are often controversial. I find it exciting when players argue about the truth behind a rule or the message it conveys. It points toward this medium's unique potential to generate meaning.

Some games are not satisfied with procedural expression, i.e., making statements with rules. They go a step further and aim to persuade or even change behavior. These games employ what Ian Bogost (2007) called *procedural rhetoric:*

> Procedural rhetoric is a general name for the practice of authoring arguments through processes. Following the classical model, procedural rhetoric entails persuasion – to change opinions or action. Following the contemporary model, procedural rhetoric entails expression – to convey ideas effectively. (...) Procedural rhetorics afford a new way to make claims about *how things work.* (pp. 28–29)

Games are particularly well suited to make persuasive arguments because of their intrinsic vividness and the direct connection between vividness and persuasive potential. Charles Hill states that "vivid information seems to be more persuasive than non-vivid information" and that "images offer greater 'vividness' than verbal narration or written description" (Bogost 2007, p. 34). Bogost (2007), in his discussion of Hill's continuum of vividness, adds,

> [...] procedural representation can muster moving images and sound, and software and videogames are capable of generating moving images in accordance with complex rules that simulate real or imagined physical and cultural processes. Furthermore, procedural representations are often [...] interactive; they rely on user interaction as a mediator, something static and moving images cannot claim to do. These capacities would suggest that procedurality is more vivid than moving images with sound, and thus earns the second spot on the continuum, directly under actual experience. (p. 35)

Procedural rhetoric employs the same expressive devices as other simulation games: they offer a point of view on a source system by selectively modeling salient aspects of it and abstracting away all the rest, and, by defining the relationships between system elements through rules, does make claims about *how things work.* However, these games have an agenda, and their claims on how things work are meant to activate, educate, and transform players in one way or another. The design process of a procedural rhetoric game is thus not primarily guided by a concern for gameplay fun but by the question "What do I want to say? How can I say it with rules and mechanics? And does the message get across to players through moment-to-moment gameplay?" *September 12th* is a popular example for a game that makes a strong statement by leveraging procedural rhetoric.

2.3.3.2.3 September 12th by Gonzalo Frasca September 12th by Gonzalo Frasca has been designed as a critical commentary to the US-led war on terror after the events of September 11 (Figure 2.5). Its main statement is *violence begets violence*, and it makes this statement by inscribing it into the game's rule system. The player controls a missile, which he or she can aim at terrorists who walk around in a Middle-Eastern village. However, the missile has a certain delay, and, once it hits, the terrorists it was aimed at have moved, and civilians are being killed. The bystanders mourn the death of these innocents and then turn into terrorists themselves. The cycle of violence continues until, after only a few minutes of gameplay, the village is destroyed and crawling with terrorists, and it is clear that the game cannot be won through shooting.

One might not agree with *September 12th*'s claim that one cannot end terror with war, but it is impossible to not get the message when playing the game. This is the power of simulation games: ideas that are inscribed in

FIGURE 2.5
Gonzalo Frasca's *September 12th*

the rule system are noticed by the player. If you sit down to play the game and have any intention of winning, you will learn the rules on the way, and, through learning the rules, you learn the arguments they contain. Learning, in this sense, should not be confused with brainwashing or indoctrination. Neither can simulation games corrupt, nor can they cure. But they can make strong arguments and leave the discussion of their validity up to the players.

EXERCISES

1. Games as simulations

Note that the process, as listed as follows, is not as neat in practice as it might seem. You will start with some system elements and go back and forth between the source system and the game system to identify the ideal level of abstraction. You might also want to experiment with the perspective from which the player relates to the system. The most obvious choice might not be the best!

Basic:

- Identify a source system in your physical, everyday environment (e.g., subway, supermarket, office, college, traffic, life with a pet, taking care of a baby, running a household, etc.).
- Identify and list the source system's salient elements.
- What can be abstracted away?
- Describe the relationships between salient elements in *if–then* rule statements.
- Transfer it into a game: how does the system become playable and engaging?
  - Who are you in the game? (What's your role in the system?)
  - What is the goal?
  - What is the conflict?
  - What are the core mechanics? (i.e., what do you do on a moment-to-moment basis?).
  - Consider the main resources in the system (e.g., energy, nerves, health, time, gasoline, fare).
- Build a playable prototype of that system; playtest and iterate until satisfied.
- Write one paragraph on which you reflect on the statements you made with the game rules.
  - What ideas does your game communicate due to the system elements you decided to include, and the rules you ascribed to them?

- Could you have made different claims? What are they?
- Did you really consider your choices carefully? Remember that nothing in a game is a given; nothing is just plain *natural*. Everything you include is your choice and reflects your values and beliefs.

Note: Aim for a simulation game that contains particularly insightful/humorous/interesting/thought-provoking statements in its rules that make players either see the source system in new ways and/or make them nod approvingly in recognition of the wisdom and observational power behind your rules.

Advanced:

Same procedure as above, but, instead of a physical source system, pick an intangible source system as the basis of the game, such as an internal process (e.g., jealousy, grieving, revenge, power dynamics)

- Make sure you continue to use a systemic approach rather than telling a story to communicate your ideas.
- Consider how you can make the intangible system and its elements concrete.

2. *Procedural rhetoric:* **Design a simulation game to make a strong statement about a personal or social issue.**

Part 1: Write a one-pager description, stating your intent for the game. Please note that one-pagers need to be exactly one page long—no more, no less.

- *Step 1:* Pick a personal or social issue you feel strongly about and that you want to make a game about.
- *Step 2:* State the issue, e.g., "One thing that bugs me…"; "I struggle with…"; "The world would be a better place, if…"; "We should do something about…", "What keeps holding me back is…"
- *Step 3:* In one paragraph, describe the issue. Address the following:
  - What is the nature of the problem?
  - Why is it relevant (to you)?
  - Who do you want to communicate the issue to? Who should know about it? Why?
  - What kind of change would you like to see regarding the issue?
  - What do you think can bring this change about?
- *Step 4:* In one paragraph, describe how a game could help to address the issue or contribute to a solution. Elaborate on the following:
  - What kind of game do you have in mind?
  - How could it help?

- What does the player do?
- What is the goal/conflict of the game?

This one-pager should help you collect ideas. It does not need to contain a fleshed-out game design. It will serve as the basis for in-class discussion and a team-based design exercise.

Part 2: Playable, physical prototype of personal or social issue game + design write-up

Based on the in-class discussion and brainstorming of last class' social or personal issues, build a playable, physical prototype.

- *Step 1:* Clearly define the problem the game should address.
- *Step 2:* Provide a statement that clearly explains how the game addresses the problem. Focus on the rules and mechanics of the game and what the player does to achieve the game's goal. Games achieve their goals by way of what players can do in them and what experiences and insights they can gain through that.
- *Step 3:* Create the prototype, and bring it to class.
- *Step 4:* Submit a written summary of the game's problem statement, the game's intent (how to address the problem) and a detailed, clearly spelled-out description of how each rule and each game element contribute to achieving the game's intent.

References

Begy, J. 2013. Experiential metaphors in abstract games. In *Think Design Play: Digital Games Research Conference Proceedings: Vol. 1, No. 1.* Utrecht, NL: School of the Arts. Available at http://todigra.org/index.php/todigra/article/view/3/1. Accessed on August 25, 2016.

Bogost, I. 2007. *Persuasive Games: The Expressive Power of Videogames.* Cambridge, MA: MIT Press. Available at http://www.gamasutta.com/view/feature/132613/persuasive_games_puzzling_the_.php. Accessed on August 25, 2016.

Bogost, I. 2009. Persuasive games: Puzzling the sublime. *Gamasutra: The Art & Business of Making Games.* Available at http://www.gamasutra.com/view/feature/4225/persuasive_games_puzzling_the_.php. Accessed on October 10, 2016.

Chandler, D. 2007. *Semiotics: The Basics,* 2nd edition. New York: Routledge.

Flanagan, M. 2009. *Critical Play: Radical Game Design.* Cambridge, MA: MIT Press.

Frasca, G. 2001. *Simulation 101: Simulation versus Representation.* Available at http://www.ludology.org/articles/sim1/simulation101.html. Accessed on October 10, 2016.

Frasca, G. 2003. Simulation vs. narrative: An introduction to ludology. In Wolf, Mark, J.P., and Perron, B. (Eds.), *The Video Game Theory Reader* (pp. 221–237). New York: Routledge.

Frome, J. 2006. Reality, representation, and emotions across media. *Film Studies: An International Review* no. 8 Film, Cognition, and Emotions (Summer 2006) (pp. 12–25).

Grodal, T. 2000. Video games and the pleasures of control. Zillmann, D. and Vorderer, P. (Eds.), *Media Entertainment: The Psychology of Its Appeal* (pp. 197–215). Mahwah, NJ: Lawrence Erlbaum Associates.

Hocking, C. 2009. Ludonarrative dissonance in Bioshock: The problem of what the game is about. In Davidson, D. (Ed.), *Well Played 1.0: Video Games, Value and Meaning* (pp. 255–263). Pittsburgh, PA: ETC Press. Available at http://press.etc.cmu.edu/content/bioshock-clint-hocking. Accessed August 25, 2016.

Humble, R. 2007. The Marriage: A computer game by Rod Humble. Available at http://www.rodvik.com/rodgames/marriage.html. Accessed on August 25, 2016.

Johnson, S. 2013. What is your game actually about? *Gamasutra. The Art & Business of Making Games.* (Reprint from February 2010 issue.) Available at http://www.gamasutra.com/view/news/193338/What_is_your_game_actually_about.php. Accessed August 25, 2016.

Juul, J. 2003. The game, the player, the world: Looking for a heart of gameness. In Copier, M. and Raessens, J. (Eds.), *Level Up: Digital Games Research Conference Proceedings* (pp. 30–45). Utrecht: Utrecht University. Available at http://www.jesperjuul.net/text/gameplayerworld/. Accessed August 25, 2016.

Juul, J. 2005. *Half Real: Video Games between Real Rules and Fictional Worlds.* Cambridge, MA: MIT Press.

Juul, J. 2007. A certain level of abstraction. In Baba, A. (Ed.), *Situated Play: DiGRA 2007 Conference Proceedings* (pp. 510–515). Tokyo, Japan.

Meadows, D. 2004. *Thinking in Systems: A Primer.* White River Junction, VT: Chelsea Green Publishing.

Peirce, C.S. 1998. *Essential Peirce: Selected Philosophical Writings*, Vol. 2. Houser, N. and Kloesel, C. (Eds.), Bloomington: Indiana University Press.

Salen, K. & Zimmerman, E. 2004. *Rules of Play: Game Design Fundamentals.* Cambridge, MA: MIT Press.

Schell, J. 2008. *The Art of Game Design: A Book of Lenses.* Burlington, MA: Morgan Kaufmann Publishers.

Tan, E. 1996. *Emotion and the Structure of Narrative Film: Film as an Emotion Machine.* Mahwah, NJ: Lawrence Erlbaum Associates, Inc., Publishers.

Wittgenstein, L. 1922. *Tractatus Logico-Philosophicus.* London and New York: Routledge Classics.

Modeling the Human Experience—Or the Art of Nailing a Pudding to the Wall

Wherein it is discussed:

- *Why we need to become conscious of our experiences to make deep games*
- *How we can structure and understand our experiences by way of multi-dimensional, experiential gestalts*
- *How we understand abstract experiences through multidimensional, structural metaphors*
- *How a knowledge of experiential gestalt structures and metaphors helps us to systematically identify the source systems of our abstract experiences*
- *How being able to identify the source system of abstract experiences allows us to model these experiences through gameplay and make games about the human condition*

3.1 Introduction

This chapter explores how to use simulation to make deep games. It is one thing to simulate restaurants and similarly observable source systems. It is yet an entirely different thing to try to model salient aspects of the human experience—the things that profoundly move us, and how we feel and think about them, e.g., the meaning of life, the inevitability of death, who we are, how we relate to others—and make them tangible in the moment-to-moment gameplay. The biggest hurdle in this regard is that the human experience resides in the realm of complex, abstract concepts. An abstract concept is any experience or idea that cannot be immediately observed or derived directly from physical reality (Lakoff and Johnson 1980). Remember Clint Hocking's Game Developers Conference rant quoted in the Introduction and how he challenged designers to make games about courage, honor, duty, and truth? All of these concepts are abstract. Love is an abstract idea. Anger and loyalty are abstract ideas. All of our inner, emotional processes are abstract. We only have direct access to their symptoms—we can see someone go red in the face, frown, or smile—but what goes on inside remains hidden from direct observation (and, very often, we are wrong with our interpretation of the visible expressions of inner processes...). Hocking (2008) claims that "[t]he mechanics of trust, are not more difficult to model than the mechanics of rope." Once you know what these mechanics are, this may be true. Identifying them, however, is not trivial at all. We have a hard time wrapping our heads around things we cannot see, touch, smell, or taste. It is hard to pinpoint the elements that constitute the experience of trust or other abstract ideas so that they can be translated into the rules of a game system. Unless they really bug or puzzle us, we usually do not bother to dissect and analyze our experiences. We go through much of our lives with a *good-enough*, and at least partially unconscious, understanding of our intangible, inner worlds.

As game designer, a merely intuitive, tacit understanding of the source system you set out to simulate is a luxury you cannot afford. If you intend to make a game about something, it is not enough to have a fuzzy sense of what that something is. You cannot be vague when you are defining rules and behavior. Rules are not like words that can tiptoe around an idea, hint at it, and make allusions. Rules lay down the law. They define how it is. Maybe no one will agree with the rules you identified to capture a source system. Maybe your rules make statements about the source system that are plain wrong. Maybe the rules fail to convey the intended experience. But rules are never vague. So you better be sure about your rules. You can only model something successfully—i.e., create a simulation that captures salient aspects of the source system—if you are able to pinpoint the crucial elements of that source system and set them into meaningful relationships to each other.

Thus, in the next section, I will suggest a systematic approach to get a grip on the source systems of games about the human experience. In other words, I will discuss how we understand and make sense of our experiences in the first place, focusing particularly on the role of metaphors to grasp complex, abstract concepts. Obviously, understanding the source system is only the first step and still a long shot from the final, playable product. A lot of other decisions will have to be made until there's a deep game, and then it's impossible to predict precisely what kind of experiences players will have when playing the game, but we will cross that bridge when we get there.

3.2 Making Sense of Our Experiences

The first step in making sense of our experiences is to practice understanding them as systemic, structured wholes (a) because thinking in systems helps to translate the experience into game rules and mechanics, and (b) this is how our conceptual system—how we think, reason, and imagine—works. We just have to become more conscious of these processes to be able to leverage them for game design purposes. According to Mark Johnson and George Lakoff, we understand our experiences (physical and abstract alike) by way of structuring and organizing them into patterns. Raph Koster talks about very similar things when he introduced the concept of *chunking* and *grokking* experiences in *A Theory of Fun for Game Design* (2005). The most basic of these patterns are what Johnson (1990) calls *image* or *embodied schema* because they arise from our physical perception of and interaction with an environment through our bodies:

> The view I am proposing is this: in order for us to have meaningful, connected experiences that we can comprehend and reason about, there must be a pattern and order to our actions, perceptions, and conceptions. *A schema is a recurrent pattern, shape, and regularity in, or of, these ongoing ordering activities.* These patterns emerge as meaningful structures for us chiefly at the level of our bodily movements through space, our manipulation of objects and our perceptual interactions. (p. 29)

As one example for the basic nature of embodied schemata, Johnson (1990) mentions the verticality schema:

> The VERTICALITY schema, for instance, emerges from our tendency to employ an UP-DOWN orientation in picking out meaningful structures of our experience. We grasp this structure of verticality repeatedly in thousands of perceptions and activities we experience every day, such as perceiving a tree, our felt sense of standing upright, the activity of climbing stairs, forming a mental image of a flagpole. The VERTICALITY schema is the abstract structure of these VERTICALITY experiences, images and perceptions. (p. xiv)

The patterns that define the abstract structure of a schema are called *experiential gestalt.* The gestalt is not the experience itself. Different, actual experiences can share a gestalt, and they are recognized and classified by virtue of that gestalt. An experiential gestalt consists of several dimensions that have a fairly obvious, physical basis:

- *Participants:* This dimension arises out of the concept of the *self* as an actor distinguishable from the actions he or she performs. We also distinguish the *kinds* of participants (e.g., people, animals, objects).
- *Parts:* We experience ourselves as having parts (arms, legs, etc.) that we can control independently. Likewise, we experience physical objects, either in terms of the parts that they naturally have or the parts that we impose upon them, by virtue of our perceptions, our interactions with them, or our uses for them. Similarly, we impose a part–whole structure on events and activities. And, as in the case of participants, we distinguish the *kinds* of parts (e.g., the kinds of objects, the kinds of activities).
- *Stages:* Our simplest motor functions involve knowing where we are and what position we are in (initial conditions), starting to move (beginning), carrying out the motor function (middle), and stopping (end), which leaves us in a final state.
- *Linear sequence:* Again, the control of our simplest motor functions requires us to put them in the right linear sequence.
- *Purpose:* From birth (and even before), we have needs and desires, and we realize very early that we can perform certain actions (crying, moving, manipulating objects) to satisfy them (Lakoff and Johnson 1980, p. 82).

The experiential gestalts of physical concepts can be directly derived from physical reality—they can be seen, touched, smelled, etc. This makes these gestalts relatively easy to model in games: their source systems can be immediately observed, and the translation of their elements and relationships into game rules is (compared to abstract concepts) straightforward.

Example: The Experiential Gestalt of *Cleaning*

Cleaning is such a physical concept with a clearly delineated experiential gestalt; it involves the person who does the cleaning (and whoever is willing to help) as its main *participant.* Its *purpose* is to convert something (the object[s] to be cleaned) from a state A (undesirable, dirty) into a state B (desirable, clean). The *parts* include at least the object(s) to be cleaned and cleaning utensils and tools (e.g., sponge, kitchen towel, soap, vacuum cleaner). The *stages* involve the preparation of the thing to be transformed from undesirable state A to desirable state B—e.g., if it is an apartment, maybe you need to move the furniture off the floor; if it is your car, you might drive it to an open area where you have access to it from all sides; if you need to polish your silver, you take it out of the drawer and lay it on the kitchen table, and, if you are cleaning yourself, you undress and step into the bathtub or shower—the act of cleaning itself, maybe a polishing stage (rubbing off with a towel, applying body lotion, waiting for the floor to dry before moving the furniture back), and a finishing stage (packing up the sparkling silver, driving the clean car back into the garage, getting dressed after the shower, putting cleaning utensils back to where they belong). The *linear sequence* pretty much follows the order described under parts. You would not polish anything before you gave it a good scrub first, and putting your clothes back on before you actually had the shower does not make much sense either and would be inconsistent with the cleaning gestalt.

The cleaning gestalt could be broken down into more details, but these five dimensions provide the structure, the skeleton that is shared by all experiences we commonly recognize as cleaning. The way we make sense of our actual experiences is by comparing them to their gestalts. This comparison happens largely automatically and unconsciously. Comparing an experience to its gestalt is a dynamic process and accounts for the fact that there are variations in experiences.

Thus, an image schema must not be understood as a template for an experience but rather as a "continuous structure of an organizing activity" (Johnson 1990, p. 29). The schema has a definite structure, yet its pattern is dynamic in two important respects:

1. Schemata are the structures *of an activity* by which we organize our experience in ways that we can comprehend. They are a primary means by which we *construct* and *constitute* order and are not mere passive receptacles into which experience is poured.
2. Unlike templates, schemata are flexible in that they can take on any number of specific instantiations in varying contexts. It is somewhat misleading to say that an image schema gets "filled in" by concrete perceptual details; rather, it must be relatively malleable so that it can be modified to fit many similar, but different, situations that manifest a recurring underlying structure (Johnson 1990, pp. 29–30).

This recognition of image schematic patterns as malleable and dynamic is crucial for the principle to be useful for game design. It acknowledges the fact that the structure of the image schema is not the experience, just like the game is not the experience.

In real life, our organizing structures have to account for variations in our actual experience to help us make sense of them. No cleaning experience is exactly the same, yet, if we understand an experience as cleaning, we do so by virtue of its gestalt—we recognize that the experience we are having right now has enough in common with our idea of cleaning that we can map it successfully onto the *cleaning gestalt*. Identifying experiential gestalts, their dimensions, and how they relate is a process of abstraction. This process of abstraction has been explained before in regard to translating a source system into a game system (see Chapter 2), but it is actually preceded by the abstraction process that happens when we abstract everything that is *noise* (i.e., does not belong to an experiential gestalt) from the flood of perceptual stimuli in real life until a pattern emerges that we can classify and recognize as an experience.

> It is by means of conceptualizing our experiences in this manner that we pick out the "important" aspects of an experience. And by picking out what is "important" in the experience, we can categorize the experience, understand it, and remember it. (Lakoff and Johnson 1980, p. 83)

In other words, to understand, structure, and remember an experience as cleaning, we need to filter out that the neighbor's dog is barking, there is a car driving by, someone mows the lawn, our knee is itching, and we are hungry. All of these things may indeed be happening, and we can be aware of them, but we also know that they are not part of the cleaning experience per se. They are filtered out and abstracted away, and, when asked what we did in the afternoon, we won't ramble on about all the individual things that happened but instead answer with "I cleaned my house."

The idea that, once identified, we can somehow recreate experiential gestalts with game systems and hope that they will evoke the original experience in players might raise some eyebrows. It is truly hard to predict what players will feel when playing a game, and that's one of the main challenges and (at least to me) attractions of designing games. In game design, we have to account for the different ways in which players interact with the structures we set up for them. As game designers, we do not create experiences. We create structural frameworks, possibility spaces that *enable* experiences. My argument is this, though; just like there are meaningful mappings between image schema and actual experience in real life, which are the basis for our understanding of our experiences, we can deliberately design for meaningful mappings between the game structure and the gameplay experience. We can create experiential gestalts with game rules and mechanics that might be experienced differently by different players, but the gestalts can never-theless be recognizable and can be made sense of and be meaningful in a similar way.* Let me refer back to *Diner Dash (DD)* once again to illustrate that point. As established before, *DD* is a game about waitressing. Its source system has been derived from the waitressing gestalt. The game models what waitressing is essentially about by letting the player enact its salient elements: seating customers, taking orders, delivering food, bringing the check, and clearing tables. Efficiency in all of these tasks is key to earn the most tips/wins. The player can enact the waitressing gestalt in several ways: being as efficient and competent a waitress as possible, or messing up, neglecting to seat customers or bring food as soon as it is ready, taking the longest route between tables and the kitchen, etc. All of these choices—like in real life—will change the precise experience of the waitressing gestalt, but they will remain recognizable as an experience of waitressing. Gestalt structures—as encountered in real life, as well as in games—are dynamic, but not mushy or arbitrary. They are coherent, unified wholes that organize our experiences and cognition, and they *constrain meaning* (Johnson 1990). The game design constrains the possible, actual experiences to be had when players engage with the game structure in the sense that a game based on the waitressing gestalt (modeling the embodied experience of waitressing) is more likely to evoke—in one way or another—some kind of waitressing experience rather than the experience of, for example, shooting, driving, or building. Note that I am not making any claims about whether players will enjoy the resulting experiences or not.

3.3 Making Sense of *Abstract* Experiences— The Role of Metaphors

While it is relatively easy to understand how we make sense of physical con-cepts such as cleaning or waitressing, the question remains: how does it work for complex, abstract ideas such as loyalty or love? The answer is it works pretty much the same way. Like physical concepts, abstract concepts also have

---

*The fact remains, however, that what someone notices as crucial or essential when engaging with a game's structure remains subjective. No matter how carefully the game has been designed to model a specific experiential gestalt, it is imaginable that the player focuses on completely different aspects of the game and that this act of individual highlighting creates an experience that overrides the carefully designed structure of the experiential gestalt the designer had in mind. Experience, after all, is a matter of attention and a point of view.

internally coherent structures that define them. The main difference is that the dimensions of those structures cannot be directly observed and derived from physical reality. To understand abstract ideas, we need metaphors:

> Certain concepts are structured almost entirely metaphorically. The concept LOVE, for example, is structured mostly in metaphorical terms: LOVE IS A JOURNEY, LOVE IS A PATIENT, LOVE IS A PHYSICAL FORCE, LOVE IS MADNESS, LOVE IS WAR, etc. The concept of LOVE has a core that is minimally structured by the subcategorization LOVE IS AN EMOTION and by links to other emotions, e.g., liking. This is typical of emotional concepts, which are not clearly delineated in our experience in any direct fashion and therefore must be comprehended primarily indirectly, via metaphor. (Lakoff and Johnson 1980, p. 85)

Making sense of abstract ideas means understanding them in terms of something concrete: "The essence of metaphor is understanding and experiencing one kind of thing in terms of another" (Lakoff and Johnson 1980, p. 5). Metaphors, in this sense, are nothing fancy. They are not reserved for poets or romantics. Metaphors are everywhere. They are cognitive, conceptual tools that are at the very foundation of our thinking, reasoning, and imagining. We use them all the time and mostly unconsciously.

> In all aspects of life, not just in politics or in love, we define our reality in terms of metaphors and then proceed to act on the basis of the metaphors. We draw inferences, set goals, make commitments, and execute plans, all on the basis of how we in part structure our experience, consciously and unconsciously, by means of metaphor. (Lakoff and Johnson 1980, p. 158)

We do not question why we think of ideas (in itself an abstract concept) as objects (a concrete and tangible thing) when we say we have *played with* or *dropped* them. Only a very small part of our understanding of the world, and our being in it as humans, stems from direct, physical experience. The rest happens by way of the metaphorical projection of these physical experiences onto abstract domains. The image schemata and experiential gestalts that are derived from embodied experience provide the physical basis our abstract, intangible experiences can be mapped onto, to make them tangible. I want to stress that these possible mappings between the source (e.g., the abstract concept) and the target (the structural metaphors) are by no way arbitrary or vague. Structural metaphors are no imaginative flights of fancy. They constrain the meaning of abstract experiences in a very precise and coherent manner, by virtue of their mutual, unified structures. For many people, who were tortured in school with obscure poetry, metaphors have a bad rep. They are perceived as esoteric, inaccessible, incomprehensible, artsy la-di-da. If you share this skepticism toward metaphors, blame it on the poets (or your teachers who did not make these poets accessible to you), not the metaphors. Metaphors are tools of cognition and understanding. Tools can be used badly. It is not the tool's fault when that happens.

Example: Metaphorical Structuring and Understanding of *Life as a Mess*

Here is an example for the use of a structural metaphor to make sense of a certain kind of life experience: *life as a mess*. The concept of *mess* is readily understood because its dimensions—participant, parts, linear sequence, stages, and purpose—can be derived from physical reality. Everybody's mess looks different, of course, so the following is my take on the subject, but everybody's mess experience shares salient structural elements that allow us to reach some kind of agreement about what we mean by mess. The participant is the person in the mess. So far, our mess experience probably corresponds. The parts (of my idea of mess) are easy to identify, too. We all know what a messy apartment looks like or can easily imagine it in its most horrendous manifestations: objects are lying around in a disorderly fashion; closets are overflowing with garments (that may not have been worn in years!); dirty dishes are stacked ceiling high in the sink; maybe there is smelly, leftover food under the couch somewhere; dust collects on the surfaces; and, if we have an extreme case of mess, the unpleasant scenery could be populated with rodents and cockroaches. Let your imagination run wild and then map what you identified onto the structural dimensions of what you perceive as a *messy life* in a more abstract sense: deteriorating relationships, stagnated job search, the lack of emotional hygiene (there is a rich metaphor there, too!), and the loss of physical fitness. The *purpose* of the mess gestalt, assumedly, is to do something about it: to clean up. However, there is an inherent conflict there; the needs and desires that determine a gestalt's purpose pull in two different directions: the need and desire for change on the one hand and the resistance to it on the other (e.g., the task seems overwhelming and requires effort, and there might be a lack of perspective as to whether investing the effort is even worth it). The stages and the linear sequence can be derived from the observation that mess accumulates over time; one dirty plate is added to another until there is a stack of unwashed dishes in the sink, which, at some point, may attract vermin, etc. This maps onto an experience of gradual decline in a messy life; mistakes pile up, and different life areas start to slowly encroach upon and affect each other. As one flees from the horrendous kitchen to the living room to eat, cluttering up that space, too, job worries may intrude on one's private life and vice versa, leading to unhealthy coping mechanisms (drinking, overeating, watching too much TV) that affect the emotional and physical well-being and so on and so forth.

This example of life as a mess illustrates how abstract ideas can be understood in terms of multidimensional, structural metaphors, by way of the consistent mappings of their dimensions to the concrete and observable dimensions of a physical concept. It makes sense to understand a messy life in terms of a messy apartment. It would not make sense to understand it in terms of a military march. This goes to show that the mappings between the abstract concept and the structural metaphor used to make sense of the concept are not arbitrary. This is crucial to keep in mind, both for the design of games—making sure that all aspects of the metaphor are coherent with the experience one wants to model—and their interpretation. While metaphorical games allow for a certain amount of interpretative freedom, you need to be able to argue your case, by way of relating the dimensions of the metaphor to the dimensions of the modeled concepts in a coherent and consistent fashion. If you cannot do that, either the metaphor has been used inconsistently, or your interpretation is standing on shaky ground.

3.3.1 Understanding Our Inner Lives through Structural Metaphors—Symbolic Modeling in Psychotherapy

While a little bit of a tangent, it is noteworthy that this strategy of exploring the human experience is also metaphorically used in a psychotherapeutic method called *symbolic modeling*. Symbolic modeling is based on the observation that the metaphorical content of our language and nonverbal cues (e.g., body language) reveal our inner landscapes and help us raise awareness for how we perceive the world and our role within it. Symbolic modeling is thus a great inspiration source for game designers interested in making deep games:

> Symbolic modeling is a method for facilitating individuals to become familiar with the symbolic domain of their experience so that they discover new ways of perceiving themselves and their world. It uses Clean Language to facilitate them to attend to their metaphoric expressions so that *they* create a model of their symbolic mindbody perceptions. This model exists as a living, breathing, four-dimensional world within and around them. When clients explore this world and its inherent logic, their metaphors and way of being are honoured. During the therapeutic process their metaphors begin to evolve. As this happens their everyday thinking, feeling and behavior correspondingly change as well. (Lawley and Tompkins 2011, pp. xiv–xv)

Clean Language—a formulaic way to ask questions that only act as prompts to explore the landscape further—is used so that the facilitator of symbolic modeling processes does not contaminate the client's symbolic landscape with his or her own metaphors, perceptions, or assumptions. If you are exploring your own inner worlds without a facilitator, this danger does not exist because whatever metaphors come to mind are yours to begin with and only tell you more about what is going on inside. Symbolic modeling understands the human experience and its corresponding metaphor landscapes as self-organizing systems that are organized into levels. While the dimensions of experiential gestalts, as identified by Lakoff and Johnson (participants, parts, stages, linear sequence, and purpose), already imply the systemic nature of experiences, Lawley and Tompkins (2011) explicitly investigate human experience as procedural.

> We distinguish four levels of organization that comprise Metaphor Landscapes: *symbols*; *relationships* between symbols; *patterns* across those relationships; and a *pattern of organisation* of the entire configuration of patterns, relationships and symbols. (...) Symbols are the tangible components of a metaphor. They form the content of symbolic perception – that which can be seen, heard, felt or otherwise sensed directly (whether physically or imaginatively). A symbol is something that exists 'somewhere' and 'somewhen'. A symbol's attributes (its characteristics and properties) give it a particular form, and its location specifies its position or place within the Metaphor Landscape. (...)
>
> When two symbols connect, co-operate, balance, fight, avoid or scare each other, they are part of a functional or logical relationship. A relationship is an interaction, connection or correlation 'between', 'across', or 'over' *two* symbols (or one symbol over two spaces or times). At a minimum, there will always be a relationship between each symbol and the perceiver of that symbol. (...)
>
> Symbols and their relationships to each other do not exist in isolation. They are part of wider contexts and larger systems consisting of higher level patterns. (...) Patterns emerge from a network of relationships. They connect components across multiple spaces, times and forms. They exist as stable configurations, repeating sequences and recurring motifs. (...)
>
> A Metaphor Landscape is more than its symbols, more than the relationships between those symbols and more than the patterns of those relationships. It exists as a unit, an identity, a whole, unified system, a pattern of patterns that specifies and describes the unique nature of the system – a pattern of organization. (pp. 29–33)

Symbolic modeling is aimed at a complete understanding of a person's pattern of organization that sheds light on who they are. As such, it goes way beyond our purposes of finding strategies to grasp the source systems of abstract concepts. It is nevertheless useful in so far as (a) it emphasizes the systemic nature of human experience and draws attention to the elements of systems, their attributes, relationships, and patterns. Nothing happens in isolation, and, to make sense of our experiences and to model them in a game, it is helpful to understand their dynamic structures. (b) It emphasizes the role of metaphors to capture the essential nature of an experience.

3.4 Applying Theory to Practice: Case Study *Akrasia*

The following case study is based on the design and development of the game *Akrasia*, which I made with a team of students in the summer of 2008 at the Singapore–Massachusetts Institute of Technology (MIT) GAMBIT Game Lab, at the MIT, Cambridge, Mass. It models a complex, abstract concept—addiction—and uses structural metaphors to make this concept concrete. The case study is meant to show the application of (neat) theory to (slightly messier) practice, particularly how the systematic approach of identifying salient dimensions of experiential gestalts corresponds with the iterative nature of game design, and the potential pitfalls of using metaphors to model abstract ideas. *Akrasia* was an *IndieCade* finalist in 2009 and can be played for free here: http://gambit.mit.edu/loadgame/akrasia.php.

3.4.1 *Case Study:* Akrasia

"Let's make a game about a complex, abstract concept that illuminates an aspect of the human experience using metaphors" (Figure 3.1). This is pretty much exactly what I said to my student team the first day of our summer program in 2008, at GAMBIT. Every game we made at GAMBIT was supposed to answer a research question, to push the boundaries of games as media. This was mine: how can we make games that are about something—that tackle abstract, instead of physical, concepts and teach us something about the human experience? I wanted my team to design a profound game: a game that makes the player think and reflect and that fostered interpretation. This should shed some light on the usefulness of the theoretical approach sketched out in Section 3.3 (i.e., how to think of experiences as systemic, structured wholes and make complex abstract concepts concrete by way of structural, multidimensional metaphors) and point toward any gaps and pitfalls when it is applied to the practice of game development.

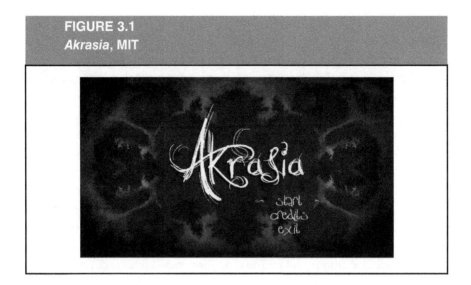

FIGURE 3.1
Akrasia, MIT

3.4.2 Conception Phase

To promote creative ownership and ensure that the team members were really behind the idea the game should model, I didn't want to suggest a complex, abstract concept to base the game on. Thus, we spent the first two weeks of our precious nine-week summer program just brainstorming and soul-searching. The concepts that resonated most strongly with the team were *identity, memory, inner demons,* and *love.* Each of them were thoroughly discussed; some were explored further in analogue prototypes, but it was very hard to reach an agreement about the experiential core of any of these concepts. What is the nature of inner demons? Should we fight or embrace them? Who are we without our memories? Is there an essence of being that is independent of our past experiences? And is love pain, safety, madness, or a walk in a beautiful field? Everyone had a different perspective, but no one's perspective seemed rich or strong enough to sustain a whole game. This goes to show that (a) our experiences are very subjective, and it is extremely hard to make these kinds of games following a democratic process. *Art by committee* just doesn't work. No perspective is better or worse than another, really, but there needs to be a unified point of view on what is to be modeled, or the rules will end up communicating contradicting messages, undermining a coherent reading of the final product. And (b) it takes a lot of practice and/ or time to become aware of, dissect, and analyze one's experiences so that they reveal themselves as truly complex, multidimensional gestalts and don't remain an isolated spark of insight.

Eventually, we settled on the abstract concept of *addiction*—specifically substance abuse—to base our game on. None of us had extensive, firsthand experience with drugs, which was both an advantage and a disadvantage (not that I'm advocating drugs here!). The advantage was that it was easier for us to reach consensus on the addiction gestalt because we based our understanding of it on portrayals of drug abuse in movies (e.g., *Drugstore Cowboy*, *Trainspotting*), as well as some medical articles, and focused on the relatively well-understood and commonly known aspects of it. No one had particularly strong feelings about one aspect of addiction or another. Related to that, the disadvantage was that the design process lacked the expressive urgency, the personal angel that comes with modeling a concept based on lived experience. Consequently, our simulation, while containing (some controversial) statements in its rules, is relatively neutral and focused on *how it works* rather than providing a unique and personal perspective on substance abuse.

3.4.3 The Iterative Process of Modeling the Addiction Gestalt

Applying the systematic approach defined in Section 3.2, we initially identified the addiction gestalt as having the following salient dimensions. Note how even a description of the experience can't get around using metaphors to make the abstract processes at work in the addiction gestalt concrete.

Addiction Gestalt, Take 1:

Participant(s): Addict.

Parts: Drugs, their effect, drug effect wearing off, health, being trapped/stuck (= the addiction itself), overdosing, an exit from the trap (= kicking the habit).

Stages: Take drugs, get speed boost (drug effect as defined by us), become trapped, take too many drugs, and overdose (= lose state); *or* stop taking drugs, their effects wear off (= speed is reduced), become able to escape trap (= win state).

Linear sequence: Implied in the above, but, if we think of the addiction gestalt as a systemically structured whole, it is not a straight line from *taking the first drug* to *overdosing*, but rather a dynamic interplay of its parts that allows for different outcomes, from kicking the habit quickly to going back and forth between taking drugs, recovery, health regeneration, relapse, etc.

Purpose: Kicking the habit.*

---

* Obviously, another valid take on the addiction gestalt would have been to say that the purpose is to *stay high:* that we decided the purpose was to kick the habit already says a lot about our perspective on the concept, and that the process of identifying its salient dimensions, is subjective.

With this good-enough-to-get-going understanding of the source system in place, we started translating it into metaphors and mapping it onto a game structure. One of the first big questions I ask when making games about complex, abstract ideas is, what is the core metaphor that will provide the main structure for the experience and enables consistent mappings between the dimensions of the source system (e.g., elements of the addiction gestalt) and the metaphorical target (e.g., whatever the addiction gestalt is represented as to make it concrete)? Games are predominantly spatial. Space in games is what characters are in traditional media: a vehicle for action. While many games have a player character, they don't necessarily need one because they have a player who acts. What games cannot do without is a platform for the player to act on, i.e., the game space. This game space can be a realistically modeled world, such as in *Myst* or *Grand Theft Auto*, or it can be a pretty abstract, rectangular playing field such as in *Candy Crush* or *Tetris*. Due to space being such a dominant paradigm, I personally like to start by identifying the metaphorical landscape the game is set in.

Akrasia aims to shed light on internal processes—the mechanics and dynamics of addiction as an inner struggle. As such, it suggests itself to be set in the mind of an addict, for which we chose the metaphor of a racetrack in our earliest physical prototype. The racetrack metaphor is well aligned with the speed boost effect of the drugs, which makes you speed right past the exit (causing you to get trapped in addiction), as well as with the *one-track-mind* focus of someone who's addicted: to score and consume drugs.

It is important to note that, by choosing *speed* as the drug effect, we did not mean to reduce the addiction gestalt to an addiction to the drug speed. What is important is the relationship between the elements *drug* and *trap*. On the most abstract level, that means consuming the drug must have an effect that prevents kicking the habit, causing the player to become *stuck/trapped*. In the first prototype, speed prevented you from exiting the racetrack, but anything that made *drug taking* and *exiting* mutually exclusive actions would have worked conceptually. Of course, every decision on how to represent abstract ideas comes with its own implications and nuances in meaning, which need to be considered. It is thus very helpful to first gain clarity on how things relate in principle, before exploring the different ways in representing them metaphorically. There is always more than one solution that theoretically works, but some are better, more intuitive, or more fitting than others.

In any case, when we playtested this first prototype, we realized a big, gaping hole in our design: the player is not the avatar, and there is no incentive whatsoever to take a virtual pill! Playtesters knew they needed to exit the racetrack. They found out quickly that the pills made this impossible. They stopped taking the pills and won. Our first attempt failed miserably at modeling dependency, a core dimension of the addiction gestalt that we completely overlooked. In other words, we had taken for granted that part so much that we abstracted it away. To make the addiction gestalt tangible to players, though—to convey the experience of *what it's like*—we needed to model dependency, too! Dependency, while part of the bigger addiction gestalt, has its own experiential structure, which consists of two main *parts*: (1) a goal you really want to achieve and (2) the thing you need to achieve that goal. With this in mind, we iterated on the dimensions of the source system as follows.

Addiction Gestalt, Take 2:

Participant(s): Addict.

Parts: Drugs, their effect, *elusive high*, drug effect wearing off, health, being trapped/stuck (= the addiction itself), overdosing, an exit from the trap (= kicking the habit).

Stages: Take drugs, get speed boost (drug effect as defined by us), *reach high*, become trapped, take too many drugs and overdose (= lose state); *or* stop taking drugs, their effects wear off (= speed is reduced), become able to escape trap (= win state).

Linear sequence: Same as above, plus *take drug, to achieve high with the help of drug effect.*

Purpose: Kicking the habit.

Based on this new understanding of the source system, the next iteration of our prototype looked as follows: the game space turned from a metaphorical representation of *the mind as a racetrack* to *the mind as a maze*. The maze has two states: a psychedelic state while on drugs and a dreary withdrawal state while off drugs. The player can go back and forth between both, depending on how frequently he or she collects the pill-shaped objects representing drugs in the maze (Figure 3.2).

The psychedelic state includes a cute but elusive dragon, representing the *high*, which is just a little too fast to catch without the pills' speed boots. By establishing catching the dragon as a goal in the game and adding a (literal!) high score, players now had an incentive to collect the pills, and, man, did they start to get trapped in their addiction, completely forgetting about the conflicting goal of kicking the habit!

Great! Now, we had overemphasized the dependency part of the addiction gestalt. Our next step was to counterbalance that by focusing more

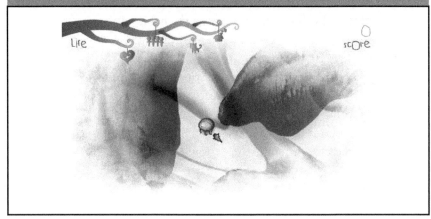

FIGURE 3.2
Akrasia, MIT: Maze/Mind in Psychedelic State with Life Tree Branch and Life Symbols

on capturing the downsides of drug consumption, fleshing out more parts of the source system. We made *health* as a more prominent resource and added the idea of a social context (family life, house, cat, friends, love), which is harmed by drug abuse. To visually represent health and the social context, we added a tree branch from which dangled life symbols. The tree branch acted as a reverse health bar that turned red when drugs were consumed (= representing being poisoned) and went back to its normal color when the player didn't collect drugs for long enough (= recovering health). When the red part had reached a life symbol on the branch (representing overindulgence), the symbol dropped from the branch and was forever lost.

The messages inscribed in these rules are (a) that there is a correlation between the intensity of drug abuse and your ability to keep your social life intact and (b) that health can be regained by staying sober (the more intense your drug abuse was, the longer it takes), but, for other parts of life, the damage is permanent. We had a lot of discussions about these statements, and they are definitely gross oversimplifications. For the sake of making a playable game within nine weeks, though, we had to sacrifice a lot of the complexity of the source system.

Finally, to complement what we defined as the core of addiction (i.e., dependency), and the consequences to health and social context, we added the withdrawal and craving phase to complete our perspective on the addiction gestalt. Withdrawal is in itself a multidimensionally structured whole, which we discerned as follows:

Participant: Addict.

Parts: Craving for the drug, relapse, withdrawal including relearning behavior, exercising willpower, and kicking the habit.

Stages: The craving can either be followed by giving in to the desire for the drug or by entering the tough phase of withdrawal, where new behavior needs to be learnt, and one needs to stay strong until one is over the habit.

Linear sequence: Implied in the above.

Purpose: Kicking the habit.

Since withdrawal is part of the bigger addiction gestalt (as defined by us), it is no wonder certain structural dimensions overlap. Adding the withdrawal gestalt, our final analysis of the source system looked like this.

Addiction Gestalt, Take 3 (Final):

Participant(s): Addict.

Parts: Drugs, their effect, elusive high, drug effect wearing off, health, *social life*, being trapped/stuck (= the addiction itself), overdosing, *craving, relapsing, withdrawal, relearning behavior,* an exit from the trap (= kicking the habit).

Stages: Take drugs, get speed boost (drug effect as defined by us), reach high, become trapped, *lose social life*, take too many drugs and overdose (= lose state); *or:* stop taking drugs, their effects wear off (= speed is reduced), regain health but not social life, enter withdrawal state, be tempted by craving, relapse into addiction *or go through withdrawal, relearn behavior, resist drugs*, become able to escape trap (= win state).

Linear sequence: No change, except social life was affected by drug abuse.

Purpose: Kicking the habit.

In contrast to the cute dragon that is being chased during the dependency phase, the withdrawal state contains a scary demon: a metaphorical representation of the craving. The craving lives in the dreary state of the maze, and it chases the player.

You can only escape it by collecting another pill, relapsing into psychedelic state. We aimed to make the demon as threatening as possible to increase the feeling of temptation. We briefly discussed that it should reduce your health when it caught up with you, treating it like any other video-game enemy. Upon closer investigation, though, that didn't make any sense. The demon is a metaphor and, as such, needs to behave according to the source it represents. Craving a drug doesn't hurt you. Giving in to the craving by taking the drug does. When the demon catches you, it means serious withdrawal has started. We decided that the logical consequence that corresponded with how craving/withdrawal worked in real life was to drastically reduce the *high* score (representing extreme sobriety) and to mess with the player controls—up is down, left is right, etc. Reversing controls represents the need to relearn behavior. It makes it extra hard not to bump into one of the pills *by accident*, because you gave in to old habits (i.e., *up* is *up*, etc.). The additional focus required to successfully navigate through the maze to the exit (the exit only exists in dreary withdrawal state, obviously, because you can't kick a habit while still on drugs!) can thus be understood as a metaphor for the willpower necessary to break out of the addiction trap.

Depending on how the player played the game—particularly how many life symbols remained on the tree branch upon exiting—one of the five endings is presented on a continuum from *happy*, no (lasting) harm done, to *lost it all except for a partner's love* (an overly romantic notion I would not subscribe to anymore) to *dead and alone in the woods*.

Table 3.1 provides an overview of all the elements of our final addiction gestalt and how we translated them into the *Akrasia*'s metaphors.

3.4.4 Conclusion

By walking through the design of *Akrasia* from beginning to end, I intended to show how getting a grip on a complex, abstract concept can be approached systematically by identifying salient elements of its experiential gestalt and translating them into metaphors. It should have become clear, though, that this process is by no means straightforward and linear. You start with an aspect of the concept that seems most prominent (to you at the time) and take it from there. There are a lot of different ways to go about this, and aspects to focus on first, and there is a constant back and forth between exploring the source system, translating some of its elements into a prototype, playtesting the prototype, finding a ton of holes and inconsistencies, and revisiting the source system to flesh out one's understanding of it further, iterating on the prototype and so on and so forth. Multidimensional gestalts often consist of several multidimensional gestalts. The structure of the addiction gestalt (as defined by us) consists of dependency, craving, and withdrawal—all in and of themselves complex, structural wholes with their own parts and elements. What to include and what to leave out are up to the game designer's discretion.

Also, when working with metaphors, it is important to remain mindful of what they represent, not get carried away by their literal meaning. As soon as

TABLE 3.1
Overview of the Addiction Gestalt Elements in *Akrasia*

Source System: Addiction Gestalt	Game Metaphors
Addict	Player avatar: roundish, little guy, representing *intent* rather than *addict as a person*.
Mind	Maze.
Mind on drugs	Psychedelic maze; contains no exit; features a dragon to be chased.
Drugs	Pill-shaped objects.
Drug effect	Speed boost upon collecting a pill-shaped object; small increase in high score.
Ultimate high	Elusive, cute dragon.
Dependency	Need pills to be fast enough to catch elusive dragon and boost high score.
Achieve high	Catch dragon, big increase in high-score points.
Drug effect wearing off	Avatar slows down.
Crash (after achieving ultimate high)	Maze transforms into dreary state.
Sober mind	Dreary maze, contains exit to quit addiction; contains a scary demon; contains pill-shaped objects.
Craving	Scary demon, chases the player avatar; reduces high-score points when catching up with player avatar.
Withdrawal state	Huge reduction in high-score points; controls are reversed.
Relearning behavior, breaking old habits, exercising willpower	Reversed controls make it hard to navigate around pills and stay on course toward exit; focus needed to adjust to reversed controls = willpower to stay sober and kick habit.
Health	Tree branch.
Health decline and regeneration	Tree branch turns red from tip to trunk, when pills are collected, representing progressive poisoning; regenerates when no pills are collected for a while.
Death	Game over; avatar death scene.
Social context	Life symbols on tree branch.
Drug abuse's impact on social context	Loss of life symbols, if too many pill-shaped objects are collected within a short time; life symbols can't be recovered, even if health is fully regenerated.

we introduced the scary demon as a metaphor for the craving, it developed a life of its own. We needed to remind ourselves that, while it looked menacing and thus raised the expectation that it could cause physical harm, it actually represented the craving, and it would not make sense for it to damage health. Metaphors always have to be checked for consistency and coherence with what they stand for.

EXERCISES

1. **Identify the dimensions of multidimensional structural metaphors:**
   - Complete this sentence with your own words: "Life is…" (e.g., "Life is a highway," "Life is a maze," "Life is a roller coaster")
     - Explore the dimensions of complex structural metaphors such as "Life is a box of chocolates," and "Life is a highway."
     - What are all the elements that belong to the second part of the sentence (e.g., a box of chocolates, highway, roller coaster…)?
       - For example, different chocolates contain different fillings; chocolate melts in your hand, so, once you grab one, you've got to eat it, or it melts; a roller coaster goes up and down; you're being strapped into your seat; you can't steer and are at the mercy of whoever designed the roller coaster; others are screaming alongside you.
     - How do these elements illuminate the experience of life expressed in the metaphor? What is relevant? What is irrelevant?
2. **Analyze a metaphorical game** (e.g., *Passage, The Marriage, Hurdles, Thomas Was Alone, Lim, High Delivery*):
   - Make a list of all game elements and describe how they work and relate to each other (their rules).
   - Explain what each element represents in relation to the game's source system (i.e., what the game is about).
   - Is the metaphor consistent? Are there aspects that don't make sense or don't seem to fit? Do you have trouble identifying the meaning of an element?
   - Remember that metaphorical meaning is open for interpretation but never arbitrary. Your interpretation needs to be sound.
   - Discuss your findings with others.
3. **Metaphorical game self-portrait**

   (Team exercise—done in pairs)

   This is an exercise in metaphorical/analogical thinking, playful self-exploration, and getting to know each other. The basic question you should ask yourself for this exercise is as follows:

   "If I were a game, what would I be?" To answer this question and use it as the basis for design, start by identifying the game components: goal, conflict, and mechanics. Go into more details: what kinds of genres are you drawn to? Why? Keep in mind that whatever you choose should relate to you as a person. If you are very curious, a game with a strong exploration component would correspond well. If you are energetic and competitive, the elements of an action game and its fast pace may be a good fit. Do your research on the different kinds of games, game genres, and game components, and do some soul-searching to find out which game design best represents *who you are.*

This is a partner exercise, so the next step is to take your partner's personality into account in the design process. The game needs to reflect both of you. Its rules, mechanics, and fiction, as well as its goal and conflict, must be informed by both of its designers. So, if one of you is very mellow, and the other is very active, how could this inform the conflict in the game? If you are both very cooperative, how can this be reflected in a game structure that fosters cooperation rather than competition?

The discussions you should have during this assignment are more important than the outcome. The goal is not to make an awesome game (even though I won't hold it against you if you do ;-)). The goal is to carefully consider how aspects of yourself can be represented by game aspects and how the dynamics between you and your fellow designer can be reflected by the mechanics and dynamics in the game. This is where the metaphorical mapping comes in. Have fun exploring!

Deliverables:

1. A playable, physical prototype of metaphorical game self-portrait. Bring to class on the due date.

2. Prepare a short presentation on your prototype (no ppt needed—just be ready to explain and demonstrate the game in 10 minutes, relating game elements to your personality traits as designers).

3. A one-page write-up that explains the metaphorical mapping between the designers and their dynamics and the game components and intended gameplay experience. Pay special attention to how each element in the game represents an aspect of you, your fellow designer, and how you relate to each other.

References

Hocking, C. 2008. GDC 2008 game designer's rant. Available at http://www.click nothing.typepad.com/click_nothing/.

Johnson, M. 1990. *The Body in the Mind: The Bodily Basis of Meaning, Imagination and Reason*. Chicago and London: University of Chicago Press.

Koster, R. 2005. *A Theory of Fun for Game Design*. Scottsdale, AZ: Paraglyph Press.

Lakoff, G. and Johnson, M. 1980. *Metaphors We Live By*. London and Chicago: University of Chicago Press.

Lawley, J. and Tompkins, P. 2011. *Metaphors in Mind: Transformation through Symbolic Modeling*. London, UK: The Developing Company Press.

4

Experiential Metaphors—
Or What Breaking Up, Getting
a Tattoo, and Playing *God
of War* Have in Common

Wherein:

- *The embodied nature of gameplay experiences is discussed, and it is explained why playing a game can "feel" like a real-life experience.*
- *The concept of experiential metaphor is introduced.*
- *A case study of* God of War II *is offered to exemplify the concept of "experiential metaphor" and to illustrate the structural parallels between the grappling hook sequence in the game and other experiences of transition (e.g., getting a tattoo or breaking up).*
- *The differences of modeling "how something works" and "what it feels like" are discussed and illustrated by way of a case study of* The Marriage.
- *The implied meaning of experiential metaphors is investigated by way of studying* Angry Birds, American McGee's Grimm: Little Red Riding Hood, *and* Left Behind: Eternal Forces. *The point is made that experiential metaphors can reinforce or subvert a game's theme or create dubious subtexts and that being mindful of their role in meaning generation is essential for purposeful design.*

4.1 Gameplay as Embodied Experience

What makes games special compared to other noninteractive media is that their simulations are not only modeled after lived, embodied experiences, but they are also *perceived* by way of embodied experiences. What does that mean? As discussed in Chapter 3, our conceptual system—the way we make sense of our experiences—is based on our physically being in the world and engaging with a tangible environment through our bodies. The game space and its objects are virtual, and made of code, and we cannot manipulate them directly, physically. How we understand what happens in a game environment, however, and form and test a hypothesis about it, is comparable to how we make sense of real-life experiences: through situated (i.e., situation-specific) and embodied action (i.e., doing). To experience something as embodied, we only need to be participants (physical or virtual) in an environment (simulated or real) that we can interact with. As Jim Gee (2004) puts it,

> When I use the term 'embodied', I mean to include the mind as part of the body. So "embodied" means, for me, "in the body" and/or "in the mind". (...) When I talk about a person's embodied experiences in the world (virtual or real), I mean to cover all the perceptions, actions, choices and mental simulations of action or dialogue. (p. 82)

Gee (2004) goes on to qualify embodied experience with this "delicious feeling of being in the midst of things" and experiencing them "a whole lot like what 'real' life is like" (p. 83). If this still sounds very much like the immersion felt when reading a book or watching a movie, I would like to draw attention to his mentioning of *actions* and *choices*, neither of which are available to the recipient of traditional media, only to game players. I am not arguing that games are better than traditional media, only that there is a crucial difference between *doing* and *witnessing*. You may be strongly emotionally invested in watching the hero being chased by the baddies, but this experience will be very different from enacting the scene in a video game, where the question whether the hero (= you) will get away hinges on your own wits and skills.* Raph Koster

---

*Torben Grodal wrote insightfully about the experience of playing a game versus watching a movie in *The Pleasures of Control* (2000).

(2005) seconds this notion of experiencing games as comparable to how we experience real life:

> But games are very real to me. Games might seem abstracted from reality because they are iconic depictions of patterns in the world. They have more in common with how our brain visualizes things than they do with how reality is actually formed. Since our perception of reality is basically abstractions anyway, I call it a wash. (p. 34)

I interpret Koster's "iconic depictions of patterns in the world" to mean *experiential gestalts* or *image schemata*, which, as explained in Chapter 3, are the abstract structures of actual experiences and can include their metaphorical projections. I want to stress, though, that, due to the player's active participation in the responsive environment of a game, all gameplay experiences are embodied, not just those of games that simulate something.

> The pattern depicted may or may not exist in reality. Nobody is claiming that tic-tac-toe is a decent mimicry of warfare, for example. But the rules we perceive – what I'll call the pattern – get processed exactly the same way we process very real things like 'fire burns' and 'how cars move forward'. (Koster 2005, p. 34)

What is important to note is that the potential of embodied experience to facilitate unique, medium-specific insights into the human condition lies in *how* it enables understanding and sense making. Its *lifelikeness* or *vividness* concerns the process of experiencing, not the content. *Tetris* is experienced in the same lifelike, vivid fashion as *Uncharted*. We understand how blocks fall and disappear in the same way we understand how to drive a Jeep or shoot a gun in *Uncharted*.

Chapter 3 explored how we can use the principles of experiential gestalts to systematically analyze our experiences and identify the salient elements of complex abstract concepts. The focus was on grasping the source systems of abstract concepts so that they can be made concrete via metaphors and modeled in the game through rules and mechanics, enabling insightful statements about relevant aspects of the human condition. The focus was on using rules and mechanics to communicate ideas about *how it works*. This chapter now focuses on the experience of playing the game as a source for meaning generation and insight into the human condition, of experiencing firsthand *what it feels like*. The notion of embodied experience generally refers to how we make sense of games—i.e., learning by doing—but it also points toward a game's potential to evoke the actual experience of real-life experiential gestalts through quasi-bodily enactment. This is especially relevant for complex abstract concepts, which are missing a physical manifestation in real life. We might feel like jumping through hoops, but we very rarely literally jump through hoops. We might feel like walking on a tight rope or on eggshells or being stuck in quicksand or being someone's punching ball or having our back against the wall or keeping the sea at bay—but, mostly, these are just figures of speech that lend substance to our otherwise abstract, inner states and help us comprehend them. Games, however, let us enact all of this. They can make abstract, inner states concrete by letting us physically enact them through our virtual bodies or other means of projection into a game environment. This opens the door for a powerful form of metaphorical mapping and meaning generation that plays a huge role in the design of deep games: *experiential metaphors.*

4.2 Experiential Metaphors—Modeling What It Feels Like

Unlike the metaphorical mappings discussed in Chapter 3, where the main concern was whether the structural metaphors that captured the source system accurately represented how it worked, experiential metaphors are a specific case of metaphorical projection. They rely on the game's affective dimension (Begy 2013). I understand experiential metaphors as an analogy between gameplay and real-life experience evoked by what the moment-to-moment gameplay *feels like*, whether these analogies were intended by the designers or not. In other words, when playing a game, we can suddenly and powerfully be reminded of another experience: "This [insert moment-to-moment gameplay] feels exactly like that [insert real-life experience]!" The following case study of the grappling hook sequence in *God of War II* gives an example for what I mean.

4.2.1 *Case Study:* God of War II, *Grappling Hook Sequence—Enacting the Art of Letting Go*

I am Kratos, the God of War, and I have reached a point in my journey where I need to cross a large, open area by swinging from one pillar to the next. As a player, I do this by identifying and activating a grip point on a pillar, then pressing R1 on the PlayStation 2 controller. In the game, my grappling hook shoots out, attaching itself to the grip point. When the connection is made, I can jump with X and start swinging. Releasing R1 on the controller releases the hook in the game. To attach to the next grip point on the next pillar, I have to press R1 again. There is always a dizzying and enervating moment of free fall between two grip points. Pressing R1 too quickly after a release latches the hook back to the former grip point. Waiting too long before pressing R1 again (= attaching) means I miss the next grip point and fall to my death. Timing is of the essence, both in terms of how long I wait before reattaching the hook and in terms of when I let go of the former grip point. If I release at the wrong time while swinging, I fly off in the wrong direction.

Playing this sequence from *God of War II* a few years ago came with a sudden, unexpected, and profound realization of what *life* felt like to me at the moment: a long relationship was ending, and I was about to leave the Massachusetts Institute of Technology to relocate to a different continent (once again), where I didn't have a full-time job lined up. Everything was *up in the air*. I didn't want to stay where I was—neither personally, professionally, or geographically—but I wasn't sure where I was going (personally, professionally, or geographically). I had to take the risk and let go of the old to be open for something new. The moment of transition, though—of being in mid-flight, neither firmly attached to the known nor connected to the new—scared the living bejesus out of me. I played the grappling hook sequence over and over again because it was reassuring to practice *letting go* and *moving on* in the safe space of the game, and it provided a much-needed mental preparation for the current challenges in real life.

Why was it possible to use jumping from pillar to pillar with a grappling hook as a way to gain clarity over and get to grips with breaking up and moving? Because—while very different on the fictional level—this gameplay sequence shared an experiential gestalt with my life situation: the *transition gestalt*. The transition gestalt can be characterized as follows:

Participant: The subject of transition (in that case, *me*).
Parts: Unsatisfying status quo A; more promising status B; need to let go of A in order to move to B; uncertainty while in transition from A to B.
Linear sequence: Implied in the above.
Purpose: Successfully transition from the unsatisfying status quo A to the more satisfying status B.

Quitting a job (before having a new offer), getting a haircut or tattoo (will it turn out OK?), moving across continents (what will it be like?), breaking up with someone (will there ever be a new love?), and the grappling hook sequence all share the same underlying, experiential gestalt of *transition*. The grappling hook sequence, however, is the only direct, physical manifestation of the gestalt among these examples. The concept of transition in my life was much more abstract, an inner process that could not be immediately observed. Playing the game, though, suddenly made it concrete. I could enact an abstract experience (apart from the mediated nature of the game itself) in a directly accessible manner. By literally letting go of an anchor point, being suspended in mid-air, and landing on the next anchor point, the game provided a structure onto which I could project my (similarly structured) internal experience, thus externalizing it and becoming more aware of it. The grappling hook sequence served as an experiential metaphor: the phenomenon of understanding a gameplay experience as a physical (however, virtual) manifestation of abstract ideas such as emotional processes or mental states.

Another famous example of this sort of experiential associations evoked through gameplay stems from seminal interactive media scholar Janet Murray (1998) when she described *Tetris* as a

> perfect enactment of the overtasked lives of Americans in the 1990s – of the constant bombardment of tasks that demand our attention and that we must somehow fit into our overcrowded schedules and clear off our desks in order to make room for the next onslaught. (...) Tetris allows us to symbolically experience agency over our lives. It is a kind of rain dance for the postmodern psyche, meant to allow us to enact control over things outside our power. (p. 144)

I believe the embodied nature of gameplay experiences is at the root of a game's wide appeal and that experiential metaphors are an underexplored yet powerful vehicle to shed light on the human experience: to provide experiential structures that make the intangible tangible; give us something concrete to play with, manipulate, and observe; and thus create distance and/or a sense of agency over inner conflicts. I believe this might be one of the (subconscious) reasons why we sometimes gravitate toward specific genres: tower defense games enable a physical enactment of *keeping the sea at bay*; the shooting gestalt is structured around a specific goal and affords highly targeted action with a powerful and clear outcome (i.e., take out the target). It thus provides a terrific antidote to the feeling of lacking impact, being frazzled, or being spread too thin—the opposite of focused, concentrated, and effective action.

4.3 Modeling What It Feels Like versus How It Works

For the deliberate design of deep games, it is important to note that a game can successfully model a complex, abstract concept via metaphors and make coherent and insightful statements about how the concept works, without evoking the actual experience of the modeled source system. An analysis of Rod Humble's game *The Marriage* clarifies the difference between modeling how it works and what it feels like.

4.3.1 *Case Study:* The Marriage

According to game designer Rod Humble (2007), *The Marriage* is his expression of "how marriage feels." I argue that this is not what the game actually models and that this is one of the main reasons the game is hard to decipher without other interpretative cues. Here is the rule summary as found on the game's Website (http://www.rodvik.com/rodgames/marriage.html):

Initially you have two squares a blue and a pink, on screen.
Soon different coloured circles will enter and leave the play space.
You have two controls.

1. When you mouse over the blue or pink square the blue square reduces in size and both squares move towards each other.
2. When you mouse over a circle it disappears and the pink square gets smaller.
   - When the edge of the blue square collides (or "kisses") with the edge of the pink square (but not when they overlap): the blue square shrinks slightly and becomes more transparent. The pink square grows slightly and becomes less transparent.
   - When the blue square touches any coloured circle but black then the blue square becomes less transparent and grows in size to a significant degree.
   - When the pink square touches any coloured circle but black then the pink square grows in size slightly.
   - When the pink or blue square touch a black circle they shrink significantly.
   - As time passes the pink square becomes more transparent.
   - When squares collide with things then a white bar at the bottom of the screen increases in size.

- When either the pink square or blue square shrink to nothing or become totally transparent then the game is over.
- The general game flow will be balancing the need to have the pink & blue squares "kiss" to insure the pink square does not fade from the marriage versus the blue square needing to touch the circles to insure it does not fade.

The rules suggest a specific perspective on marriage and make the following statements about it: for one, partners have slightly different *needs*, and both have to be satisfied for the relationship to work out. The game is hard, suggesting that keeping a marriage going is not a trivial task. It takes several attempts to figure out what to do, which is still no guarantee that one always does the right thing. The rules further make a statement that the equality of partners is important to have a mutually beneficial relationship. If one square gets too big, kissing edge to edge becomes impossible, the other square fades, and *The Marriage* fails. The game does not leave the option to lead an unhappy relationship. This implies an emotional rather than formal perspective on marriage. The marriage can theoretically still exist on paper, but what counts is the personal commitment.

The Marriage does an excellent job at conveying ideas about marriage (whether you agree with them or not) via its rules and mechanics. It does not, however, model *what marriage feels like*, as Humble claimed, but rather his view on how it works. When playing the game for the first time and being unaware of its title, I had no clue what it was about. Its fictional surface is abstract (circles and squares for partners and events), and the gameplay experience—the affective dimension evoked by the game mechanics of mousing over circles and squares, making the former grow and the latter disappear—did not, in any way, parallel the experience of being in a relationship. (Just as a comparison, even *Pong*, while, of course, much more simplistic and lacking the expressive depth of *The Marriage*, would do a more accurate job at modeling the experience of relationship because, at least, it allows the player to enact the interplay between two partners from the perspective of one of them!) Knowingly or not, Humble identified salient elements of (his experience of) marriage as a source system by systematically exploring its experiential gestalt. The translation process of these elements into the game, though, shifted the focus away from the lived experience of marriage to an observation and reflection on its dynamics. These dynamics are *informed* by what marriage feels like, but the way they have been translated into the game shifts the perspective to an outside view on marriage—how it works—rather than portraying the experience from the inside, what it feels like. The main indication of this shifted perspective is that you don't interact with the game from the point of view of one of the partners—as is usually the case in a relationship—but as an ominous agent of love, "trying to make the system of marriage work" (Humble 2007). If we model a source system from a different perspective, it changes its experiential gestalt dramatically to something that is unrecognizable or (worse!) something that feels completely different, possibly undermining or, at least, interfering with the game's theme and message.

The case study of *The Marriage* illustrated how games whose source systems are derived from very subjective, firsthand, lived experience do not necessarily recreate those experiences through gameplay. The reason is that, while we inevitably start with an exploration of how something feels like (because that is the only thing we have direct access to)—e.g., when we are trying to make sense of jealousy or envy or bliss—we often have to move away from the radically subjective, absorbing, immediate feeling to get a better understanding of what's going on. In the process of fleshing out the experiential gestalt; identifying its various elements; and seeing it as a complex, multidimensional, structured whole, we gain distance to it. Such is the nature of reflection. We look at the issue from different sides, and, by doing so, we gravitate toward an understanding of how it works, away from purely looking at what it feels like, an oscillation between the two. This is good and productive and one of the main reasons why a game design can help us make sense of ourselves, life, and our role within it, and how we relate to others. To give an example, to someone with obsessive–compulsive disorder (OCD), the anxiety feels very real that something bad might happen when a pencil isn't perfectly aligned with the edge of the desk. Yet, at the same time, the person with OCD can know that this is just a feeling. I might start by exploring the stab of jealousy, but, by doing so, I discover a connection to the element of self-esteem. Suddenly, I am modeling a system that portrays how jealousy works, not what it feels like, and I'm making a very different game from what I originally wanted to design.

This tension between what it feels like and how it works is a major challenge when designing games about the human condition. Negotiating it takes a careful consideration of what the game should really be about, what its purpose and message is, and how to best go about fulfilling this purpose and communicating the message.

4.4 Impact of Experiential Metaphors on Meaning Generation—Potentials and Pitfalls

Every game has an affective dimension and evokes some kind of emotional response that is tied to the game's structure. Aki Jarvinen has written at length and most insightfully about a game's affective aspects in his book *Games without Frontiers—Methods for Game Studies and Design* (2009), where he emphasizes the meaning of goals for the player experience.

> When we are talking about player emotions, we are talking about players' appraisals and actions in relation to goals. [...] Universality of goals for human psyche has been widely accepted, and therefore their role and function has been promoted into high status among emotion theorists. (p. 127)

The notion of experiential metaphors implies that games' affective dimension is another source for meaning generation: one that is particularly relevant to bear in mind in regard to the design of fictional, representational games. These games are about something. So far, we discussed how procedural expression and rhetoric—ideas expressed through the rules and mechanics—are the main vehicles for meaning (before the game's fiction). If the gameplay experience itself—the interconnected web of emotions it evokes—can also carry semantic freight, we need to take this into account when designing games with a communicative goal. The meaning implied in a game's experiential structure is often overlooked in the design process because the statements made by rules and fiction are so much more obvious (and a little less dependent on subjective experience).* The following case studies aim to illustrate how a game's affective dimension can support (*Angry Birds*) or undermine (*American McGee's Grimm: Little Red Riding Hood*) a game's theme and overall communicative goal

---

*The game's structure can mirror an experiential gestalt from real life, but whether that gestalt is recognized depends on what the player focuses on. As designers, we can only create the conditions for an experience to be evoked. Whether players have this experience depends on factors on their side we don't have any influence over. As in real life, engaging in an activity that is connected to an experiential gestalt does not mean that this is where our attention is. The activity is happening on one level, but, if we are internally occupied with something else, our experience of that moment is likely disconnected from the activity. For example, if I'm cleaning the house, but I am busy thinking about an oppressive work situation, the work situation is the experience I'm focusing on and trying to make sense of, not the cleaning, although cleaning has its own characteristic gestalt. Same with a game: I might be clearing off blocks in *Tetris*, and I'm registering that activity on some level, but I'm really thinking about what's for dinner. In that case, I won't be actively engaged in *Tetris'* intrinsic experiential gestalt of clearing tasks off my desk, as Murray described it.

and/or create an ethically charged subtext that makes a game's message even more concerning than it might have appeared at first glance (*Left Behind: Eternal Forces*).

4.4.1 *Case Study:* Angry Birds—*Mechanics of Vengeance*

Before the actual gameplay starts, the player learns through a narrative sequence that the birds are angry because the pigs stole their eggs, and the birds now want revenge. Vengeance is thus the game's declared theme, and, as we shall see, this is perfectly aligned with and substantiated by its experiential gestalt. The gameplay consists of the player loading a slingshot with birds of different sizes, pulling it back, aiming and unleashing the feathery fright in the direction of the pig's housings, and aiming to destroy them with the bird projectile. The rules mainly model the laws of physics: how the force with which the slingshot is pulled back and the angle at which it is released impact flight curve and determine where the bird lands and whether and how much damage it does. Beyond that, the rules do not make any statements or communicate ideas. The game's meaning lies mostly in its experiential gestalt and how well it meshes with its fiction.

Angry Birds leverages what Mark Johnson has identified as one of the seven most basic and pervasive force gestalt structures in our physical experience of the world: the *removal of restraint*. He defines the removal of restraint as follows:

> When the door is opened, we are free to come into the room. When the fence is taken away, the dog can visit its canine neighbors, if it so chooses. The removal of a barrier or the absence of some potential restraint is a structure of experience that we encounter daily. The relevant schema is thus one that suggests an open way or path, which makes possible an exertion of force. (Johnson 1990, p. 46)

The removal of restraint gestalt matches *Angry Birds'* vengeance theme perfectly:

1. A force is being built up by pulling back the slingshot = anger is being cultivated and nourished by mulling over how one has been wronged.
2. The player lets go of the slingshot, thus removing restraint to the force = whatever constraints held the anger back are now removed; self-control and social constraints are overridden by the built-up emotion.
3. The force is unleashed = anger is unleashed in a stroke of righteousness, unstoppable.

The removal of restraint gestalt, however, is in itself neutral or—as Johnson calls it—nonpropositional. It is not "a rich image or mental picture; rather, it is a more abstract pattern that can be manifested in rich images, perceptions and events" (Johnson 1990, p.2). Successfully writing a test (studying = force/knowledge buildup; test writing = removing restraint, unleashing force/knowledge on paper; impact = impressing the professor), finally eating that chocolate bar (growing craving = force buildup; giving in to craving = removing restraint), or opening a dam (water = force buildup; opening dam = removing restraint) all share the same gestalt, yet they all represent something different.

In the case of games, the fiction goes a long way to contextualize the abstract structure of an experiential gestalt and give it its specific nuances of meaning. In the case of *Angry Birds,* the gestalt is contextualized as vengeance, not just through the narrative introduction but also by way of how vengeance is enacted through gameplay. The slingshot mechanism goes beyond a simple removal of restraint (such as opening a door) by including the aspect of *rebound.* Revenge is an enactment of *what goes around comes around.* First, you might get pushed back—pigs may steal your eggs—but you'll get back at them with ferocious, feathery force. Further, the removal of restraint gestalt, as materialized in the slingshot experience, is accompanied by a moment of lack of control. While the bird projectile is in the air, there is nothing one can do. This mirrors the experience of loss of self-control when pushed over the edge (that which actually triggers the removal of restraint). You just know you're super mad, and whatever clever reply you had prepared in your mind (when you loaded the mental slingshot with a mean fudge-muffin of a bird) develops a life of its own and is outside your control once you confront your adversary. You started hurling (!) insults, and, once they've been spoken, it's too late—you can just hope for the best. Unless you're really, really good at *Angry Birds,* unleashing a bird is not like a surgical strike; it's mayhem, it's madness, and, when you miss and those stupid pigs smirk at you, you're ready to do it all again and again and again. Speaking of myself here: the madder I get, the worse my ability to aim properly and hit anything. I'm stuck in the mechanics of vengeance.

When a game's experiential gestalt is perfectly matched and contextualized by its fiction, even the most shallow-looking, purely fun game can achieve conceptual depth. The *Angry Birds'* design is a stroke of genius not just because it's so addictive but also because it could not have coupled gestalt and fiction more fittingly and meaningfully. In contrast, there is a tension in *American McGee's Grimm: Little Red Riding Hood* between its experiential structure and its fictional theme.

4.4.2 *Case Study:* American McGee's Grimm: Little Red Riding Hood—*Mechanics of Cleaning*

Grimm, a dwarf as smelly as he is sarcastic, has gotten fed up with the brainless, saccharine sweetness of fairyland. The game begins with a noninteractive narrative sequence in which Grimm gives a scathing analysis of the tale of Little Red Riding Hood. He points out the implausible granny–wolf confusion, and granny's and Little Red Riding Hood's even more implausible rescue from the belly of the beast by an anatomy-savvy lumberjack. To set the record straight, Grimm embarks on a fouling mission that spreads chaos and darkness all over fairyland. This is what you do in the game: you run around as Grimm, contaminating the environment with your griminess, turning it and its inhabitants from cute and clean to dreadful and disgusting. Obviously, this rude romping around is met with resistance by fairy creatures, who desperately try to clean up after you. To stun them, you can butt stomp: you jump and land on the ground with your butt, immobilizing the neat freaks around you for a little while. You can also move by jumping. Grimm's idle animation is peeing.

While the game's graphics are delightfully dark and gloomy, communicating a rebellious and anarchic subversion of fairy cuteness, playing the game felt nothing like it to me. Why? Because playing the game felt exactly like cleaning to me. Cleaning is arguably the most common or obvious manifestation of the conversion gestalt, which looks as follows:

Participant: Someone converting something from status A to B.
Parts:
- There is an undesirable status quo A (with a spatial component).
- There is a desirable status B (with a spatial component) that takes status A's place.
- There is an element of resistance that undermines the conversion efforts.

Stages:
- Undesirable status A is the initial state.
- An action needs to be taken to change status A to B.
- The conversion from A to B requires effort.
- The element of resistance undermines conversion efforts.
- Desirable status B is achieved.

Linear sequence: Implied in above.

When this gestalt manifests as cleaning, the undesirable status A is the dirty apartment, and the desirable status B is the clean apartment. The element of resistance consists of people walking over the freshly scrubbed floors or dust collecting again on the sparkly surfaces. Very rarely is the conversion gestalt applied to making something dirty, but it principally works exactly the same way. The gameplay experience in *Grimm* is *reverse* cleaning. The gestalt is recontextualized through the fiction of making fairyland dirty, but the experience remains the same right down to the feeling that you must not *miss a spot*. I expected the game to feel liberating, dismantling the orderly surface of fairyland to reveal its seedy underbelly in a rebellious, anarchic sort of way. Yet, due to the conversion gestalt, there is an obsessive–compulsive quality to the gameplay experience, a rigor and righteousness that seem mismatched with playing as the unshaven, stinky, subversive Grimm.

The last example also features the conversion gestalt, but, this time, the mapping between the game structure and fiction creates an ethically charged subtext that might very well be aligned with the message the developers wanted to send. This case study is not aimed at pointing out a mismatch but rather at how a game's gestalt structure can impact its messages and, in this case, reinforce an already dubious theme, making it even more problematic.

4.4.3 *Case Study:* Left Behind: Eternal Forces—*Mechanics of Cleaning Contextualized as Religious Purge*

Left Behind: Eternal Forces (LBEF) is a Christian real-time strategy game based on the *Left Behind* novel series. The game's premise is that the Tribulation Force (Christians' angelic army) is fighting against the Antichrist, represented by Nicolae Carpathia and his Global Community, in an end-of-days battle in New York City in the aftermath of the Rapture, an event where millions of people disappeared from the earth and were beamed straight to heaven. The game's main goal is to build the Tribulation Force and its infrastructure. One of its core aspects is converting the baddies and nonbelievers to the Christian faith, so no one is left behind during the apocalypse (although, if it doesn't work, you can kill them, too). Conversion is achieved by clicking on nonbelievers to raise their spirit points until they start praying. People's faith, however, wears off if it is not reignited every once in a while. To prevent them from falling back into the Antichrist's clutches, you have to make sure they pray in regular intervals by clicking on them again. Again, the underlying experiential gestalt is that of conversion, and I argue that it is this experiential structure that really makes *LBEF* problematic, not so much its individual mechanics. Why? Let's have a closer look at the implied meaning of the gestalt structure and how it impacts the game's affective dimension:

- Status quo A is declared undesirable and denoted negative.
- Status B is declared desirable and denoted positive.
- According to Jarvinen, our emotions are coupled to our goals, and thus the emotional experience of the gestalt is coupled to the goal of converting status A to status B.
- Hence, the antagonistic force (nonbelievers or the wearing-off of belief over time) is easily and clearly established as *the enemy* and thus can be met with righteous anger for undermining one's efforts to change states from A to B.
- Since clear values of good and evil have been ascribed to status A and B, reflection and doubt are eliminated.
- There is one right course of action that must not be questioned, and there is no need for persuasion or even considering the other's perspective. It is a simple matter of changing states from A to B (or it wouldn't be the conversion gestalt anymore).

All of this follows that *LBEF* aims to brainwash. Different views do not need to (and, in fact, cannot) be taken into account. When you're cleaning, you are not waiting for the dirt to make an argument for its existence and to hear its side. Cleaning is a straightforward activity. If you apply the cleaning gestalt to the conversion of religious or political views, you create an analogy between *the others who need to be converted* and *dirt* and eliminate every option for dialogue or negotiation. This message was probably intended by the developers, but, without being aware of gestalt structures and the role they play for meaning generation, it is hard to put one's finger on why exactly this game is so ethically charged. Deliberate design and a thorough and conscientious game analysis need to consider all of a game's expressive channels. The experiential gestalt is one of them.

EXERCISES

1. **Identify experiential gestalts in real life.**
   - Pay attention to your experiences in the course of the day.
   - Identify two to three experiential gestalts.
   - Clearly describe the abstract structure of each by breaking it down into its various elements (participants, parts, stages, linear sequence, purpose).

- Find at least three more concrete experiences for each of the abstract gestalt structures you identified.
- Map each concrete experience dimension for dimension with its corresponding abstract gestalt structure.
- Submit a write-up that includes the following:
  - A brief reflection on what it was like to pay attention to your experiences throughout the day.
  - What was it like to identify experiential gestalts—was it easy or hard? Why? Did this change in the course of the day, and, if so, how?
  - List the abstract experiential gestalt structures you identified with a breakdown of their dimensions.
  - Juxtapose each of the abstract experiential gestalt structures with three concrete experiences. (This can include the original experience that made you notice the gestalt structure.) If you can't find another experience that matches 1:1, chances are you have not found a gestalt structure.

2. **Identify the experiential gestalts of casual games.**
   - Play at least four to five casual games (or as many as needed beyond that to find at least one with a recognizable experiential gestalt) that are representational on the fictional level (i.e., not abstract games, as defined in Chapter 2).*
   - Pay particular attention to what playing each game *feels like*.

Note: Some games might not feel like anything to you because either they don't have a recognizable gestalt, or it doesn't resonate with you at the moment, and you can't perceive it.

- Once you have found a game whose gameplay experience strongly reminds you of an experience from real life, systematically map the game's structure to the structure of the experience it reminds you of. The more games you can find with identifiable experiential gestalts, the better.
- Analyze how well the game's structure matches its fictional theme. Does it reinforce the theme, undermine the theme, or create a dubious subtext? Is it disconnected from the theme? Be specific and provide examples from the game to support your arguments.

---

*Casual games are particularly useful for this exercise because you can access many different gameplay experiences in a short time.

- Submit a write-up on the due date that includes the following:
  - A two-to-three-sentence description of each casual game played.
  - A one-paragraph statement: which of these games felt like a real-life experience, and which did not?
  - For games with a recognizable experiential gestalt, provide a systematic analysis of the gestalt including a dimension-for-dimension mapping with the real-life experience it reminded you of.
  - A detailed analysis of the relationship between the game's theme, its fictional surface, and its experiential gestalt.

3. Metaphorical game design

Step 1: In preparation of the design exercise, read the following texts:

- George Lakoff and Mark Johnson: *Metaphors We Live By.* pp. 61–96.
- Steven Pinker: *The Stuff of Thought: Language as a Window into Human Nature.* pp. 235–278.
- Doris C. Rusch and Matthew Weise: *Games About Love and Trust?* Available at http://gambit.mit.edu/readme/papers/games-about-love-and-trust-har.php.

Step 2: In groups of three, pick a complex, abstract concept, e.g., dignity, trust, faith.

Step 3: Explore and identify the concept's dimensions/elements.

- What is its multidimensional gestalt?
- What is the system? How do the various elements/dimensions relate to each other?
- What is/are the metaphor(s) you are using to represent the abstract concept?
- From which perspective will the player explore the system?

Note: Step 3 will need to be revisited and refined while you are building the prototype. Fleshing out the multidimensional gestalt, the system, and its metaphorical presentation is part of the iterative process of game design.

Step 4: Identify your approach: do you want to model what it feels like or how it works?

Step 5: Create deliverables, including the following:

- A one-paragraph statement of intent:
  - What is the abstract concept you intend to model?
  - What is the core metaphor you are using to capture the abstract concept?
  - What is your approach: modeling how it works or what it feels like?

- An analog prototype that tackles the abstract concept in a meta-phorical way.
- A summary of the game's elements and rules including an explana-tion of their metaphorical meaning—how does each element cor-respond to the multidimensional gestalt of the underlying abstract concept?

Step 6: Bring the prototype to class.

Step 7: Submit a statement of intent and rules with an explanation of metaphorical meaning by the due date.

4. Game of Love

Make a card game for two to four players that models salient aspects of love/relationship. The *Game of Love* exercise challenges you to base a game on a complex abstract idea, namely, *love*, by using metaphors and no other material than playing cards.

Use a deck of traditional playing cards to capture aspects of the con-cept *love* in the game rules. The resulting game can either model what aspects of love/relationship *feel like*, or it can focus on how aspects of love/relationship *work*. Questions you might want to explore to get you started could be, "How do partners interact?"; "What are the challenges and obstacles love can overcome?"; or "Is there a goal in love (or a rela-tionship)? What would such a goal be, and how could it be achieved?"

The first approach—modeling what it feels like—aims to evoke an experience associated with love in the player (e.g., the player experi-ences feelings of *caring, longing,* or *jealousy*). The second approach—modeling how it works—enables a more cognitive understanding of the *rules of love* without the immediate emotional engagement (e.g., the player explores the mechanisms of caring as an important aspect of a certain kind of love through the game's system but without experienc-ing feelings of caring himself or herself while doing so).

In order to translate your ideas about love into a game and concrete mechanics, ask yourself what the parallels are between your concept of love and the structure games usually take: is there a goal, and, if so, what is it? Is there a winning/losing condition? What is the conflict/challenge? Should the game be competitive or collaborative? Stay within the metaphor as much as you can, to make sure that all your game rules and mechanics support your concept/interpretation of love as a game.

The challenge:

- Design with intent: decide whether you want to model *what (aspects) of love feel like* or *how (aspects) of love work.*

- Identify the aspects of love you want to focus on, and write them down.
- Identify metaphors to capture the identified aspects of love with playing cards/the card game rules.
- Design a card game about love that uses metaphors to make salient aspects of love emotionally tangible and/or cognitively understandable to players.
- Playtest your game with players.
- Interview your players about their experience playing the game, and ask them to describe the ways in which the game made them think about love.
- Iterate on your design by revising the rules and interaction until the game models either what it feels like or how it works.

Rules of the challenge: Use only a traditional card deck. You can use a subset of the card deck but no additional materials. The game can be for two to four players. Each element in the game needs to support the love metaphor you identified. The metaphor needs to be coherent, and there must be no element/rule/mechanic in the game that is unrelated to the metaphor.

Challenge complete:

- Provide a paragraph explaining your design intent: what aspect of love did you intend to capture in the game and how (focusing on modeling what it feels like and/or how it works)?
- Create a playable card game about love.
- Provide a list of all the game rules/mechanics, and explain how each rule/mechanic represents an aspect of love you are trying to capture in the game.
- Explain how the game's dynamics are either intended to evoke an experience you associate with love and/or enable the player to understand certain mechanisms of love.
- Protocol playtesting results and design iterations: what have you learnt through the process?
- Once complete, submit on the due date.

Review criteria:

- *Cohesion:* Is there an alignment between the game rules/mechanics and the love concept underlying the game?
- *Tangibility:* Is the metaphor emotionally and/or cognitively tangible to players?
- *Resonance:* Can players relate to your interpretation of love?

References

Begy, J. 2013. Experiential Metaphors in Abstract Games. In Mäyrä, F.; Zagal, J.; Waern, A.; Juul, J. and Consalvo, M. (Eds.) *Transactions of the Digital Games Research Association, Vol. 1, No 1.*

Gee, J. 2004. *What Video Games Have to Teach Us About Learning and Literacy.* New York: Palgrave Macmillan.

Grodal, T. 2000. Video games and the pleasures of control. In Zillmann, D. and Vorderer, P. (Eds.), *Media Entertainment: The Psychology of its Appeal* (pp. 197–215). Mahwah, NJ: Lawrence Erlbaum Associates.

Humble, R. 2007. The Marriage: A computer game by Rod Humble. Available at http://www.rodvik.com/rodgames/marriage.html. Accessed on September 5, 2016.

Jarvinen, A. 2009. *Games without Frontiers: Methods for Game Studies and Design.* Saarbrücken: VDM Verlag Dr. Müller.

Johnson, M. 1990. *The Body in the Mind: The Bodily Basis of Meaning, Imagination and Reason.* Chicago and London: University of Chicago Press.

Koster, R. 2005. *A Theory of Fun for Game Design.* Scottsdale, AZ: Paraglyph Press.

Murray, J. 1998. *Hamlet on the Holodeck: The Future of Narrative in Cyberspace.* Cambridge, MA: The MIT Press.

5

Allegorical Games—
Or the Monster Isn't a
Monster Isn't a Monster

Wherein:

- *The potentials of allegorical games to evoke deep gameplay experiences are discussed, such as*
  - *Allowing to make inner processes tangible,*
  - *Creating a "magic" door to a deeper theme,*
  - *Avoiding distractions from the theme, and*
  - *Making players think and providing an incentive to keep playing.*
- *These potentials are exemplified by way of a comparative analysis of four allegorical games:*
  - Silent Hill 2
  - Papo & Yo
  - Spirits of Spring
  - Journey
- *Three design approaches are then proposed, each emphasizing another function of metaphor use in allegorical games:*
  - *Metaphor as message*
  - *Metaphor as mystery*
  - *Metaphor as muse*
- *To apply theory to practice, guidelines are presented on how to go about designing allegorical games:*
  - *Suggesting the "hero's journey" as an organizing structure*

- *Identifying the communicative goal (i.e., metaphor as message, mystery, or muse)*
- *How to playtest and iterate depending on the communicative goal*

5.1 Introduction

The approaches of deep game design described so far focused on how we can use experiential gestalt structures to model complex, abstract ideas to provide insight into what salient aspects of the human experience *feel like* or *how they work*. Obviously, this is not the only way to make games that teach us something about ourselves, that make us see the world with different eyes and leave us pondering profound questions about life. Titles such as *Journey, Silent Hill 2 (SH2), Papo & Yo,* and *Spirits of Spring* all have deeper meaning. They are about something beyond their immediately visible, fictional surface, and they all use metaphors to communicate their messages. These metaphors, however, are extended and combined to larger narratives rather than portraying the games' underlying complex, abstract concepts as one individual gestalt structure. This makes these games allegories. According to Dictionary.com, an allegory is "A story that has a deeper or more general meaning in addition to its surface meaning. Allegories are composed of several symbols or metaphors." Allegories include characters and events that stand for abstract ideas. *Journey* depicts one character's travel through the desert to a mysterious beacon, but, in truth, it is a more general contemplation of the hero's journey, identity, growth, and search for meaning. *SH2* is not really about a man looking for his dead wife in a creepy, foggy town filled with monsters, but rather a metaphorical portrayal of a psychotherapeutic process to recover and come to terms with the repressed truth about the wife's death (Rusch 2009). *Papo & Yo* is a young boy's fantastic journey through the Brazilian favelas whose goal is to lead the monster that accompanies him to a shaman to cure it of its frog addiction. In truth, the game is about the young boy's struggle with his alcoholic father. *Spirits of Spring* tells the story of Chiwatin, a young native, who is the guardian of spring. Spring is taken away by the evil crows, and Chiwatin and his friends, Rabbit and Bear, set out to get it back. The game uses this fictional surface to explore issues of bullying and the role of friendship in surviving it.

By way of a comparative analysis of these four example games, the following explores the potentials of allegories to create deep gameplay experiences.

The discussion then shifts to three allegorical design approaches, each emphasizing a different way in which metaphors can make you think and pursue their expressive and communicative goals: (1) *metaphor as mystery*, (2) *metaphor as message*, and (3) *metaphor as muse*.

The last part of this chapter applies the insights won from game analysis to the practice of designing allegorical games, including a brief introduction to narrative structure and an overview of decisions that need to be considered throughout the design process to define and achieve the game's purpose and experience goal. The example games have been chosen because they span a wide spectrum of metaphorical game design, tackle salient aspects of the human experience (e.g., personal growth, guilt and forgiveness, letting go, abuse, and bullying), and are relatively well known. It is important to note that this is an exploratory, exemplary study that does by no means claim comprehensiveness. It is possible that there exist other approaches than those discussed here. To get the most out of this chapter, it is recommended to play the games before reading on because analyzing them in detail goes beyond the scope of this book. Also, there will be spoilers!

5.2 Potentials of Allegorical Games

Why should we make allegorical games? How can they facilitate gameplay that is meaningful, thought-provoking, engaging, and provides insight into the human experience?

5.2.1 Reason 1: Making Inner Processes Tangible

As described in Chapter 3, Section 3.3.1, metaphors allow us to make abstract, inner processes tangible, providing inside views into someone's emotional landscape. Of the five examples, this aspect is most emphasized in the horror survival adventure game *Silent Hill 2*. *SH2* is set in the main character James Sunderland's psyche, which, due to overwhelming guilt and emotional trauma, has truly become a horror survival environment. His journey through the town in search for his dead wife is a journey through his subconscious to recover his repressed memories, namely, that he killed his terminally ill spouse to relieve her from her suffering. The puzzles and roadblocks encountered on the way represent the psychological obstacles that have to be overcome in search of the truth. The lock-and-key puzzles share analogies with the process of psychotherapeutic discovery: another session, another door is opened, and another part of the emotional land-scape becomes accessible. The ubiquitous fog can be understood as a men-tal fog that needs to be lifted (and is lifted in the end of the game, when the mystery about Mary has been cleared up). The monsters that lurk in the fog can be understood as torturing thoughts and feelings that are haunting James. Pyramid Head, the game's boss monster that keeps appearing but remains unbeatable until the end, stands for how James perceives himself: a faceless (heartless) executioner. Only once James comes to terms with what he has done and is able to forgive himself does he become able to face Pyramid Head and eliminate him/James' distorted perception of himself from his inner world. To find out what happened to Mary, the journey leads from the cemetery (a recollection of death?) into town (a surface explora-tion of the emotional landscape) to the historical society (digging deeper into the past) and across the lake (analogous to the river Acheron that leads to the land of the dead) to the hotel that used to be James' and Mary's special place (representing a more thorough examination of their relation-ship), and, from there, deeper and deeper down into the earth through a grave (!) and seemingly never-ending vertical tunnels (deeper into James' subconscious), until the final confrontation with Mary where the truth is revealed and Pyramid Head can be overcome.

With its metaphorical treatment of the psychotherapeutic process, *SH2* allows the player to experience the tensions of an uneasy mind; the frustra-tions of getting lost in the fog or being stuck with a puzzle; and the feeling of loss, helplessness, and outrage when Maria—James' sexy fantasy version of his wife Mary—is (seemingly) killed by Pyramid Head, repeating the trauma of losing a lover to the executioner, the powerlessness in the face of this overwhelming foe, and the feeling of resolution and closure at the end of the game when the mystery is solved and Pyramid Head is done for. A literal approach to the therapy theme could not have evoked these feelings because it could not have depicted what it feels like on the inside. Also, it would have been hard-pressed for an interesting game mechanic. Playing a guy who's sitting on the couch and talking for the whole game doesn't sound very appealing…

Papo & Yo by Minority Media is a similar case, since it also uses meta-phors to provide an inside view into what it is like for a child to live with an abusive, alcoholic father. How the child perceives his father as a monster is probably the most obvious aspect of this. Even more insightful, however, is the metaphorical nature of the core mechanics: to navigate the Brazilian favelas the game is set in, one can create pathways by interacting with chalk marks on buildings and sidewalks, or stack houses onto each other to build bridges from one area to the other. These core mechanics metaphorically represent the inner process of imaginative play and make its importance to retain a sense of agency in a disempowering, abusive relationship tangible through gameplay. The toy robot Lula is another piece of the metaphorical vocabulary related to imaginative play. It enables Quico to jump very high or reach otherwise inaccessible places in the environment. Lula can also be understood as Quico's mother who protects her son, but is destroyed when getting between him and Monster, leaving Quico even more vulnerable and robbed of Lula's empowering function (until Lula is revived later on in the game). While the metaphors in *Papo & Yo* provide a glimpse into Quico's inner experience of life with his alcoholic father, the game's allegorical nature also serves another purpose (Figure 5.1).

FIGURE 5.1
Minority Media's *Papo & Yo*

5.2.2 Reason 2: Creating a "Magic Door" to a Deeper Theme

According to the creative masterminds of Minority Media, Vander Caballero and Ruben Farrus, metaphors provide a magic door to topics that are otherwise hard to stomach or potentially unappealing to a gamer audience. Who really wants to play a game about bullying or dealing with abusive parents? Probably fewer people than those who are attracted by rich, imaginative narrative experiences set in mythical environments far removed from everyday life, in which players can engage in actions a simulation that was firmly anchored in a literal depiction of a theme would not allow for. In his 2013 Serious Play conference talk "Secrets to Amazing Transformational Games," Jesse Schell mentions seven ways to make the player care about a game, one of them being "make me care by connecting with my fantasies."

Metaphors are a great way to transport the mundane into the magical, to stimulate imagination, and to provide a fantasy that draws players in. By doing so, they also offer a new way of seeing and experiencing a topic, thus enabling a player's fresh engagement with and unbiased exploration of it. Neither *Papo & Yo* nor *Spirits of Spring* give away their themes right away. It is by building relationships with game characters, establishing a conflict, and exploring the gameworld that the player slowly discovers the underlying meaning.

In both games, experience comes first: *Papo & Yo* makes the player care about Monster, who, in the beginning, seems harmless enough. He sleeps a lot, and Quico can use his big belly as a trampoline to jump to high places. Monster follows Quico from one area in the game to another, evoking a companionship idea. Only when Monster consumes the first frogs (metaphors for alcohol) does he turn into a flaming inferno of rage that slaps Quico around. This is when the game shows its serious side, but, at this point, one is already invested in Quico, hooked by the whimsical mechanics of traversing the favelas, and hopeful that one can possibly cure Monster of his frog affliction to save him as a companion.

Spirits of Spring is equally sneaky about introducing its theme. It starts by presenting the player character Chiwatin and his two friends, Rabbit and Bear, in a pleasurable nature environment. Chiwatin's job is to guard spring by tending to special trees that keep spring anchored and stable. He/the player does so by collecting the spirits of spring, which dance around flowers, and delivering them to dead spring trees to bring them back to life. If a spring tree is not brought back, permanent winter takes over. Collecting the spirits also creates a spirit string that floats after Chiwatin. He can send the string out to collect faraway spirits and use it to build bridges across water. The more spirits, and the longer the string, the farther its reach. Reviving a spring tree obviously uses up spirits, and new ones have to be acquired to elongate the string again.

The first few minutes of this short game are dedicated to learning the core mechanics, building a relationship with Rabbit and Bear, and simply enjoying the pretty spring landscape. A very desirable status quo has been established that is suddenly endangered when the evil crows appear. They are shown stealing the spirits of spring from the trees, converting the landscape into a hostile, icy desert. Soon after, one sees that the crows have also destroyed the beaver camp, establishing them as a serious enemy and a threat to the other animals in the game, such as Rabbit and Bear. Now, there is double motivation to do something about them. There is no particular reason for the crows to steal spring or harm other animals, other than to be mean. The game does a great job at making you really angry at those birds, wishing to teach them a lesson, but feeling powerless and weak. A successful alignment has been created between the player and someone who is being bullied, but without outright saying that this is what the game is about. The rest of the game explores more experiences related to bullying, and the theme is made more and more explicit: the temptation of resorting to violence yourself (a shifty fox gives you a power up that not only makes you strong but also destructive), switching sides, from being a victim to being a bully, hurting your friends in the process, realizing that you have become a bully yourself, making amends with friends, reconciliation, and the triumph of friendship over the bullies.

The game deals with salient aspects of the bullying experience (albeit in a very linear fashion that does not give the player many choices in how to handle the situation) but without immediately evoking bullying associations through its setting (e.g., schoolyard), or the depiction of characters (e.g., nerds versus jocks). Leveraging allegory to create a magic door to a particular topic also promotes creative freedom in regard to the game's core mechanics, goals, and conflicts, opening up new opportunities for meaning generation that can reinforce the theme and provide multiple layers of depth.

5.2.3 Reason 3: The Theme and Nothing but the Theme

What would the gameplay be like in a game about bullying that was set in a schoolyard? What would the player do? Stand around? Chat with friends? Play catch? Would the bullies steal your lunch box, and would you try to get it back? What would be the bigger goal? The conflict? Maybe you and your nerd friends are trying to organize a comic book fair, but the bullies are sabotaging your efforts. Sure, it would be possible to design such a game. Taking a literal approach, though, can easily distract from the core theme, from the essence of the experience the game aims to convey. If organizing the comic book fair is what you are trying to do, it is easy to shift the focus on this task, withdrawing attention from what bullying really is about. A literal approach is also very limiting in terms of the core mechanics, goals, and conflicts it affords; they have to be realistic, observable, and anchored in the physical world. Due to its allegorical nature, *Spirits of Spring* remains true to its theme across all levels of meaning generation. Moreover, it reinforces its theme through its core mechanics: goal and conflict. Chiwatin's job of guarding spring in the gameworld can be understood as analogous to someone who manages the emotional climate of his environment: someone who makes sure things remain sunny and bright and everything/everyone flourishes, and who cultivates a sense of play for himself or herself and others. The crows spoil that emotional climate. They take away the fun and playfulness and bring about the winter everyone fears. The goal is to reestablish the previous condition (spring/emotional well-being/sense of play), but, of course, that isn't easy because the crows interfere all the time. After trying to eliminate the crows (and thus neglecting spring guardian duties!), the conflict is resolved by shifting the focus from the crows back to one's friends (arguably an oversimplified solution to the problem, but one way of looking at the issue).

The metaphorical approach enables an insightful abstraction from and the distillation of reality; there are no distracting details or actions that could draw attention away from the core theme onto other ideas. It gets right to the point: what is bullying *really* about? It's not about stealing a lunch box or interfering with the organization of a comic book fair, or crashing a poetry reading. It's about threatening emotional balance and making you feel powerless to do something about it. That's what all physical manifestations of bullying have in common when you shift from an outside view—what is physically observable—to an inside perspective—what it feels like. Bullies disturb an inner springtime. By using allegory to cut straight to the core, one can ensure that every aspect of the game is *on theme* and supports and reinforces the intended message: the core mechanics, the goal, the conflict, the setting, the characters, and the narrative.

A metaphorical treatment of a topic further provides the creative freedom to invent metaphorical core mechanics that would not be possible, if the

FIGURE 5.2
Minority Media's *Spirits of Spring*—Building Bridges
with a Strong Spirit

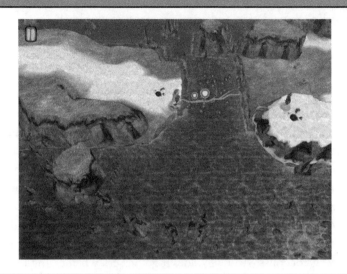

game had to be realistic.* Metaphorical core mechanics, if informed by the theme, can add another layer of meaning. It is certainly no coincidence that one of Chiwatin's main abilities is to build bridges with the spirits of spring. He connects. By taking away the spirits, the crows disconnect (Figure 5.2).

This is in line with the isolating effect of bullying. Bullies destroy social connectedness. You feel like an outcast. In the game, friendship is the key to overcome bullying. Friendship is about building bridges, about connection, and about a feeling of togetherness. The bridge-building mechanic would not have made sense in a realistic, literal game environment, yet it adds another layer of meaning, communicating another insightful message about the experience and effects of bullying.

Admittedly, one could argue that I have no proof this meaning was intended by the developers, that I'm just making this up. Well. As stated in Chapter 3, p. 53, metaphors tend to be open for interpretation, but possible interpretations are never arbitrary. One needs to be able to make a case for the proposed meaning, to clearly show the analogies between the metaphor and what it represents. I believe I have done that, and my reading makes sense.

---

*This does not mean that metaphorical core mechanics must always be unrealistic. It just means that they are not bound by the expectation of how things work in real life.

Other readings could be valid, too, and that is a good thing. Interpreting metaphors is not about finding that one ultimate truth. It is about inquiring a semiotic possibility space, thus gaining a deeper, more complex understanding of the concept the metaphors represent. I see this as another strength of metaphorical game design and another reason to employ it.

5.2.4 Reason 4: Allegories Make You Think

According to Schell (2013), another way in which games can make us care is by engaging our curiosity. Allegorical games are exceedingly good at that. Why? Because they are about something else than what they present on their fictional surface. There is something underneath that surface that is the game's true theme. This makes these kinds of games *deep* in a very literal sense of the word: you need to dive below the surface to discover their hidden meaning. Metaphors raise questions; their hidden meaning calls out from *down below*. In *Papo & Yo*, we wonder, who is this monster? Why does it live in a house? What's its relationship to the boy? Why does Monster fall asleep when eating coconuts? And why does it go berserk when eating frogs?

SH2 very openly starts with a mystery: how can a dead woman write a letter? The game is full of clues that hint at its underlying meaning. There is so much symbolism about its locations alone; there are all these strange notes you find. When you save the game at one of the red marks, James Sunderland thinks that it "feels like someone's groping around in my mind," hinting at the psychological aspect of the game. Somehow, one knows that this is not just a horror game, and the monsters are not simply enemies to give the player something to hit with a crowbar. They represent something. But what is it?

There is an exquisite pleasure in slowly uncovering a metaphorical game's hidden meaning, in putting the pieces together and trying to make sense of it all. Even if one never arrives at one coherent reading, if the game feeds you enough clues that you think the key to it all is just around the corner, this can create an enormous pull. Media scholar Henry Jenkins wrote in his book *Convergence Culture* (2006), "fandom, after all, is born of a balance between fascination and frustration" (p. 247). Applied to allegorical games, the tension between being fascinated with a game's promise of a secret message and the frustration of not quite getting it (yet) can be a powerful vehicle for a player's investment into and continued engagement with a game. Just look at the many articles, blog posts, and forum entries that populate the Web with speculations about what metaphorical games, from *Braid* to *The Path*, are about.

5.3 Metaphor as Mystery, Message, and Muse— Three Ways to Make You Think

As stated in Section 5.1, metaphors make you think. You have to work to uncover their hidden meaning, and, from a design perspective, it can be hard to find the right balance between fascinating and frustrating the player. Different allegorical games go about revealing their true theme differently, depending on their expressive and communicative goal. Some state explicitly what they are about (e.g., in the title, at the end of the game); others remain opaque throughout, leaving the player scratching his or her head. Some games intend to convey a specific message; others focus more on evoking ideas, prompting self-exploration, and allowing the player to find his or her own meaning. Being aware of these different approaches can facilitate purposeful design, from helping to clearly define the game's goal to informing playtestings, particularly in regard to game comprehension.

5.3.1 Approach 1: Metaphor as Mystery—Stimulating Curiosity

SH2 uses a metaphorical approach to leverage the engaging qualities of the mystery genre; it presents the player with an intriguing puzzle and then provides clues throughout the game that promote hypothesis building and the hope that, eventually, it will all make sense—the horse will get its carrot. Indeed, in the end, the game reveals what happened: James killed Mary and needs to forgive himself to be able to leave his private purgatory, the town of Silent Hill. *SH2* prevents frustration by framing the game with a big mystery and its reveal. Whether one can make sense of everything else in between is not so important as long as it seems that there is a deeper, unifying meaning that ties it all together to one coherent whole. The game thus allows for a more casual engagement with its story but rewards the player, who digs deeper with an extremely detailed and coherent mapping of all the game's elements with the psychotherapeutic process of uncovering repressed memories and coming to terms with emotional trauma and guilt. (For an in-depth analysis of the game and its metaphors, see Rusch [2009]). There is an interpretative key that unlocks a whole treasure trove of meaning, but it is not crucial for the enjoyment of the game.

5.3.2 Approach 2: Metaphor as Message—
Achieving a Communicative Goal

Papo & Yo and *Spirits of Spring* are metaphorical games with an agenda. Their communicative purpose—telling a personal story and creating empathy for children with abusive parents/children who experience bullying—requires a successful decoding of their metaphorical meaning. These games want their message to get across. The metaphor is supposed to create interest and lure players in, not to obscure the true theme. Hence, both games become more and more overt over time about their underlying meaning. *Papo & Yo* intersperses nonmetaphorical, narrative sequences that reveal the game's literal meaning and help make the connection between a monster and a father, frogs and alcohol, etc. *Spirits of Spring* uses a voice-over narrator to openly address the bullying theme later on in the game, leaving no doubt about what the game really is about. The game trailer to both games combines live action sequences with in-game footage, making the literal meaning behind the games' metaphors explicit. Some players (e.g., some of my students who play and analyze the games as home assignments) object to this approach. They feel the games would be more meaningful if the onus of interpretation fell on the player. They feel cheated of an opportunity to be smart. From the designers' perspective, it's a trade-off between limiting some player's enjoyment of their own cognitive abilities and risking a lot of people *not getting it*. If the game's intent is to communicate a message, it makes sense to reduce that risk by helping game comprehension along.

5.3.3 Approach 3: Metaphor as Muse—What Does It Mean to "Me"?

In a way, *Journey* is exactly what the title promises it to be: a journey. It qualifies as an allegory because it is about more than the one concrete journey afforded by the game. The game's theme is the quintessential journey through life in its most universal sense. This interpretation is supported by the fact that one plays a nondescript character in a nameless desert who works his or her way to an equally nameless mountaintop. Every element in the game can be read as the epitome of whatever it is it represents: the desert is life's possibility space in which we make connections and experience things; the mountaintop manifests the very idea of *destination*; and the creatures and other obstacles that get in your way stand for *obstacles* and *setbacks*. Decoding the glyphs and wall paintings can be understood very generally as our search for meaning: of trying to figure out our history; to learn where we came from; and how that informs who we are, what we are doing here, and what our purpose is. *Journey* further parallels the concept of *life trajectory* with its dramatic structure: you are being thrown into an environment without knowledge of who you are nor what your purpose is; you start to get your bearings and find your way through the desert; on the way, you might meet others (i.e., other players when playing in multiplayer mode); depending on your encounters, you might feel lonely or supported; and you gain experience and abilities, live through setbacks, get carried away by the moment, face and survive rough times, and resurface with a newfound appreciation for life until you arrive at the mountaintop, your final destination: the completion of your life's journey in death/game over.

By cultivating vagueness through designing every game element as a projection screen for the player, *Journey* uses metaphor as muse to inspire self-exploration rather than to make the player chase a prepackaged meaning the designer hid underneath the game's fictional surface. Unlike metaphor as mystery or metaphor as message, metaphor as muse is about the player, about enabling contemplation and facilitating insights that are personally meaningful, rather than creating a meeting of minds with the designer. As Jenova Chen, *Journey*'s game director, said in an interview with Dean Takahashi (2013) on venturebeat.com, "People get more out of it, if they put themselves into the game."

Playing *Journey* prompts questions such as, what's my journey? Who are my people? Where am I going? What do I hope to find there? How do I deal with my own relative insignificance in the vastness of the desert? What do encounters with others mean to me? Who are those who help me through the desert and make the journey significant? What happens to me when I die?

5.4 Designing Allegorical Games

Section 5.3 has shown that not all allegorical games are created equal. They tap into different potentials of metaphors to convey ideas, reinforce a theme, draw the player in, and illuminate salient aspects of the human experience. They can further pursue different expressive and communicative goals, emphasizing or de-emphasizing game comprehension. The following section applies the insights won from game analysis to the practice of designing allegorical games.

5.4.1 From Theme to Story

As stated in Section 5.1, allegories are a form of narrative that uses metaphors to convey a deeper or more general meaning. Their intentional design thus requires an understanding of metaphor, as well as storytelling.* I would like to propose the hero's journey as a productive way of structuring allegorical game stories. As Joseph Campbell illustrated in his numerous works on the subject, particularly *The Hero with a Thousand Faces* (2008), the hero's journey is a monomyth: a narrative structure of personal development and growth that underlies myths and stories from the dawn of humankind. While narrative functions differently in games than in traditional media, the hero's journey as an overarching dramatic structure remains valid in the interactive form and is used by many games, including the four examples. In fact, it is particularly suitable for allegorical games, since it is itself an allegory. Regardless of what the story is on the surface, underneath, it's always about the hero's personal transformation. The hero's journey is the ultimate allegory for inner growth—arguably the perfect structure for narratives that aim to teach us something about ourselves.

The journey's stages, in a nutshell, are as follows. For a more detailed account, I recommend Christopher Vogler's book *The Writer's Journey: Mythic Structure for Writers* (2007).

1. *Ordinary world:* Vogler describes it as "the context, home base, and background of the hero" (p. 87). This is where it all begins. The things to come are strange and extraordinary in comparison to this starting point. *SH2* begins in an ordinary parking lot. No monsters, yet. It is explained that James Sunderland came here to look for his dead wife. While this is already a bit weird, it is nothing in contrast to the creatures and locations he is about to encounter soon. *Papo & Yo* starts with Quico coming home, hiding in the closet—probably a place where he often seeks refuge from Monster. From there, he launches his adventure into a fantastical world. *Spirits of Spring* establishes Chiwatin as the guardian of spring in his normal environment, going about his everyday business where all is well with the world before the crows show up.

---

*Storytelling in video games is a complex-and-contested field. There has been a scholarly dispute from the beginning of game studies between the so-called ludologists and narratologists about whether games are narratives at all (narratologists say games can be powerful vehicles for narrative experiences) or something else altogether (ludologists argue that games should be treated as their own form, not a subset of narrative). I am not interested in regurgitating this dispute here.

Journey doesn't present much in the way of a background, but it clearly demarcates the desert as a home base, possibly even the graveyard that is shown in the intro cut scene: we come from nothing, and we'll go back to nothing. The ordinary world is where the theme is established.

2. *Call to adventure:* The main character has been introduced; now, something must happen. In games, the call to adventure usually occurs soon, to jumpstart the action. *SH2* presents the inciting incident that gets the story rolling at the very beginning in the form of Mary's letter that called James to Silent Hill. *Journey* presents the mountain in the distance as the call to adventure. It is the game's only tangible goal. In *Spirits of Spring*, the crows show up and threaten the ordinary world, and *Papo & Yo* provides a sudden escape from the dreary reality of Quico hiding in the closet by way of Quico's imagination that opens a portal to a different world.

3. *Refusal of the call:* In many stories, the hero is reluctant to leave the ordinary world and embrace change. Unsurprisingly, this stage of the hero's journey is underused in games, since, usually, the player is eager to play, and it would be silly to force him or her through a refusal stage where he or she doesn't want to leave the ordinary world.

4. *Meeting with the mentor:* In a broader sense, this stage is not just about meeting a helpful person but also preparing for the journey in general. It's about gathering supplies, getting ready, and finding sources of wisdom that will make it possible to overcome the obstacles ahead. In games, a tutorial can serve such a function: learning special abilities, acquiring a map, etc.

5. *Crossing the threshold:* Now, the hero fully commits to the adventure, leaves the ordinary world, and enters a new, special place.

6. *Tests, allies, enemies:* This is the core of the gameplay: the player overcomes obstacles, fights enemies, finds clues, solves puzzles, navigates the gameworld, and meets other characters. In *Spirits of Spring*, Chiwatin's main test is the destructive powers he gets from the shifty fox. Rabbit and Bear warn him against taking the fox's help, but Chiwatin is filled with a desire for revenge and doesn't listen. He goes after the crows, all fired up and creating a path of destruction in his wake. Of course, things backfire on him, and he finds himself all alone and more miserable than before.

7. *Approach to the inmost cave:* The tension builds up; the stakes are raised, and the confrontation with the main enemy or obstacle is about to happen. In *SH2*, James Sunderland crosses the lake into the land of

the dead, to the hotel where he spent his honeymoon with his late wife, Mary. Allies and mentors cannot follow into the inmost cave. It's a place where the hero needs to go alone.

8. *The ordeal:* "Now the hero stands in the deepest chamber of the Inmost Cave, facing the greatest challenge and the most fearsome opponent yet" (p. 155). In *SH2*, this is James Sunderland's confrontation with his guilty conscience, manifested as the long-anticipated encounter with Mary. The inmost cave is where the biggest treasure is guarded by the biggest fear. In this case, James' fear is to find out he killed Mary. The biggest treasure is to come to terms with this fact and forgive himself. "The Ordeal in myths signifies the death of the ego. The hero is now fully part of the cosmos, dead to the old, limited vision of things and reborn into a new consciousness of connections" (p. 171). It's when Quico realizes he can't cure the monster and needs to let him go, and when Chiwatin finally understands that friendship is more important than standing up to the bullies and makes amends with Rabbit and Bear.

9. *Reward:* This is quite straightforward; the hero gets to celebrate his victory over death. The hero perceives things differently and has gained new insight. Things look good for a while.

10. *The road back:* While the hero has been transformed, the final challenge is yet to come on the way back to the ordinary world. The villain might have recovered from the blow and strikes back stronger than before. For example, after Chiwatin has been reunited with his friends, there is one final encounter with the crows.

11. *The resurrection:* "This is the climax (not the crisis), the last and most dangerous meeting with death. Heroes have to undergo a final purging and purification before reentering the Ordinary World" (p. 197). James shows his transformation by finally defeating Pyramid Head. Quico has changed, too, because he is now ready to let go of monster, to free himself of his burden and move on. Chiwatin stands up to the crows because he knows he has his friends at his side. The climax provides catharsis.

12. *Return with the elixir:* The transformed hero brings a special gift to the ordinary world to share with others. Their newfound identity makes the world around them a better place. While, in games, this part might be cut short because there is nothing left to do, it cannot hurt to consider what the hero is taking home with him after having lived through the journey of transformation.

Once the designer has identified the game's particular theme, the hero's journey can help to create a rough level structure and plan a player's spatial and emotional trajectory through the game from beginning to end. Playtesting can then ensure that the experiential goals for each stage are being met.

5.4.2 Define the Communicative Goal and Playtest to Achieve It

It has to be noted that the metaphor as mystery, metaphor as message, and metaphor as muse approaches described in Sections 5.3.1 through 5.3.3 are not mutually exclusive or principally different. It's a difference in degree and emphasis. Each game that employs metaphor as muse also bears a mystery simply by virtue of being metaphorical (*Journey* does bring up the question of what it all means and what its individual elements stand for), and each metaphor-as-message game also evokes emotional experiences and might prompt players to ask personally meaningful questions (e.g., *Spirits of Spring* will likely remind players of instances where they were bullied themselves and how that felt, how they went about it then, and how they'd go about it now). For the sake of intentional game design, it is helpful, though, to know which aspect the game emphasizes: what is most important for the game to achieve its main purpose? If the metaphor is used as a vehicle to convey a message, cognitive comprehension is crucial. If the metaphor serves the main purpose of facilitating emotions, and if those emotions are meant to inspire deeper insights into the human experience and to learn something about oneself, then what players feel at various points in the game is the essential measure of success.

5.4.2.1 *"Metaphor as Mystery" Design Takeaway*   Using metaphor to leverage the engaging qualities of the mystery genre starts with having a very clear vision of the source system the game should model. Much attention needs to be paid to creating accurate mappings between the source system and its metaphorical representation. Just because something is mysterious doesn't mean you can make stuff up. It needs to follow an internally coherent logic. It also facilitates the design process by allowing the designer to refer back to a solid understanding of the source system and let it inform how things work in the game and how they should be depicted. Further, to tap into the player's curiosity about what it all means, you need to be mindful about the number and quality of hints you give to keep the player actively invested in the process of building and testing hypothesis. If there are not enough hints,

the story will recede into the background, and the player will lose interest in it. If you give too many or too obvious hints, you're doing the player's job of decoding the message, reducing interest as well. Curiosity can only be sustained if the gap between the known and the unknown is just right (see May's [2009] *In Pursuit of Elegance: Why the Best Ideas Have Something Missing*). Playtesting of such games thus needs to pay particular attention to the player's hypothesis-building processes: are they trying to make sense of the hints and metaphorical game elements? Do they feel like they are getting somewhere, or are they just lost in the woods the whole time, and do they get exceedingly frustrated? It is not essential that players really decipher the meaning of all game elements (the way you interpret them) as long as they remain engaged in the hypothesis-building process overall. It is up to you as designer to decide how much to reveal in the end. Sometimes, leaving things open and keeping players guessing beyond the actual gameplay can be more powerful than affording closure by spilling the beans. This only works, however, if you provide enough leads in the game to stimulate curiosity.

5.4.2.2 "Metaphor as Message" Design Takeaway This approach is for games with a clear communicative agenda. It is important to ensure players get the message. Inserting quotes that make the theme explicit, adding non-metaphorical cut scenes, giving the game a title that points toward its true meaning (e.g., *Papo & Yo* already hints at a relationship between a father and a son), and designing contextual materials (e.g., a Website with explanatory text, game trailer, etc.) that help to connect the metaphor with the concept it represents—all these are measures that can be taken to increase game comprehension. It is further advisable to keep the metaphor/allegory relatively straightforward. Find the very essence of what you want to communicate, and focus on modeling that. *Papo & Yo*'s metaphors are close to their source: the setting, characters, and actions are very easy to connect to their literal meaning. *Spirits of Spring* is a bit further removed from usual associations with bullying (a mythical native landscape rather than a schoolyard), but the crows themselves (their humanoid representation) and the experiences the player has with them are a direct model of the social dynamics of bullying, facilitating game comprehension.

Remember that it is hard to be obvious in metaphorical game design and much easier to create something obscure. Many things that make perfect sense to the design team, because they are overly familiar with the theme and have already bought into the metaphor, do not make sense to players. If it requires a lot of explanation to draw the parallels between a metaphorical element and what it represents, it is very likely players won't understand it. Obscure or elaborate connections between metaphor and its source do not make for a clever game; they make for an incomprehensible game. The depth of a metaphorical game comes from making sure every element supports the message—setting, characters, core mechanics, puzzles, obstacles, enemies, goal, and conflict. Once you have the interpretative key, the meaning of every game aspect should seem obvious. If the designer needs to argue and explain how things fit into the bigger message, the metaphors are too complicated and counterintuitive. Use playtesting to see whether whether people *get it*. Ask open questions about what players think the game's theme is and what game elements mean to them. You can gage whether you are getting closer by giving them the interpretative key, e.g., by telling them what the game is about and explaining the core metaphor (e.g., in *SH2*, the theme is psychotherapy, and the core metaphor is Silent Hill as James' subconscious) and see whether knowing the theme helps them find the parallels between the metaphors in the game and what they represent. You can test for how each of the game's communicative layers supports the theme, from the audiovisual design to the core mechanics to the experiential gestalt of the gameplay itself. Be wary of asking leading questions, though. When people start to associate structurally similar experiences with your game, but don't identify the exact theme you had in mind, you still know you are getting very close and just need to tweak the fictional layer, rather than the game's structure and mechanics. When we made *Akrasia*, players associated the gameplay experience with consumerism, workaholism, and possessive love. All these experiences are structurally very similar to substance abuse because they share the addiction gestalt. If we wanted to make sure people got the specific kind of addiction we were going for, we would have had to be more explicit in terms of our audiovisual representations.

Testing for meaning is difficult because you need to know how to analyze your playtesting data. What does it mean if people don't understand? What do they not understand? Why do they not understand it? For example, usability issues can interfere with sense-making processes. If people have trouble interacting with your game, they will have trouble understanding what game elements do, how they connect to each other, etc. Since this is essential to make sense of a gameplay experience, you need to first address the usability issue before you change your metaphors.

5.4.3.3 "Metaphor as Muse" Design Takeaway Playtesting a game that employs the metaphor-as-muse approach does not need to pay attention to game comprehension the same way the metaphor-as-mystery or metaphor-as-message approaches demand, since it's not about *being understood* in that left-brain kind of way. The game's deeper meaning becomes accessible mainly through the emotional experiences it affords. It is thus more important how particular game elements and the game as a whole make the player feel than what they stand for. These feelings prompt associations to concepts outside of the game and make it more universally meaningful. In *Journey*, the mountain, as the final destination of a journey into the light, can be read as death or enlightenment, but the vehicle for this reading is the experience evoked by the traversal through the game, the mechanics, and the audiovisual design: the mountain is huge, and making your way up there is cumbersome. Strong wind is blowing against you, and it's almost as if you could feel the fatigue of death, which prepares you for the sweet relief or ecstasy, brought by stepping into the light in the very end.

How can you make sure you create evocative experiences that enable insightful associations beyond the confines of a particular game? Vander Caballero explains in his 2012 Game Developers Conference talk "Empathetic Games Are Here to Stay! What's Next?" that, at Minority Media, they create a beat chart: an overview of all the elements in specific parts/levels of the game and the emotions they should evoke, e.g., fear, sorrow, anger, frustration, power, shame. Having such a beat chart is incredibly important in order to craft the desired experience. The beat chart informs playtesting goals and ways to analyze and interpret playtesting data. It shows whether the game design is going in the right direction experientially, even if players are not making the *right* connections between the game's fiction and its underlying meaning.

These are just some pointers about the potentials and pitfalls of creating allegorical games. There is no recipe, and, as always, the only way to design one powerful game is by creating a ton of mediocre or outright bad ones. Hopefully, the following exercises will help.

EXERCISES

1. Allegorical game analysis

Suggestions for allegorical games to play: *Braid, Shadow of the Colossus, Ico, Brothers—A Tale of Two Sons (http://www.brothersthegame .com/about-the-game), The Path, Aether, Binding of Isaac.*
Step 1: Play the game all the way through at least once.

Step 2: Take notes as you are playing:
- What do you think the game is about (= its underlying theme)?
    - What are the questions the game raises in regard to its deeper meaning?
    - What are clues it provides to decode its deeper meaning?
- What is the core metaphor it uses to convey that theme?
    - What are other metaphorical means used to reinforce the theme, e.g., audiovisual design, characters, settings, obstacles, goal, conflict?
- What are the core mechanics? (What do you do on a moment-to-moment basis?)
    - Do they reinforce the theme, too, or are they disconnected from it?
- What are salient emotions evoked during gameplay?
    - Be specific; take note of particularly memorable passages of the game and your emotional response to them. Pay attention to detail.
    - Consider how your emotional response to the game relates to its content and mechanics.
- How is metaphorical approach used in this game: metaphor as mystery, metaphor as message, or metaphor as muse? Remember that these approaches are not mutually exclusive, so it is possible the game applies to more than one. Make sure to point out whether there is a bias toward one approach over another, and argue your case by bringing concrete examples from the game.
- Is the game's deeper meaning revealed at any point or left obscure?
    - How does that impact your gameplay experience?
    - How do you think the way the game promotes game comprehension (or not) supports its overall experience goal?
    - Are there any noticeable inconsistencies in the game's metaphor(s) that prevent a coherent reading? What are they?

Step 3: Now, sort and structure your notes to write an insightful analysis that focuses particularly on the game's metaphorical approach, its metaphorical coherence and depth, how it handles game comprehension, and how this supports or undermines the game's assumed or explicitly stated deeper theme. Close with your observations of what you learnt from playing the game about the practice of metaphorical game design:

- How you can apply your observations to your own game design practice?
- What do you think could have been done better and how?

Step 4: Submit a 1,000–1,500-word analysis of an allegorical game of your choice.

2. Designing allegorical games

Step 1: Pick a theme that resonates strongly with you. Ruben Farrus, the design director of *Spirits of Spring*, recommends to start with a self-exploratory question to identify a personally meaningful theme: "What's your pain?"

Step 2: Decide your game's communicative goal: Do you want to communicate a concrete message (metaphor as message)? Do you want to use metaphor to create a mystery? Do you want the game to inspire the player to explore themselves (metaphor as muse)?

Step 3: Explore possible metaphors for the theme. Draw on the self-exploration tools introduced in Chapter 1, to coax imagination.

Step 4: What's the story? Map the metaphor onto the hero's journey. Feel free to adjust the structure to the needs of your game.

Step 5: Create a beat chart. Define how you want players to feel at which point in the game and how you can make that happen: what challenges, obstacles, and helpers will they encounter where?

Throughout: prototype, playtest, iterate.

Step 6: Deliver a prototype, a statement of intent, and a reflection on the design process: What's the theme? What's the intended experience you were going for, the game's communicative goal? How did playtesting inform iteration? How well do you think your game achieved its goal? What would you do differently?

References

Caballero, V. 2012. *Empathetic Games Are Here To Stay! What's Next?* Presented at Game Developers Conference, San Francisco, CA. Available at http://gdcvault .com/play/1020598/Empathetic-Games-Are-Here-to. Accessed on September 5, 2016.

Campbell, J. 2008. *The Hero with a Thousand Faces*, 3rd ed. Novato, CA: New World Library.

Dictionary.com. "Allegory in culture." Available at http://www.dictionary.com/browse /allegory?s=t. Accessed on September 5, 2016.

Jenkins, H. 2006. *Convergence Culture: Where Old and New Media Collide.* New York and London: New York University Press.

May, M. 2009. *In Pursuit of Elegance: Why the Best Ideas Have Something Missing.* New York: Broadway Books.

Rusch, D. 2009. Staring into the abyss—A close reading of Silent Hill 2. In Davidson, D. (Ed.), *Well Played 1.0: Video Games, Value and Meaning* (pp. 235–255). Pittsburgh, PA: ETC Press. Available at http://press.etc.cmu.edu/content/silent -hill-2-doris-c-rusch.

Schell, J. 2013. Secrets to amazing transformational games. Presented at *Serious Play* Conference, Redmond, WA, Aug. 19th-22nd 2013. Available at http://www .slideshare.net/jesseschell/secrets-of-amazing-transformational-games.

Takahashi, D. 2013. An interview with Jenova Chen: How Journey's creator went bankrupt and won game of the year. Venturebeat.com. Available at http:// venturebeat.com/2013/02/08/an-interview-with-jenova-chen-how-journeys -creator-went-bankrupt-and-won-game-of-the-year/4/.

Vogler, C. 2007. *The Writer's Journey: Mythic Structure for Writers.* Studio City, CA: Michael Wiese Productions.

6

Designing with Purpose and Meaning—Nine Questions to Define Where You're Going and Make Sure You Get There

Wherein the topics covered in the previous chapters are summarized and presented in the form of nine questions to identify a game's vision and guide its purposeful design. The questions are as follows:

- *What is the game about?*
- *What is the game's purpose/communicative goal?*
- *Literal or metaphorical approach?*
- *Does the metaphor fit the game's experiential gestalt?*
- *Should the game model "how it works" or "what it feels like"?*
- *How encompassing should the system that shall be modeled in the game be?*
- *From which perspective should the player interact with the system?*
- *Do the core mechanics reinforce the game's meaning?*
- *Are the player and the avatar well aligned?*

6.1 Introduction

After filling our toolbox with approaches and techniques to design deep games, this chapter serves as a summary of the key points that need to be considered to define a vision for a project and stay on track throughout the development process. It happens time and time again that we set out to make a game about X and end up modeling something completely different. Game design is a decision-making process, but many decisions are made semiconsciously. Having an overview of questions that raise awareness for decision points helps to minimize the gap between intent and outcome because decisions are made more deliberately. It further encourages experimentation in the design process—to ask *what if*—rather than go with what seems like the obvious solution.

The questions presented in this chapter have been derived from my own lessons learned from making deep games. I also see them at the root of problems in my students' games, when there is a discrepancy between the intended and actual experience. The questions mostly address the conceptual, preproduction part of game design (rather than the design decisions that come up when implementing the game), and they don't claim to be comprehensive. The fact that I am presenting them chronologically is owed to the linearity of the medium I'm writing in. The iterative nature of game design demands tentative, preliminary answers that get revised as the vision for the project takes shape over time and as more questions are investigated. In other words, answering the following questions is a process, and it is as iterative as design itself.

6.2 Question 1: What's It About?

An obvious starting point to the design process is to ask what the game should be about. I have come across three different conceptual frameworks that give rise to deep games and can help define their theme: (1) another media source, e.g., a book, a film, or a painting, that serves as a source of inspiration for the game (2) somebody's personal experience (doesn't have to be the designer's), or (3) a cause.

6.2.1 Based on Another Medium

The most relevant question when making a game that is based on another medium is, what stands out about the original work that you want to capture in the game? It is not possible; neither is there a point in trying to replicate the original. Due to its medium-specific characteristics and the designer's unique interpretation of the work the game draws on, the game can add a meaningful complementary reading that increases insight into the source and adds a new perspective.

6.2.1.1 Case Study: Oedipus Rex/Seer When Abe Stein, the audio director at the Singapore–Massachusetts Institute of Technology (MIT) GAMBIT Game Lab, approached me about collaborating on a game about Sophocles' (2006) play *Oedipus Rex*, it was unclear which aspect of the original the game should cover. We started exploring the text to identify what resonated most with us. Questions of fate occupied us for a long time: what if Oedipus' parents had not given him away? What if Oedipus had decided to never sleep with or kill anyone? So did the concept of tragedy: the noble hero who is trying to live up to an ideal and, by doing so, brings about his own downfall. Could we make a game in which the player worked toward one goal, e.g., keeping the enemies out, only to discover in the end that he or she had trapped himself or herself in the process—that the protective fort was actually a prison? Eventually, what got to us the most was the fact that, even after Oedipus had done all the things he did, he could have been fine if he had just stopped searching for the truth. If he had heeded the blind seer and stopped asking who angered the gods (namely, Oedipus himself), he could still have lived with himself (Figure 6.1).

It took almost a whole semester in which we prototyped various ideas that explored fate and tragedy to arrive at the conclusion that we wanted: to make a game that allowed players to ponder the notion of *ignorance is bliss*. The

FIGURE 6.1
Seer, MIT

final game *Seer* (whose design and development I was no longer a part of) features King Oedipus in a rubber ducky, navigating a sea of ignorance. The player makes his way to various lighthouses (beacons of truth) to shine their light on the ignorance, bit by bit revealing a mysterious and increasingly negative text. With every lighthouse, the player character Oedipus looks more menacing, growing horns and an evil tail. There are rapids that hinder progress from one lighthouse to another. Persisting against the rapids is a metaphor for Oedipus overcoming the blind seer's resistance to telling Oedipus the truth. The player can stop at any time, but, when he or she keeps going until the bitter end, the harsh truth will be revealed as writing in the water, and the Oedipus player character will have fully transformed into a monster.

What is helpful to consider when defining what a game based on another medium could be about is (a) what are games good at? How can the game enable a complementary experience that enriches a reading of the original? In the case of *Seer*, the game allows the player to explore for himself or herself whether he or she thinks ignorance is bliss or whether she'd press on until the bitter end to find the truth, even at the cost of her own well-being. (b) What are the different themes in the original, and which one resonates most strongly with us as the design team (or, at least, the design vision holder)?

6.2.2 Based on (Somebody's) Personal Experience

Ask five people what they mean when they say "Let's make a game about relationship," and you get at least seven different answers. There are no straightforward concepts. What do you want to model? The butterfly stage? The dynamics between people? The love? The heartache? The process of breaking up? When making games about personal experiences, someone needs to own the theme and infuse it with authenticity. I had a student team that started with an already well-defined aspect of relationship—unrequited love—and ended up prototyping a beautiful contemplation of the connection between finding true love and self-love: the process of clinging to someone, letting go of that person, making it through a time of darkness and despair alone, coming to terms with oneself and appreciating one's own company, and ending with seeing many possibilities and potential partners to choose from. The theme was one student's personal experience, which the rest of the team added to, helped to flesh out, and developed further. The sense of unity and coherence, however, was achieved by one person sharing something personal and the others respecting that and supporting the vision. Art by committee doesn't work, and just because you didn't provide the original idea does not mean you cannot contribute creatively to how this idea takes form as a game.

6.2.3 For a Cause

Having a cause that informs the game can give valuable guidance in defining the exact theme. I collaborated on *Elude*, the depression game, with a child psychiatrist, Atilla Ceranoglu. We started out just wanting to make a relevant game together, a game that tackled an aspect of the human experience that remains inaccessible to many people but that would benefit from being made more accessible. Depression is a very common issue with severe health consequences, so we settled on that. Deciding to make a game about depression didn't tell us much about what kind of game it should be, yet. We had only narrowed down the illness but not our concrete approach to it. The most productive questions in our discussions to define what the game should be about were, where could a game have the biggest impact? What aspect of depression as a social problem has been underexplored and deserves attention? What do games do best? As explained in Chapter 4, Section 4.1, games are really good at enabling embodied experiences. A game can allow you to explore *what something feels like* from within. A big social issue related to depression is a caregiver's anger and frustration because they don't understand what their loved ones are going through. (How could they if they don't suffer from depression themselves?) Hence, we decided to make a game that models what depression feels like to promote understanding and dialogue between people with depression and their caregivers and decrease stigma, anger, and frustration. You know whether you are getting closer to having a clearly defined theme for your game when you are able to complete the following sentences suggested in the inspiring book *Challenges for Game Designers* (Brathwaite & Schreiber 2006): "this game is about...", "this game deals with...", "this game explores...", "this game teaches...", "this game simulates the experience of...".

6.3 Question 2: What Is the Purpose/ Communicative Goal of Your Game?

Your game's purpose determines your design approach, as well as how you playtest, to make sure you are achieving your purpose (see also Section 5.3).

Sections 6.3.1 through 6.3.5 present a list of possible goals you might want to pursue with your game. They are not necessarily mutually exclusive, although it makes sense to determine what is prioritized.

6.3.1 Personal Games for Self-Expression

You might want to make a game to make sense of or share an experience. Anna Anthropy's and Mattie Brice's biographical games *Dys4ia* and *Mainichi* are the examples of personal games whose main purpose is self-expression. As stated on Anthropy's Website (http://wizardofvore.itch.io/dys4ia), *Dys4ia* is a "journal game about the six months of my life when I made the decision to begin hormone replacement therapy." Mattie Brice writes about *Mainichi* on her Website (http://www.mattiebrice.com/mainichi/): "This is an experiment in sharing a personal experience through a game system. It helps communicate daily occurrences that happen in my life, exploring the difficulty in expressing these feelings in words" (Figure 6.2).

Personal games have become *a thing* over the last few years, enriching games' thematic scope with so far underexplored ideas, pushing our understanding of what games can be and introducing new and diverse voices. They also challenge the primacy of player-centric design and iteration. As Brice

FIGURE 6.2
Mainichi, Mattie Brice

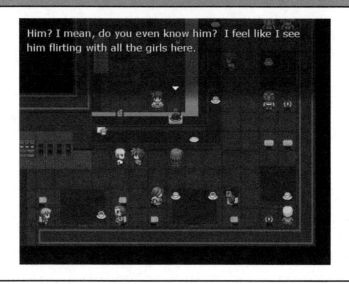

said in an interview on the different perspectives on personal games with Leigh Alexander (2013) for *Gamasutra*,

> I feel games also can, and maybe should sometimes, resist players. If there's such a thing as 'death of author', I think there should be 'death of the player.' Players shouldn't have to be… the most important thing for games, especially as we live with an audience that's so homogenous.

Making a personal game for self-expression gives you a lot of freedom, but that doesn't mean it's easy. You may not want to playtest it because you do not care whether others think it's *fun*, but creating something you feel is true to yourself and really captures what you want to say is not without its challenges. The goals we set for ourselves are sometimes the highest. An iterative approach might be useful in so far as it silences the inner critic and allows you to simply start somewhere and then tweak until you're satisfied. Brice compares personal game design with creative writing. In both cases it is true that we first make a mess, then we clean it up.

6.3.2 Raising Awareness

Games can raise awareness for social and personal issues by creating empathy, provoking discussion, stimulating emotions, etc. There are many different ways in which one can go about it, but the important point is that you can't raise awareness for a topic if people *don't get it*. Game comprehension is thus a major factor to playtest for. People need to at least understand what the game is about. It also helps if they become emotionally invested in the cause the game aims to raise awareness for: Tiltfactor's *Layoff* game prompted a lot of discussion among its players, as well as various media channels that reported about it.* In this *Bejeweled*-like tile-matching game, you play from the perspective of management that has to cut jobs before the backdrop of the financial crisis in the United States. Laid-off workers are dropped into an unemployment line on the bottom of the screen. The gameplay alone, however, would hardly be enough to make people care much about the issue. Hence, the laid-off workers were given biographies. Suddenly, you didn't just fire *job groups* but also real people with kids, spouses, dreams, and debt. This design decision considerably increased the game's emotional impact.

---

* See the controversy around the *Layoff* game in the embedded video on the Website: http://www .tiltfactor.org/game/layoff/.

The mental health games we made as part of the interactive documentary *For the Records* were meant to raise awareness for mental health issues. We deliberately did not aim to present the illnesses we portrayed from a clinical perspective but rather to capture the subjective experience of them: what it feels like to live with attention deficit disorder, bipolar disorder, eating disorder, or obsessive–compulsive disorder.

6.3.3 Object to Think With

Games that raise awareness for a cause do not necessarily teach the player much about that cause (e.g., *For the Records* only communicates salient aspects of what certain mental disorders feel like, but it doesn't teach the player anything about how to diagnose or treat them). Their main goal is to bring a topic to the player's attention with whatever means are most effective. But, sometimes, our purpose might be to promote a more encompassing understanding of an issue, to teach players *how it works*. In that case, the game serves as an object to think with. Seymore Papert (1980) coined the term *object to think with* to describe an object that promotes a sense of inquiry and thus stimulates learning by doing. Games are ideally suited to be objects to think with as they afford the player to exercise freedom along five different axes, enabling learning in a self-directed, intrinsically motivated way. Players have the *freedom to fail*, which means they are free to do things at play that would look like failure in other contexts. They have the *freedom to experiment*, which relates closely to the freedom to fail and means that, within the play space, players have room to maneuver and invent new approaches to whatever task is at hand. An important point is the *freedom to fashion identities*. Play allows us to explore the nature of physical and social worlds and our identity within them. That identity is not a fixed thing but is itself *in play*. By trying on different identities, we define ourselves. Play allows *freedom of effort*. In play, one does not have to *keep it up* but can freely alternate between intense and relaxed play. Finally, there is the *freedom of interpretation:* no two players ever play exactly the same game, since the individual, social, and cultural motivations of any player affect what is experienced through play, and no two players ever experience the *same* game. This creates a challenge for those looking to games to provide a standardized context for learning (see Klopfer et al. 2009). It would go far beyond the scope of this book to explain in detail how to design a successful learning game, but, if the goal is to promote an understanding of how something works, the game needs to be designed as an object to think with; it needs to afford the aforementioned freedoms of play and integrate the lessons to be learned within the rules and mechanics so that there is no disconnect between what the game is about and what the player actually does on a moment-to-moment basis.

6.3.4 Changing Behavior/Perception

An often-called-for-but-very-tricky goal to achieve is to design for behavior or perception change. For one, we don't really know why people change their minds. Sometimes, a lover's casual remark is all it takes. Other times, we need to be bombarded by various channels over a long period of time for our values and beliefs to be affected (see Howard Gardner's insightful book on *Changing Minds* [2006]). It is equally tricky to assess whether a real change occurred because it might only be temporary. Behavior change is closely connected to a change in values, and our values are connected to our sense of identity (see Bers 2001, 2008). Someone might stop smoking for a year or longer, but, if this behavior change is not accompanied by a change of identity—e.g., seeing yourself as someone who is truly health conscious—the chances of relapsing are high. Changing perception is more attainable. It doesn't need to go as deep as changing who we are, but a game that makes us see things differently, and makes us notice something we have not noticed or paid attention to before, can plant the seed for a more lasting transformation. Tiltfactor's social card game *Buffalo* is such a game. According to the Website (http://www.tiltfactor.org/game/buffalo/), it's

> A card game of quick wits and zany combinations, *buffalo: the name dropping game* asks you to name-drop faster than your friends, collect the most cards, and win! How fast can you name a vain artist? How about a glasses-wearing heartthrob? Don't be surprised if you find yourself surrounded by curious players eager to name an annoying conqueror or perky religious figure!

The combinations of adjectives and professions draw attention to what is usual—e.g., white, male chemists—and what is unusual—Afro-American, female chemist. As you mull over the last play session or prepare for the next one, you'll seek for unusual combinations in real life, and this raises the following questions: why are there not more glasses-wearing heartthrobs?

Where is the diversity among pop stars?, etc. If your goal is to change perceptions, consider how the actual gameplay achieves that, paying particular attention to bridging the gap between games and real life.

6.3.5 What You Do Is What You Get

Some games are designed to achieve their purpose immediately, meaning they don't require a transfer of insights from screen to real life. Playing them is the change—what you do in the game is what you get. Any kind of physical game has an end in itself; the game is about making players healthier, and it happens by playing the game. Beyond exercise games, games with a social component lend themselves to this approach. *Way* by Coco & Co, a student team at Carnegie Mellon that developed the game in one semester, is about creating meaningful connections with strangers. According to the Website (http://www.makeourway.com), it's about how "two strangers learn to speak." This is facilitated wonderfully by the design: in this two-player puzzle game, challenges need to be overcome together. Each player has only half the information necessary to advance. By only using gestures, players can point to solutions and help each other across levels. This creates understanding beyond language, an experience of collaboration, and, eventually, friendship. The relationship that is being established with a complete stranger is real and points toward the power of collaborative play and the relative unimportance of cultural differences or language barriers.

This overview of purposes does not claim to be complete, but it covers the most common ones. There are many ways to go about achieving them, and you might want to adjust your course in the iterative design process. It is helpful, though, to settle on the purpose early on because it becomes your game's *true north*, which you judge all design decisions and playtesting results against. There is no intentional game design without a clear purpose one tries to achieve. I recommend Jesse Schell's "Lens of Transformation" from his excellent book *The Art of Game Design* (2008) and the accompanying card deck to help determine the game's purpose.

Games create experiences, and experiences change people. To make sure only the best changes happen to your players, ask yourself these questions:

- How can my game change players for the better?
- How can my game change players for the worse? (Schell 2008)

6.4 Question 3: Literal or Metaphorical Approach?

I've advocated strongly for the use of metaphors to make deep games, but, obviously, whether you do it or not is a choice. Nonmetaphorical games can provide thought-provoking, insightful experiences that teach us something about ourselves as well. Most people gravitate toward a literal approach, not even considering the metaphorical route, so stressing the benefit of metaphors has been one of the major goals of this book. In all fairness, though, both approaches are valid and can be highly effective. Let's compare two games about depression: *Depression Quest* and *Elude*. Both games aim to raise awareness for the illness by modeling the experience of what it's like to live with it. *Depression Quest*, made with the interactive narrative tool Twine, takes a literal approach. The Website (http://www.depressionquest.com) describes it as follows:

> Depression Quest is an interactive fiction game where you play as some-one living with depression. You are given a series of everyday life events and have to attempt to manage your illness, relationships, job, and pos-sible treatment. This game aims to show other sufferers of depression that they are not alone in their feelings, and to illustrate to people who may not understand the illness or the depths of what it can do to people.

Elude pursues a very similar goal, but is metaphorical. Instead of modeling an everyday environment that contains specific daily tasks and challenges, one is placed in the inner landscape of someone struggling with depression. The game revolves around the simulation of different mood states—neutral, happy, depressed, as well as transitions between them—and the limitation of agency in regard to achieving, maintaining, or escaping these states. At their core, both games intend to convey the experience of powerlessness when it comes to mood management or simply *getting things done*. In *Depression Quest*, certain choices at the bottom of the screen get crossed out; the further one's mood declines.

In *Elude*, you get sucked into a dark and claustrophobic underworld with no means of escape for as long as it takes until that phase subsides. Both games have gotten considerable recognition for what they are trying to do and how they are doing it, yet they are very different. The advantage of being literal about one's subject matter is that people have a much easier time understanding what the game is about. *Depression Quest* does a great job at combining the power of language to describe situations and evoke empathy, with the potential of interactivity to make the lack of choice and dwindling motivation in depression experientially tangible. The scenarios the game presents are vivid and highly relatable. You learn a lot about what goes through a depressed person's head when you explore this interactive fiction. On the other hand, a literal approach requires an ad-hoc interest in the subject to be willing to play a game about it. In the case of a Twine game, it also requires a lot of reading, which might turn some players off. A metaphorical game has better chances at making people curious and luring in those without a preexisting interest in the topic (see Minority Media's *magic door* theory from Chapter 5). Even if it is clear what the game is about (*Elude*, while metaphorical, isn't very secretive about its subject), people might still play it to try and decode the metaphor.

A literal approach benefits from an observable source system, which also means that a literal game can only portray symptoms, not the cause. *Depression Quest* takes away those choices that would be available to a healthy person. By doing so, it tells you, for example, "if you're depressed, you can't just pull yourself together to get some work done." It makes you feel the frustration of this symptom by limiting your agency. We can infer the illness from the symptoms.

Metaphors can get past the symptoms to the cause, an inside view. *Elude* focuses on modeling the mood struggle itself (Figure 6.3).

FIGURE 6.3
Elude, MIT

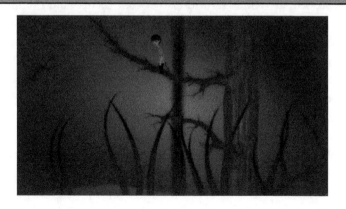

It tries to convey the essence of what depression feels like, instead of spelling out various instances in which the illness manifests that exemplify the experience. I do not want to decide which approach is better. They do different things; they emphasize different aspects of the disorder and provide different perspectives. Which one is more appropriate depends on one's goals, the game's purpose, the audience, and the designer's aesthetic ambitions. *Depression Quest* is more informative, nuanced, and a better, concrete portrayal of how depression plays out in daily life. *Elude* aims to get a dialogue going between the friends and relatives of people with depression and their loved ones by creating a very focused, shared experience of restricted agency. Its main goal is to convey the feelings of anger, loss, frustration, and hopelessness at being at the mercy of one's mood. The blanks—how it all impacts daily life—are supposed to be filled in by those with the lived experience. Gabriel Garcia Marquez writes in *Of Love and Other Demons* (1995): "Crazy people are not crazy if one accepts their reasoning" (p. 35). It means we can possibly understand everyone if we just believe what they report about their experiences. *Elude* intends to help others understand the *reasoning* behind depression symptoms: if you were incapable of envisioning a (joyful) future, would you be able to get out of bed?

To summarize, the literal approach is easier to understand and relate to for players, is more concrete, and has an observable, more easily accessible source system. The downside is that it narrows interpretation, might require preexisting interest, and bears the danger of getting stuck with the obvious. The metaphorical approach creates curiosity, is more open for interpretation and projection, and enables a contemplation of the abstract experience itself instead of only communicating its visible symptoms. Its downsides are a hard-to-grasp, elusive source system, the difficulty of ensuring coherence across all game elements, and higher barriers to game comprehension.

6.5 Question 4: The Right Metaphor for the Experiential Gestalt?

As discussed in Chapter 3, designing metaphorical games includes a careful analysis of the experiential gestalt the game should model. One experiential gestalt (the game's skeleton) can be represented by several metaphors (the flesh that is put on the skeleton). Every metaphor, though, comes with its own nuances of meaning. (The flesh can drastically change the appearance of the whole.) One has to be careful that the metaphor one settles on does not introduce unintended ideas into the game's message.

To give an example, when we made *Elude*, we knew we wanted to leverage the common spatial metaphor of *up* is *good* and *down* is *bad* to capture the two extremes of the mood spectrum (e.g., *feeling high* versus *feeling low*). We also knew we wanted to make the mood struggle tangible by introducing a downward force (= depression) that worked against your attempts of achieving the up destination at certain times in the game. This is the skeleton, the experiential structure, decoupled from a concrete visual representation. We made three prototypes that attempted to put flesh onto the skeleton. Each visual representation was a metaphor in its own right, though, and came with its own meaning implications.

Prototype 1: In this prototype, players had to jump from platform to platform in order to reach a goal in the upper-left corner of the screen. The downward force was built into the platforms themselves; they automatically descended from the top of the screen to the bottom. If you were carried off-screen by a descending platform, you entered the *depression phase.* There were two things that made this prototype problematic: (1) It was actually engaging to fight against the downward-moving platforms. The mood struggle was experienced as a welcome (because perceivably beatable) challenge by players, not something that made them feel helpless and out of control. (2) The platforms defined the inner world the game modeled. They were its essential architecture, the very structure of the internal landscape. To me, this sent the message that there was no way to separate oneself from the disorder. It's who you are. It's not just an element that sometimes takes over, that's disruptive, stifling—it's the very foundation of your inner makeup. While it might feel like that sometimes, I disagreed with this message and wasn't comfortable designing the game this way.

Prototype 2: In this version, the player started out at the bottom of a waterfall and had to work his or her way up. The waterfall represented the antagonistic force that pushed you back down into the deep, dark pool at the bottom. Depression is sometimes described as a drowning feeling, and being hit by a waterfall certainly conveys the idea of helplessness or being overwhelmed. What did not sit right about this design was that the downward force came from above! Up was meant to be positive. It couldn't be both depicted as the desirable destination and the origin of the struggle. It didn't make sense. It's not the existence of happiness that causes depression—thus, they should not both live in the same place.

Prototype 3: The player finds himself or herself in a forest. The goal is to jump from the ground up onto tree branches and work his or her way to the top of the trees, where, above the tree crowns, he or she will find happiness. The tree branches are taking the place of the moving platforms from prototype 1, only that they are stable in this version. The downward force is represented by black vines that reach out to the player from down below and drag him or her into underground caverns. The vines are the arms of depression that lies dormant below, and that comes after you when it awakens, enveloping you in its inescapable embrace and dragging you into the darkness. It made sense to us to think of depression as a lurking, subterranean beast that is part of the inner landscape, not its foundation, and who comes for you from time to time, but who also releases you again after a while.

In daily life, when trying to express our intangible thoughts and feelings, metaphors come to us spontaneously and effortlessly. In game design, however, it's a bit more complicated. Metaphors that can sustain a whole game (not just illuminate a salient aspect of an experience), provide a game structure, and afford game mechanics more often need to be constructed. This construction is a dialectic process that goes back and forth between exploring spontaneously appearing images and understanding the underlying experiential gestalt the game shall be based on until a good match has been identified that also works as a game. It is important to keep a close eye on the emerging metaphorical landscape to make sure it still matches the experiential gestalt and is consistent and appropriate in its meaning.

6.6 Question 5: How It Works versus What It Feels Like?

Games that model what something feels like usually imply how it works, whereas games that model how something works do not necessarily convey what it feels like. This difference has been discussed in Chapter 4, Section 4.3.1 by way of Rod Humble's *The Marriage*. The game models how salient aspects of marriage work (as perceived by Humble), but the moment-to-moment gameplay does not really convey what it feels like. The perspective from which a player relates to the system plays a crucial role in the experience, and, in *The Marriage*, one takes the unusual perspective of the love of force between two people instead of taking the role of one of the partners.

In contrast, the grappling hook sequence in *God of War II*, as described in Chapter 4, captures what transition feels like, as well as how it works, which stages it entails, etc. It is useful to come up with an ideal player story to determine whether the game should focus on how it works or what it feels like. When we made *Akrasia*, the substance abuse game, the only consideration in the beginning of the design process was that the game should capture the mechanisms of addiction metaphorically. We thus focused on how it works first. Soon, we found out players didn't understand what they should do or why, and we realized that our ideal player story was to make them feel the different aspects of addiction: wanting to chase the high, craving, temptation, and withdrawal. We had to model what it feels like, and, to achieve that, we needed to dissect the experiential gestalt further and recreate it through design. It is important to keep in mind that, if the goal is to model what something feels like, the experience players have when playing has to be carefully monitored in playtests. Just because the rules express the desired statements doesn't mean the experience gets across.

6.7 Question 6: *Zooming In* versus *Zooming Out*—How Much Shall Be Modeled?

This question regards the complexity of the source system the game should model. Some messages are best conveyed by zooming in, modeling only a small part of a real-life issue to make a very poignant statement. Gonzalo Frasca's *September 12th* doesn't bother with a nuanced portrayal of the conflict with Iraq. It only models how violence breeds violence. *Hush*, a short single-player game from the University of Southern California's interactive media division, aims to raise awareness for the 1994 slaughters in Rwanda. It is set during a Hutu raid on a Tutsi community. You play as a mother who has to keep her baby calm by singing a lullaby. The mechanics are inputting the lullaby text on-screen as it appears. When you mess up, the baby starts to cry and draw the raiders' attention. *Hush* zooms in very far and focuses on the mother's subjective experience of terror as a means to address the issue of genocide. Molleindustria's *McDonald's Videogame* takes a different approach. It zooms out to show how McDonald's operates from every conceivable angle: from clearing rainforests to make room for cows and soy fields, to injecting cattle with hormones, bribing environmentalists, and hiring and firing employees, to slaughtering the cows and selling burgers.

The zoomed-in perspective lends itself to a more subjective approach, either modeling what it feels like or making a succinct, provocative statement. The zoomed-out perspective appeals more to a cognitive appreciation of the dynamics of complex systems, thus gravitating more toward the procedural rhetoric of how things work.

6.8 Question 7: From Which Perspective Shall the Player Interact with the System?

We often assume that there is a *natural* perspective from which the player will relate to the game system. What happens if you challenge your assumptions? Playing around with perspective can help you get unstuck when you hit an impasse in the design process. It can also give rise to fresh, out-of-the-box game ideas. What if you played a substance abuse game from the perspective of the craving, trying to get the addict to take more drugs and finding ways to weaken his or her willpower? What if you played a relationship game from the perspective of the nosey neighbor witnessing the comings and goings of the partners and overhearing conversations, bedroom activities, and slammed doors?

What is important when choosing a perspective is that the system element, which should become the player's agent, is meaningfully connected to many other elements and has some means of action. This should not lead to hasty exclusions of unusual perspectives. It just means one might need to think a bit harder about the game's goal, conflict, and gameplay verbs. Designing a game about a frat party, where the player plays from the perspective of the couch, is certainly a challenge but could inspire some interesting ideas. Maybe it's a magic couch that can change its appearance, the fabric with which it's covered, the tightness of its springs, etc., thus enticing party guests to sit on it or making them get off of it. Maybe the couch's goal is to live vicariously through others. It is a romantic at heart and wants to bring couples together who will fall in love. It observes the people at the party, decides who'd be a good match, and then changes itself to look inviting to the right person, getting rid of the wrong folks who are taking up too much space by poking them with its springs. When a drunk passes out on you, you've lost, so beware!

Obviously, changing the perspective changes the experience. When you experiment with a new point of view, you need to revisit your ideal player story.

6.9 Question 8: Do Core Mechanics Reinforce Meaning?

Obviously, every game needs to answer the question of what the player does on a moment-to-moment basis. The core mechanics are one more way of reinforcing the game's theme. A good question to keep in mind is thus, how do the core mechanics help to convey the theme and generate meaning? Mechanics themselves can be metaphorical—the gameplay verb can stand for something else. In *Spirits of Spring*, using the spirit string to build bridges and reach otherwise inaccessible areas supports the idea of social connections as an antidote to bullying. In *Ico*, one plays a young boy with horns, Ico, who has been banned to a ramshackle castle by his village that thinks he's a demon. He meets a ghostlike girl—Princess Yorda—also a prisoner in the castle. Together, they are trying to escape. Apart from climbing, swinging on ropes, letting down drawbridges, and other ways of navigating the environment, handholding between Ico and Yorda is an essential mechanic. It is fascinating how much this simple gesture, integrated into various gameplay aspects, reinforces the idea (and feeling) of companionship, responsibility, and caring. Holding Yorda's hand while fighting the smoke demons makes Ico stronger. You pull Yorda out of dangerous smoke portals by grabbing her hand. Yorda is a bit absentminded and tends to wander off, so holding her hand while traversing the castle keeps her by your side. Handholding also makes the PlayStation 2 (PS2) controller vibrate gently, as if you were feeling Yorda's heartbeat.

In *Braid*, the time manipulation action is so closely intertwined with the game's story and deeper meaning that it is hard (impossible?) to imagine the game with a different core mechanic. The game forces the player to enact obsession and perfectionism by constantly going back and fixing mistakes until one gets it perfectly right. In *Perfection* (one of the four *For the Records* games, which deals with anorexia nervosa), a core mechanic consists of scrubbing away slugs brought about by watering a garden (another core mechanic). Watering stands for eating, and the slugs represent unwanted emotions. Scrubbing—performed by mousing over a slug, clicking and holding the left mouse button, and scrubbing over the slug as if it were a stubborn smudge you were trying to eradicate with a sponge—is a metaphor for exercising. It is meant to be a bothersome activity that is enacted with grim determination and followed by a feeling of relief when a slug has been expunged. According to our user studies, the mechanic indeed elicited these feelings, and players had a hard time giving up on it even after they learned they needed to accept some slugs as part of a healthy garden.

In *High Delivery*, one of my favorite games of all times, one steers a bottle hanging on a balloon upwards through the air to collect flowers. The so-acquired bouquet is finally delivered to a gate in heaven. It is one of the most beautiful metaphors for remembering a departed loved one I've ever seen and a profoundly touching experience. Its core mechanic—the way one steers the balloon carrying the bottle—perfectly fits with the theme: one moves the mouse cursor, which is represented as a little propeller, next to the bottle. This gently blows the bottle and the balloon in the direction the propeller is facing (e.g., moving the propeller to the left of the bottle blows it toward the right and vice versa; moving above the balloon and blowing downwards blows the balloon downwards; moving beneath it blows it upwards, etc.). The indirect, slightly wonky controls capture the longing inherent in thinking of a dear departed: there is no way of directly getting in touch, only the memory that is more or less vivid still and shifts in and out of focus.

6.10 Question 9: Player–Avatar Alignment?

When designing games about the human experience, a very common pitfall is to assume an ad-hoc mental/emotional alignment between a player and an avatar. I cannot stress this enough: just because you know the role the player takes in the game is that of a person with, for example, obsessive–compulsive disorder, or someone who's lovesick, or an addict, or whatever personality/ situation you envision the player to step into when playing the game does not mean the player experiences any of these things! You have to deliberately design for it. For a player to empathize with the character, to walk in his or her shoes, he or she needs to be put into the mind-set of the person he or she is meant to empathize with. Their goals, struggles, wants, needs, opportunities, or lack thereof need to be aligned, made tangible through the rules and mechanics in the moment-to-moment gameplay. The character's strengths and limitations need to be the player's strengths and limitations, or they won't be felt in this embodied sense games are so good at evoking. In the horror survival game *Silent Hill 2*, you are playing as the journalist James Sunderland who is called to the town of Silent Hill by a letter from his dead wife, Mary. The whole game revolves around unraveling the mystery of what happened to Mary and the part James played in her death. (It turns out James had killed his wife because she had a terminal illness.)

As much as I love *Silent Hill 2*, it really bugs me that the game interprets some of the player's actions as expressions of James Sunderland's mental state and gives you a different ending based on it. For example, at some point in the game, you take away a knife from another character who is suicidal. Like any other object you can pick up in the game, you can examine the knife. However, in this case, the game interprets this action as James' desire to commit suicide himself, whereas the real motivation behind examining the knife from the player's perspective was probably just curiosity! The player does not experience repressed guilt for having killed his or her wife. The player is just playing a game. The experience of guilt hasn't been designed into the game as part of the gameplay experience. The player and James are only aligned in regard to the emotions that surround uncovering the mystery and being scared of what's lurking around the next corner, because that experience is shared through gameplay.

When we made *Akrasia*, the substance abuse game, we assumed the players would certainly want to collect the virtual drugs, and it would be hard for them to stop, because they were stepping into the shoes of addicts, after all. In retrospect, that was a completely silly assumption. Even if the player knows which role he or she is taking in the game, it won't matter if the rules and mechanics don't reinforce it. In the case of *Akrasia*, we had to model the addiction gestalt with rules and mechanics, and give players a goal they could only achieve when taking the drugs, thus creating the experience of dependency and constructing an experience of *withdrawal* and *craving* when off drugs to evoke the *temptation* of taking them again.

When I first started concepting *Elude*, the depression game, I only focused on the experience of depression: what it was like to feel a lack of agency, being trapped, and hopeless. I conjured up the darkest scenarios—a quicksand of despair, enclosing cave walls, being buried alive—and they resonated with me, but something always appeared to be missing. When I spoke to my good friend and colleague at the MIT, Konstantin Mitgutsch, about it, he said, "Looked at from the outside, depression is just boring, you know? These scenarios are just boring. Nothing happens." He was right. The scenarios (if at all) would only resonate with people who already had experience with the disorder, who were already mentally/emotionally aligned with their avatar in the game. To help someone who didn't have lived experience with depression understand what it was like, I couldn't focus on the mere absence of agency, hope, passion, and joy. I had to focus on their loss. Hence, the design was iterated on to capture different mood states—normal, happy, and depressed—and the gameplay concentrated on the struggle between a personal desire for happiness and a limited ability to achieve it. That way, players got to experience the loss of happiness and the inability to achieve it firsthand, and the depression phases gained meaning through this contextualization.

A game that does an excellent job creating alignment between a player and an avatar is *Fahrenheit: Indigo Prophecy*. Among other characters, one can play as policewoman Carla, who suffers from claustrophobia. Just claiming that that was her issue wouldn't make the player feel claustrophobic. The scenes where her claustrophobia comes to bear thus require the player to push the R1 and L1 buttons of the PS2 controller in a regular rhythm to simulate controlled breathing while completing some other task (e.g., navigating through a confined space and moving bookshelves to recover some files). If you fall out of the regular breathing pattern (push buttons too quickly or neglect them for too long), Carla hyperventilates or holds her breath. In either case, she freaks out and runs out of the room in a cut scene, and one has to replay that part of the game. Of course, the stress experienced during gameplay is not claustrophobia itself, but it is recontextualized through the game's narrative, causing a false (but effective) attribution of the gameplay tension to this disorder. It's as close as you can get to simulate this kind of affliction in a game and align a player with an avatar.

The nine questions mentioned in this chapter help to define a vision for your game and to facilitate deliberate decision making in the design process. They do not, however, provide a way around playtesting. If you want to know whether your design decisions successfully addressed your questions and the game achieves its experiences goal, start testing even the roughest, first paper prototype and continue until there is a fully playable digital build.

EXERCISE

1. Questions in Action

Step 1: Pick an existing game, preferably something small-ish. The great sources for suitable games are the following sites: (a) http://www.gamesforchange.org/play/, (b) http://www.indiecade.com/2015/games, and (c) http://www.igf.com.

Step 2: Use the nine questions in this chapter to analyze the game:
- What is it about?
- What is its purpose/communicative goal?
- Does it use a literal or metaphorical approach (or a mixture of both)?
- If metaphorical, does the fictional surface the metaphor provides match its underlying experiential gestalt?

- Does the game model how it works or what it's like (and is that consistent with its purpose/communicative goal)?
- How big is the modeled system: does the game zoom in, getting a close-up of the situation, potentially emphasizing a subjective, emotional experience, or does it zoom out, trying to grasp the complexities of a bigger issue?
- What perspective does the player take in the game?
- Do the core mechanics match, and maybe even reinforce, the game's meaning, or is there a disconnect between what one does in the moment-to-moment gameplay and what the game is about?
- How does the game put you in your character's shoes? Are the player and the avatar well aligned, or are there discrepancies between the role you take in the game and your experience as a player? What measures does the game take to help the player step into the player character's shoes, into his or her world?

Step 3: What if…?

Now, use the questions in step 2 to help guide modifications of the game that provide different answers.

- What if the game tried to change behavior instead of raising awareness?
- What if it used a literal instead of a metaphorical approach (or vice versa)?
- What if the game modeled what it's like rather than how it works or vice versa?
- What if you zoomed in or zoomed out?
- What are the potential characters in this game, and what if you played from a different perspective (e.g., playing as the monster in *Papo & Yo* rather than the little boy)?
- What if you changed the core mechanics? What other core mechanics could you think of that match the theme just as well or maybe better?
- What other ways might there be to create/improve player–avatar alignment?

Experiment with one question at the time. See how one different answer can lead to a completely different game with a different experience and message. This goes to show that every design decision, even small ones, matters. That's why making them deliberately and intentionally is so important to minimize the gap between intent and outcome.

References

Alexander, L. 2013. Four perspectives on personal games. *Gamasutra: The Art & Business of Making Games.* Available at http://www.gamasutra.com/view/news /191406/Four_perspectives_on_personal_games.php. Accessed September 05, 2016.

Bers, M. 2001. Identity construction environments: Developing personal and moral values through the design of a virtual city. *The Journal of the Learning Sciences,* Vol. 10, No. 4 (pp. 365–415). New Jersey: Lawrence Erlbaum.

Bers, M.U. 2008. Civic identities, online technologies: From designing civic curriculum to supporting civic experiences. In Bennett, W.L. (Ed.), *Civic Life Online: Learning How Digital Media Can Engage Youth* (pp. 139–160). The John D. and Catherine T. MacArthur Foundations Series on Digital Media and Learning, Cambridge, MA: The MIT Press.

Brathwaite, B. & Schreiber, I. 2006. *Challenges for Game Designers: Non-Digital Exercises for Video Game Designers.* Boston: Course Technology.

Gardner, H. 2006. *Changing Minds: The Art and Science of Changing Our Own and Other People's Minds.* Boston: Harvard Business School Press.

Klopfer, E., Osterweil, S., & Salen, K. 2009. Moving learning games forward: Obstacles, opportunities and openness. An Education Arcade paper. Available at http://education.mit.edu/wp-content/uploads/2015/01/MovingLearning GamesForward_EdArcade.pdf. Accessed September 05, 2016.

Marquez, G.G. 1995. *Of Love and Other Demons.* London: Penguin Books.

Papert, S. 1980. *Mindstorms: Children, Computers, and Powerful Ideas.* New York: Basic Books.

Schell, J. 2008. *The Art of Game Design: A Book of Lenses.* Boca Raton, FL: CRC Press.

Sophocles. 2006. *Three Theban Plays: Oedipus Rex, Oedipus at Colouns, and Antigone.* Dover Thrift Edition, Dover Publications. Mineola: NY.

7

It's Not Always about You!—
Lessons Learned from Participatory
Deep Game Design

Wherein:

- *The concept of participatory design (PD) as a political statement of the empowerment of various stakeholders is introduced.*
- *A point is made that, in the case of nonfictional, deep games, the most important stakeholders are the people with lived experience of the subject (= subject-matter experts) that is being portrayed in the game.*
- *A comparative case study of four short games on mental health issues is presented that shows the potentials and pitfalls of working with people with lived experience who have varying degrees of game knowledge, design skills, and team involvement.*
- *The following PD takeaways are summarized:*
  - *The importance of preproduction.*
  - *Identifying a common vision for the project.*
  - *Enabling non-game-savvy subject-matter experts to explore and express their experiences in a medium they feel comfortable with, before moving toward game design discussions.*
  - *The importance of dividing responsibilities: subject-matter experts guard the "authenticity" of the experience to be modeled in the game, and game designers make sure the game "works," keeping an eye out for playability, game comprehension, and appeal.*

7.1 Introduction

My parents, who are in their seventies by the time I'm writing this, had just moved to South Africa after having lived in Austria for 40 years. When I asked my dad during a phone call how he was doing, he laughed and said, "How could you possibly understand how I was doing? I am an old man who has just moved to Africa!" He had a point. Regardless of how reflective we are or how deep we delve into our souls, our experiential horizons are ultimately limited to the known shores of our own little worlds. Even the most empathetic person can never truly know someone else's lived reality. It's important to admit that. The biggest hurdle to truly understanding others is thinking we already do.

What does that mean for deep games' design? Can we only make games about ourselves? What if we want to expand our creative practice to include the aspects of the human condition we don't have firsthand experience with? One approach is to use our observations of others, self-knowledge, empathy, research, and the power of imagination to put ourselves into someone else's shoes and *make something up*. Traditional media have done a most wonderful job at enriching our understanding about human nature without the authors always having firsthand knowledge of their character's inner lives or their circumstances. There is no reason game designers shouldn't do the same. Sometimes, however, there is an argument to be made for a nonfictional approach. Nonfiction, as defined by the Merriam-Webster Online Dictionary, is "writing that is about facts or real events."*

Imagine you are a middle-aged, middle-class, heterosexual, white woman, and you are charged to make a game that portrays the experiences of young, gay, black, homeless men as part of a bigger research project on resilience and health behavior.† The game's goal is to raise awareness and educate the broader public about a social issue. You are dealing with a group whose lived reality is very different from your own. Moreover, there is an expectation that your game is anchored in reality. Now, what you create does not just need

---

*http://www.merriam-webster.com/dictionary/nonfiction. We can expand the notion of *writing* to include any kind of media creation such as film and game design.

†This is a real, National Institutes of Health–funded research project conducted by Douglas Bruce at the health sciences department at DePaul University. Douglas approached us to indeed make games about the experiences of young, gay, black, homeless men, and we were faced with the question of how to go about it. It seemed obvious that we had to get to know the people whose lives we were supposed to make games about and ideally include them actively into the design process (http://csh.depaul.edu /faculty-staff/faculty-a-z/Pages/health-sciences/douglas-bruce.aspx).

to *ring true*. As nonfiction, it demands as much authenticity as can be mustered.* According to the Merriam-Webster Online Dictionary, "authentic" is defined as "real or genuine: not copied or false; true and accurate; made to be or look just like an original" (http://www.merriam-webster.com/dictionary /authentic). When we create nonfiction work, to just make something up would be morally objectionable. Granted, it is never possible to capture *the truth* as every documentary filmmaker or nonfiction writer knows. The source system itself is not a given but rather a subjective construction by whoever aims to capture it,† and it is then further transformed, distorted, and abstracted in oh-so-many ways in the process of communicating it to others and translating it into design. But, just because creating something authentic is challenging and there are many caveats to consider doesn't mean we cannot or should not uphold authenticity as a core value. We owe it to the audience to go for a genuine portrayal of *what it's like*, as well as to the subjects whose experiences we aim to communicate: in this case, the young, gay, black, homeless men. One possible way to increase authenticity is to invite people with firsthand knowledge of the experiences to be communicated to make games with us in a process of participatory game design. As transmedia activist Lina Srivastava puts it, "We have to stop treating other people's stories as if they are ours for the taking and shaping. We have to recognize that agency and self-representation are crucial to social change and people's perceptions of their own situations matter" (http://henryjenkins .org/2016/01/telling-stories-lina-srivastava-talks-about-transmedia-activism -part-two.html).

7.2 Participatory Game Design

What is participatory design (PD)? PD is a method borrowed from interaction design. Traditionally, it advocates for the inclusion of stakeholders— particularly software end users (*user* being defined as someone who uses a software application to *get a job done*)—into the design and production

---

* Just to clarify, a well-told, complete fictitious story can ring true, whereas a story based on true events or personal experience can be delivered poorly and seem disingenuous.

† The notion of *constructing* the source system is derived from the constructivism as a philosophy of education that claims that we generate knowledge and meaning from an interaction between our experiences and our ideas. We don't witness an objective *reality* but rather a construction thereof based on our sociocultural backgrounds and predispositions. Jean Piaget is credited with founding constructivism as a school of thought. One of its most prominent and radical proponents was Austrian-American philosopher, philologist, and psychologist Paul Watzlawick.

process. Users get a say in the kind of software application that is being created because they are the ones who have to work with it. They are the experts of their own experience. It makes sense to consult them about their needs and to include them into the process of solving their problems. PD, in this sense, is an act of empowerment where all stakeholders get a say in what is being created. It is as much a political statement as it is a creative method.

The proceedings from an early PD conference held in Seattle state it as follows:

> Participation stands in contrast to the cult of the specialist. In the specialist model, an expert is sought out. The question is presented to the Expert who will eventually produce the Answer. With this approach, those most affected by the conclusion must sit idly by, waiting patiently for enlightenment. PD, of course, demands active participation. PD, however, is not *against* expertise. There is no reason or motivation to belittle the role of expertise. (…) In the participatory design model, however, this special expertise becomes yet another resource to be drawn on – not a source of unchallenged power and authority. A partnership between implementers and users must be formed and both must take responsibility for the success of the project. (Schuler & Namioka 1993, pp. xi–xii)

PD doesn't have a strong track record in the games industry. While games are software, too, they do not have the same goals as utility applications, such as Microsoft Word. Entertainment games are not played to get a job done. Like literature and movies, games are creative, artistic expressions; thus, their design process has been firmly in the hands of professional game designers.* Due to the complex nature of games and the impossibility to anticipate exactly how someone is going to interact with them, designers bring in playtesters to gather feedback and fine-tune the experiences they want to evoke. This, however, is normally done later in the process when there is already a playable version of the game. Using player feedback to inform design iterations and find bugs is very different from cocreating a game from scratch with player input. In recent years, however, entertainment game designers have also started to involve players into the design process earlier on (Sotamaa et al. 2005; Danielsson & Wiberg 2006; Mazzone et al. 2008; Isbister et al. 2010; Tan et al. 2011; Lange-Nielsen et al. 2012; Vasalou et al. 2012). Serious games are a little different. They are a hybrid technology that aims to entertain as much as it aims to educate, and to get a job done, in one

---

*This is starting to change a little bit, and even entertainment games are bringing in players earlier, as described by Khaled & Vasalou (2014).

way or another. PD approaches have thus found more traction in the serious games domain. An increasing number of serious game designers are involving the representatives of their target audience into the design process early on. For more information on PD approaches in serious games, see Khaled & Vasalou (2014).

So far, the focus of PD was on including end users/players into the design process because they were the ones *most affected by the product to be created*, and thus most needed to be empowered through cocreation. In other words, they had the highest stake in it (at least in terms of quality, not financial success). The higher the stakes for a specific group, the more important it is to get their input so that the project most effectively fulfills their needs. This opens PD up to other stakeholders than end users/players and becomes a question of assessing stakes. I suggest to ask the following: (a) What's the problem to be solved? (b) For whom is it a problem? (c) Who do we need to make the game for to address this problem? (d) If the game fails to address the problem, who suffers the most negative consequences? Answering these questions should identify who needs to be involved in a PD process. For utility software answers, questions b through d tend to point exclusively toward end users. The same is true for most serious games based on subjects other than personal experience: e.g., for a health education game, the problem is *bad eating habits*. That's a problem that most directly concerns people with bad eating habits. To educate about bad eating habits and potentially improve them, the game needs to address people with bad eating habits. If the game fails in its mission, the people who most directly suffer the negative consequences are people with bad eating habits. Insurance companies, society at large, the friends and family of people with poor eating habits, etc., are other stakeholders, but, arguably, they are less immediately and severely affected than the person who might get sick if he or she doesn't start making better food choices. Ergo, the most important stakeholders are the intended players, and getting their input on why they eat poorly, what they need to learn to make better food choices, what would help them change their behavior, and what kind of game would get them excited so they'd actually play it is paramount for the creation of an effective product.

Coming back to nonfiction deep games. There, the stakeholders who most need to be included in PD are not necessarily the players. For example, if the problem the game tackles is the lack of awareness, understanding, and empathy for an aspect of the human experience, the people for whom most is at stake are those with a lived experience of this aspect. This corresponds with Lina Srivastava's answer in response to the question, "What criteria should

we be using to measure or assess the impact of transmedia activism cam-
paigns?", which follow similar goals as nonfiction deep games and thus lend
themselves for comparison:

> The primary focus should be on the impact of a campaign with the
> affected community. (…) Concentrating on the effect on audiences is
> a lesser criteria, not to be ignored, but in my opinion not to be given
> primacy unless the audience is itself a target of the campaign (e.g. in
> public health or consumer choice campaigns, rather than in human
> rights). (http://henryjenkins.org/2016/01/telling-stories-lina-srivastava
> -talks-about-transmedia-activism-part-two.html)

If a math learning game gets the facts wrong, that's mostly bad for the
players. When math is misunderstood or ignored, it doesn't get its feelings
hurt. We don't have a moral obligation toward math to *get it right*. We
have a moral obligation toward the players. But, if a game is about what
it's like to have Alzheimer's disease, survive a bad car accident, have a
mental illness, be in an abusive relationship, etc., we have an even greater
moral obligation toward those whose experiences we aim to convey. If
we intend to raise awareness, increase understanding and empathy, and
decrease stigma, the people who suffer most from an unsuccessful game
are not the players. It's the people who continue to be ignored, misunderstood, alienated, stigmatized, and not helped, for whom most is at stake.
It is these kinds of games that I have in mind when I discuss PD in the
context of deep games.*

Enabling people with lived experience—a special kind of subject-matter
experts (SMEs)—to shape what is being created based on their genuine experiences is thus well aligned with PD's values of democratization and empowerment. It further justifies privileging the value of the authenticity of the
represented experience over player input. If you want to understand someone
else's lived reality, you've got to let them tell you about it first, on their own
terms, in their own ways. Already coming in with demands about what you
want to hear about and how you want it to be expressed is not a great basis

---

*It is important to note that this is not the only possible reason to use PD in deep games and
that deep games can have different purposes than to communicate aspects of the human experience
to others. Their design can be motivated by self-expression or a therapeutic purpose. In that case, we
are also dealing with PD—e.g., a designer working with people with lived experience of an issue they
seek to come to grips with—but we don't need to take a player's side into account because the focus
is on the process rather than the product, and expressing the experience through design is exclusively
for the benefit of the people with the experience (more about this application of deep game design in
Chapter 8).

for this kind of dialogue. Obviously, to increase understanding, there has to be a *meeting of minds* between both sides at some point. Hence, players' feedback is still very important. Giving feedback to a modeled experience, though, is very different from cocreating it. The main power of expression still remains with SMEs. Balancing player feedback and SME's input can be tough, particularly when a game element an SME is very fond of is confusing to players. This discussion will resurface in the case study in Section 7.3 and requires careful consideration on a case-by-case basis.

There is no point denying that PD is challenging. Being an expert of one's own experiences is one thing. Being able to translate them into something playable is quite another. Serious game designers have struggled with including representatives of their target audience into the design process because they lacked either domain knowledge or design knowledge or both! (Khaled & Vasalou 2014). PD in deep games has similar issues: while we can assume our design participants have domain knowledge—they are the experts of the experiences we aim to capture—they are not necessarily game-affine or may not understand design. Unfortunately, there is no recipe for successful PD. Every project needs to find its own approach depending on its participants, development context, and design challenge. It is the designer's job to identify generative tools and techniques that enable the productive involvement of users/players/SMEs in the ideation, conception, and development.

> The onus is on designers to explore the potential of generative tools and to bring the languages of co-designing into their practice. Designers will be integral to the creation and exploration of new tools and methods for generative design thinking. Designers in the future will make the tools for non-designers to use to express themselves creatively. (Sanders & Stappers 2008, p. 15)

The examples for tools identified by designers to facilitate codesign span a wide range, including idea generation through brainstorming, storyboarding scenarios, and prototyping. It would go beyond the scope of this chapter to provide a detailed overview of PD methods, since they are so varied and dependent on the nature of each individual project. Instead, I want to focus on how PD can be leveraged for deep game design specifically. The following section is a case study of *For the Records (FtR)* (http://fortherecords.org). While this project focused on making games about mental health disorders, the lessons learned from the participatory design process with SMEs can be applied to a broad range of nonfiction deep game designs.

7.3 Case Study: *For the Records*—Potentials and Pitfalls of Participatory Game Design

FtR is an interactive, transmedia documentary project about mental illness. It was conceived by documentary filmmaker Anuradha Rana and myself. It includes short films, interviews, photo essays, animation, and games that revolve around four mental health issues: (1) obsessive–compulsive disorder (OCD), (2) attention deficit disorder (ADD), (3) bipolar disorder, and (4) the eating disorder (ED) anorexia nervosa. The project was produced at DePaul University with students and recent alumni over the span of one year. All pieces complement and provide context to each other and are embedded into the Website http://fortherecords.org.

FtR is inspired by research on the phenomenology of mental illness conducted by Mona Shattell et al. at DePaul's School of Nursing (see Jones & Shatell 2013; Schrader et al. 2013; Jones et al. 2014; Shattell 2014). The goal of *FtR* is to capture what living with mental illness feels like in order to foster dialogue and promote understanding. Many social problems surrounding mental health issues are founded in an insufficient understanding of the fullness of experience, not merely the cognitive understanding of symptoms or physiopsychological mechanisms. The lack of experiential understanding often burdens relationships between people with mental health issues and their social environment. To authentically portray what living with mental illness is like, we chose a participatory design process that included working closely with people with lived experience of the modeled mental health issues and involving them actively into the conception and design of all media pieces.* We identified our five SMEs by conducting interviews during the annual National Alliance on Mental Illness (NAMI) Walk in the Fall 2013, and drawing on our personal network. Their expertise included OCD, ADD, bipolar disorder, and ED (anorexia nervosa), which is why we chose to focus on these issues. To create the various media pieces, we split into a game development and a film group. The game development group was further divided into four teams of three to eight members, each team working in parallel

---

*We do not aim to make blatant generalizations here. We acknowledge that what the lived experience of a mental health issue for one person doesn't need to be exactly the same for another. We assume there are salient parallels, though, that allow people with similar issues to identify with someone else's experience, at least to an extent. When we speak of an *accurate representation* of a mental illness or *authenticity*, we mean specifically that our representation aims to be *genuine* and *authentic* for the person we worked with.

under faculty supervision. The film group similarly formed four teams, each responsible for the production of one experimental short film. Preproduction and development of games and films spanned Summer 2013 to Spring 2014. This case study focuses on the participatory design process of the four games: (1) *Into Darkness* (OCD), (2) *It's for the Best* (ADD), (3) *FLUCTuation* (bipolar disorder), and (4) *Perfection* (ED).

7.3.1 Game Synopses

All four games are single-player, browser-based experiences that require between 5–15 minutes of playtime. They are best played in Google Chrome. *Into Darkness* is a game about OCD and focuses on the compulsion to perform rituals in order to fend off anxiety. The player navigates a maze without exit, a metaphorical representation of the disorder itself. As the player aims to find the exit (i.e., leave the disorder behind), darkness encroaches from all sides accompanied by scary music. Performing a ritual – walking in circles five times by pressing the arrow keys – staves off the darkness. This provides temporary relief from anxiety, but at the same time prevents the maze's exit from appearing. This models one of the core conflicts of OCD: the desire to escape the compulsion, but dreading the anxiety that comes with it. Once the player resists the compulsion to perform the ritual, an exit appears, allowing the player to escape and win the game. OCD is a mental illness that can be overcome, which is why this game has a win state (Figure 7.1). Other mental issues, such as ADD or bipolar disorder, can be effectively dealt with, but the affliction will always remain, which is why the games tackling these experiences have no win state.

It's for the Best is a game about ADD. According to the experience of our SME, ADD is usually considered *not a big deal* as far as mental health issues go. This underacknowledges the troubling feelings of worthlessness ADD can bring with it and the self-doubt that accompanies the need for medication to function. By modeling a personal take on the ADD experience, the game aims to promote a mindful way of communicating the need for medication to ADD patients. In the game, players try to keep up with assignments represented by papers that flutter onto the screen with increasing speed. Clicking on papers makes them disappear and is accompanied by a satisfying sound effect, but the onslaught of papers is so heavy that one cannot possibly keep up. Unfinished assignments start to pile up in the background and to clutter up the screen. Choosing to click the pill featured prominently in the middle of the screen clears off the papers but diminishes the experience of agency

FIGURE 7.1
Into Darkness, Play 4 Change

and self-reliance. The game is accompanied by unnerving whispers of "You're not good enough." The experience ends after a certain in-game date has been reached. There is no win state, since ADD is a lifelong disorder that can only be dealt with but not *won* (Figure 7.2).

FLUCTuation intends to communicate the incomprehensible behavior of people with bipolar disorder to their friends and families in order to alleviate alienation from loved ones. The game consists of three phases that have been modeled after three phrases our SME used to capture his experience with the different states of the disorder:

> *Phase 1:* The onset of mania: "Why can't they [e.g., friends] keep up?" This phase is briefly represented by an introductory party scene in which the player character starts out as *the heart of the party* who is first imitated by others, but then shoots off through the ceiling into the sky, leaving everyone else behind.

> *Phase 2:* Mania (Figure 7.3): "It feels like architecting a divine plan. Everything is in sync and coming together in perfect unison." This

FIGURE 7.2
It's for the Best, Play 4 Change

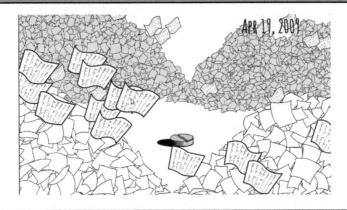

FIGURE 7.3
Manic Phase in *FLUCTuation*, Play 4 Change

phase has been implemented as a platformer in which the player character is catapulted higher and higher up by jumping onto glass platforms that shatter underneath his feet. The shattering glass represents the damage done due to bad decisions made in mania (e.g., irresponsible relations, overspending). Some platforms carry people. Jumping on those platforms is accompanied by rainbow sparkles, representing not only the intense gratification of social interactions during mania but also the potential damage done to the people one interacts with in that state. Game control decreases over time. Simultaneously, a fractal image grows in the background, which represents the feeling of being part of a bigger whole. Mania ends suddenly and plunges the player into depression.

Phase 3: Depression (Figure 7.4)—"It feels like wading through mud, lost in the company of others." The player finds herself in the deep, dark ocean of depression, where the broken shards from the manic phase platforms conglomerate to block her path to the surface. The player's agency is restricted to painfully slow up, left, and right movement (like wading through mud). The people positioned to the sides of the screen send out lights that gravitate toward the player character. These lights stand for well-meant but overwhelming questions such as "How can I help you?" A depth meter shows how far one is from the surface, but it is unreliable and cannot be trusted. There is no way of knowing when depression will be over. This last phase of the game transitions into an ending cut scene that represents the end of a manic-depressive cycle and return to normality. Each part of the game is timed to decouple it from the player skill. It does not have a win state, since bipolar disorder can only be managed, not won.

FIGURE 7.4
Depression Phase, *FLUCTuation*, Play 4 Change

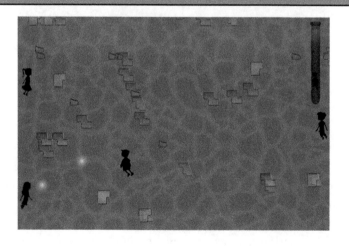

FIGURE 7.5
Perfection, Play 4 Change

Perfection (Figure 7.5; http://fortherecords.org/perfection.html) is a game about the ED anorexia nervosa, a phenomenon that is often highly incomprehensible to people without firsthand experience and fraught with misconceptions (e.g., persons with anorexia do not eat simply to look *better*). It aims to align the player's mind-set with that of a person with anorexia by suggesting a (false) win state (i.e., perfection) whose pursuit has devastating side effects. The game's core metaphor is the body as a garden. The game suggests that a perfect garden is devoid of slugs and weeds. To achieve perfection, the player is asked to eliminate these unwanted elements until only the main plant in the middle is left. The conflict of the game revolves around garden saturation. Watering the garden increases its saturation; the main plant flourishes, but so do the weeds and the numbers of slugs rise (i.e., representations of unwanted emotions). Eliminating slugs by moving the mouse over them in a scrubbing motion (i.e., a metaphor for exercising) decreases saturation, as does parching the garden. Desaturation further kills the weeds, but it also damages the main plant. The game is structured in three stages in which an increasing number of weeds must be eradicated (i.e., representing increasingly higher weight-loss goals). At the end of stage three, when no more weeds are left, the *Perfection* ending is reached. This ending, though, has come at the cost of a healthy main plant and equals *starvation*. It turns out that the *Perfection* ending is not a true win state after all. There is another ending, though—imperfection—hidden in the game. This ending represents the true win state and encourages the player to challenge his or her previous assumptions and change his or her behavior. To reach it, players have to consistently keep their garden within an ideal saturation range, learn to accept the slugs and weeds, and nurse them back to health. While the ED may never fully be *forgotten*, there are good chances to overcome it, which is why this game has a win state (Figure 7.5).

7.3.2 Participatory Design with SMEs

In the case of *Into Darkness* and *It's for the Best*, the SMEs (people with OCD and ADD) were part of the development team. Out of respect for his desire to remain anonymous, I won't disclose which role the SME had on the team of *Into Darkness*. On *It's for the Best*, the SME was one of the two designers and took a role as artist. This raises the question whether this case can still be considered PD. *Perfection* and *FLUCTuation* did not have a person with lived experience consistently embedded on the team. Also, neither of these games' SMEs possessed extensive game knowledge, let alone game design skills. They had, however, a strong, personal interest in *FtR* and were well versed in other forms of artistic expressions. The SME for *Perfection* is a dancer who was training to become a dance therapist at the time (and successfully completed her studies in the meantime). The SME for *FLUCTuation* is a sociologist and filmmaker with an extensive documentary filmography. One could say the participatory design process of the four *FtR* games happened on a continuum of involvement and design control where *It's for the Best* is on one side of the spectrum and *Perfection/FLUCTuation* is on the other side, and *Into Darkness* is in the middle.

The following is a comparison of how PD played out in each project and how PD impacted (a) the identification of the game's communicative goal, (b) finding the core metaphor, and (c) making design decisions about game elements. It concludes with a summary of the lessons learned and thoughts on how to address challenges of PD in nonfiction deep game design. Since these games were made with the purpose of increasing the player's understanding of the lived experience of the modeled issues, the players' responses to the games are part of the reflection on the strengths and weaknesses of the PD process as applied in the four example games.

Any statements made about whether and in how far the games resonated emotionally with players or increased their understanding of the portrayed issues are based on weekly playtestings performed throughout the design and development process with DePaul faculty and students from different disciplinary backgrounds, including, but not limited to, game development, film, animation, and nursing. We further conducted an Institutional Review Board (IRB)–approved in-depth, qualitative user study on the completed games with a group of 17 mental health care providers in the greater Chicago area. From the start, we aimed to make sure the games evoked the intended emotional experiences by testing for the player's responses to the games overall, the conflicts the players experienced, the goals they felt they should pursue within each game, and how they felt toward individual game elements (e.g., in *Perfection*, how did an increase of slugs make them feel? The intended experience was that they'd want to avoid the slugs and thus chose not to water the garden because that increased their numbers). We also aimed for a cognitive understanding of the modeled disorders and how this understanding was promoted or hindered by the game structures, as well as individual game elements. Each test of the user study began with a demographic interview that assessed the tester's preexisting experience with the mental health issues modeled in the games. Gameplay was then observed by the researchers conducting the test (a group of Human Computer Interaction [HCI] grad students with experience in qualitative data collection and evaluation). The gameplay session was followed by a debriefing interview, which included a *prompt list* that contained all the elements of all four games. After asking the players for their general interpretation of the game, the researchers went through the prompt list to assess whether the meaning of each element was clear. Since these findings have been published in Harris et al. (2015), I don't want to bog down this chapter with numbers.

7.3.2.1 Identifying the Communicative Goal   The phenomenology of mental illness is complex. Each team had to decide which aspects of their particular disorder they wanted to model and why. What was the communicative goal? We found a clear correspondence between the intensity of SME involvement in the design process, SME design knowledge, and how much of a *clear voice* a project had. The more involved, and the more design understanding, the stronger the voice and statement the game made. As a result, playtesting showed that more players understood the message and were able to empathize with the modeled experience.

Out of all four games, *It's for the Best* is the most personal in the sense that it takes a very specific view on attention deficit hyperactivity disorder (ADHD)—the feelings of self-doubt and frustration associated with the need for medication—and was driven by the strongest desire to say something about it. There was a clear addressee for the game, namely, the parents who administered (with the doctor's orders) medication from the time the SME was eight years old. The game doesn't want to make a claim that ADHD medication is bad, but that it matters greatly how its need is communicated to the patient/child to avoid making him feel like he or she needs to be *fixed*. This project also had the longest history. It started as a physical prototype in my deep games course, while the designer/SME was still a student. He came back to work on *FtR* as an alumni a year later because I invited him to create a digital version of the game as one of the four interactive pieces. That means *It's for the Best* also had the longest production time due to all the thinking and contemplation that already went into creating the prototype as part of the class. The goal of the assignment was to make a game about a *personal issue*, and the SME settled on his struggle with ADHD medication. As a result of having taken the deep games class, this SME/designer was the most aware of strategies on how to express inner experiences because he had practiced them on numerous projects for a whole quarter. This is an ideal case and probably very hard to replicate in other PD projects, but it goes to show that the combination of firsthand knowledge of the topic to be modeled, a strong, personal agenda, significant design skills, and time spent honing and iterating on a prototype is most conducive to the creation of powerful deep games. At the end of this section, I am going to suggest strategies on how similar results can be achieved without ideal conditions such as these.

Into Darkness went through several concepts and prototypes over the course of the summer leading up to development, before its communicative goal was firmly established, namely, that "fear's grasp is only as strong as you allow it to be." As a witness to the team's process, my hunch is that the lack of the SME's preexisting communicative agenda, paired with his strong game design/development knowledge, might have slowed down the identification of a clear message. The SME and the lead designer, who started the brainstorming and concepting before the rest of the team joined in in the Fall, were tackling the questions of how to model what the experience of OCD is like and how to make a game about that at the same time. In an email the lead designer, William Guenette, sent to me in July 2013, he states, "One of the main things is, we are trying to avoid a puzzle game which seems like it's too blunt and obvious. Is that something we should worry about or is it fine to hit people over the head with the point?" This shows a game design–centric approach—which genre could fit our purpose?—rather than considering the message first. This is not necessarily wrong, but it can lead to premature self-censoring of ideas for the sake of design feasibility and prohibit a really unique and authentic voice to come through. My response to the team was to trust the personal images that come up for their SME when he thinks of his OCD and worry about the design later. This should encourage a metaphorical approach and promote leveraging personal insight and experiences to guide the design process instead of the other way around. Upon the completion of the project, the lead designer reports in regard to employing a metaphorical approach:

> All metaphors were useful in being able to understand the inner experience itself, though most would not translate well into a game format. The ones that really helped understand feelings were key to understanding what we wanted the player to feel, and those that were structural helped us create the design for the gameplay itself.

This shows an emphasis shift from a design-centric view to an *inner-experience* approach, where metaphors were used as a *conceptual glue* to reconcile the message with gameplay. By September, the team had settled on the maze metaphor and identified the compulsive performance of rituals as the main manifestation of OCD and a method of keeping the anxiety at bay. What the SME impressed upon the team was that the ritual had to feel cumbersome. The design goal was thus to create an experience in which players truly felt compelled to repeatedly perform an action they hated to perform, because the consequences of not doing so would feel even worse.

Perfection and *FLUCTuation* both started with extensive, in-depth interviews with the external SMEs. Interviews were conducted in informal settings—parks, coffee shops—and with little structure to allow the SMEs to lead the way and talk about the things that seemed most relevant to them about their experiences. The initial question for each SME was "Can you tell me what it's like to have an eating disorder/bipolar disorder?", and then we took it from there. Each initial interview took about 2 hours to complete and was followed up with email correspondence. This email correspondence began with the designer/interviewer summarizing the main findings from the face-to-face conversation to double-check whether the most important aspects of the SME's lived experience of the disorder had been captured and to gather any additional thoughts that may have occurred to the SME in the meantime. While we were able to identify the core themes for both *Perfection* and *FLUCTuation* through interviews and follow-up email correspondence, there was less time in the production process to really hone in on one clear message.

The following provides excerpts from the interview with the SME for bipolar disorder in June 2013 and leads through the process of identifying the game's main motifs. Note how metaphors emerged naturally in the conversation, sometimes in the form of *emotional snapshots* (e.g., feeling like a gutted fish in the down phase of the disorder), sometimes as bigger metaphorical structures that described the disorder in a more encompassing way.

> *SME:* Manic phase feels like there is a purpose, like one is architecting a divine plan. It involves a loss of control, an inability to exercise free will in an effort to calm down. It's the meteoric rise of a solitary runner. You're alone in your mania, propelled forward. There's an intoxication that comes with operating at great heights. There is a multi-sensory perception of shit coming together as if planned by God, like erratic cacophonous sounds shaping themselves into a symphony. The fall from manic is a jagged descent. You're trying to hold on to it when you feel it is about to end. The inability to do so reminds me of a child's futile mid-summer's attempt to sustain the glow of lightning bugs trapped in a jar. No matter how vigilant the stewardship, no matter how many air holes you drill into the jar's lid, the light burns out in a dishearteningly desultory fashion.

The metaphorical description of the depression phase focuses first on the issue of social relationships, highlighting this as a salient aspect of the experience.

> Everyone is staring, hoping something will change. I am a dead, empty, gutted fish. People ask how you're doing, and it feels so fraught with obligation. Like a chorus of a thousand screeching prayers amplified through an electric bullhorn. There is an intense feeling of isolation as one realizes the pain one has caused others during mania. Interventions from other people are not received the way they are intended. You cannot respond to them the way you should, because the realization of this pain that you caused fuels an increased sense of isolation/detachment, as well as anger and resentment toward the ones who've been harmed during mania.

The interview then shifts to the distorted sense of proportion in the depression phase where every task seems bigger than it is:

> A pile of three dishes becomes a pile of 3000 dishes. The individual problems you created for yourself in manic form a huge heap of problems that seems insurmountable in depression. Whatever you need to tackle, you can't tackle because it's too big and has spiraled out of control. It feels like wading through mud or quicksand. There is a sense of

suffocation when stuck in depression, and there is no way of knowing when it is going to end.

This interview provided the basis for a follow-up email discussion between the designer and the SME in which we identified the main themes to be communicated with *FLUCTuation*: a sense of loss of control in both mania and depression, as well as alienation from self and others.

Perfection started with an in-depth conversation with the SME that clarified the role of food and emphasized that ED is really about control and the idea of perfection. The SME understood perfection as not only having the perfect body but also (and maybe more importantly) having perfect control over one's inner life. We learned that the intake of food opens the door to unwanted emotions, and that all emotions—bad and good—are unwanted because they seem incontrollable. To feel means to discover needs, and there is always the danger that the needs are not being met, so it is better to suppress feelings altogether and strive for total control. As our SME explained in an email after the initial interview, "Control of food 'equates' to control of what feels uncontrollable, aka emotions, life, specific situations, anxiety, OCD, etc." We further learned that exercising is not just a means to lose weight but also to regain control over one's feelings and that that was central to the SME's experience.

Another salient aspect for her was the *eating disorder voice*: an inner voice that urged her toward *perfection*. As a dancer, the SME had a dance coach whom she experienced as very critical of her physicality, and thus she identified her ED voice with him and his harsh comments. To the game team (and me as its lead designer), the themes of perfection and control were so prominent that they overshadowed the ED voice as its own element in this initial brainstorming phase. Early concepts introduced an ED voice in the beginning of the game as a primer to the player, but then focused on modeling a system that seduced the player to achieve a *perfect* state that would coincide with the game's lose condition. This corresponds to the conflict inherent in ED where perfect control—the ability to stop eating altogether—is equivalent to death. To people without a firsthand experience of ED, this strive for perfection and control at the cost of one's health seems so incomprehensible that we thought being able to make players enact this conflict, and fall into the ED trap themselves through how we set up the game's rule structure and conflicting messages, would promote a powerful embodied understanding of the disorder. While our SME agreed with and supported this approach (or we would not have moved forward with it), it became clear later in the process that the aspect of ED that was most salient to her was her struggle with the ED voice and learning how to *talk back* to it with the voice of health. This became apparent with the dance our SME choreographed and performed for the experimental film that complemented the game in the bigger *FtR* project. The film is called *Re-Embodied*, and, in it, the SME dances and narrates her personal story of struggle with and recovery from the ED voice with the help of a firm therapist who wouldn't give in to the ED voice.

I still think our design approach wasn't wrong and that what we created has merit. But we (design team) made a decision about the game's communicative goal that was guided by our interests rather than the SME's. When we started brainstorming and concepting, our SME hadn't had a chance yet to really think about what she wanted to say about ED and thus spent most of the initial conversations educating us about more general aspects of ED (as experienced by her).

We designed a game based on what was new and thus interesting to us, rather than giving the SME a venue to express what it's like for her to live with ED. The game is accurate in so far as there is not a single rule or element that wasn't derived from the collaboration with our SME, but it's not as authentic as it could be in regard to its voice.* If our SME had created the dance beforehand, it would have given us a different basis for collaboration. Her thoughts would have been more fully formed, and she could have guided the game design process more clearly to capture her experiences more authentically. I am convinced that this would have led to a stronger, more relatable project.

Playtesting and user study showed that we hit the mark with the experiences we wanted to evoke in players. When we asked players for an interpretation of the game's content or the meaning of individual elements, they often drew a blank until we at least revealed the core metaphor of *body as garden*. In a way, you already had to understand ED in order to understand the game. I believe this would not have happened, if our SME had a stronger, expressive agenda at the beginning of the project and had articulated what she wanted to say as she did with her dance performance and voice-over narration.

Lessons learned: there is a strong correlation between the ability of finding a clear, communicative goal and giving SMEs a voice and time spent in preproduction. It takes time to figure out what one wants to say. Evidence

---

*Granted, it is not always possible to find such a clear voice at all, no matter how much time is allotted for it and what methods are being employed. In these cases, one just has to go with one's best instincts on what aspects of the experience are most relevant, what to include in a systemic representation, and what to abstract away. Having design knowledge certainly helps to make these calls.

indicates that encouraging SMEs to form their thoughts in a medium they are most familiar with—be it dance, poetry, film, or drawing—before any game design considerations take place is a highly productive method. If the medium the SME is most familiar/comfortable with is game design, then he or she needs to make sure this medium is harnessed as a tool for self-exploration/ expression and that the priority isn't to *make a good game* at this point. Once the purpose and message have manifested themselves, and a vision statement or an expressive goal has been clearly articulated, the collaboration with the design team can shift toward making a game. At that stage, it is helpful to either be working with SMEs who have game design knowledge or to spend some time discussing the characteristics of the medium with them, so that designers and SMEs can make informed design decisions together.

7.3.2.2 Finding the Core Metaphor   Each of the four *FtR* games aimed at identifying a *core metaphor* as the basis for the design. The function of a core metaphor is to provide a conceptual framework, a larger metaphorical structure, into which all other game elements can be embedded. This helps to keep all aspects of the game coherent, in line with one possible reading, thus promoting interpretation and sense making. Without a solid core metaphor, there are always bits and pieces of the concept and/or experience that do not quite fit.

Into Darkness and *It's for the Best* settled on their core metaphors quickly. *It's for the Best* could already build on a physical prototype, and the *Into Darkness* team had developed their core metaphor in tandem with their communicative goal: OCD as a maze. For *Perfection* and *FLUCTuation*, finding a strong conceptual frame was much harder. We used a variety of methods, such as brainstorming core metaphors with SMEs who represented the disorder to them. Brainstorming sessions were mostly verbal but encouraged SMEs to also draw their thoughts or find images that reminded them of their disorders. This method fostered mixed results. A game's core metaphor needs to be complex enough and have multiple dimensions to support a game structure. It is enormously helpful to have game design experience to identify what works in that regard. Since the SMEs of *Perfection* and *FLUCTuation* didn't have game design knowledge, we had to change our strategy. For *FLUCTuation*, we invented a method I'd like to call *metaphor archeology*. This is a process of analyzing interview transcripts for traces of salient dimensions of bigger, structural metaphors. For example, the SME spoke of the "intoxication of operating at great heights" in mania, and the "jagged descent" when "coming down" from it, and described the depression phase as feeling "submerged" without knowing how long this state would last, when you could "come up" again. The structural metaphor we could derive from these dimensions was the well-established *up-is-good, down-is-bad* dichotomy. The SME further emphasized physical movement metaphors to capture the emotional experiences of manic and depressive state: being propelled forward in mania and wading through mud or quicksand in depression. This already implies gameplay variables to tinker with: movement speed and sensitivity to player input. The quality of movement in each state further determined the metaphor for the game space in mania and depression: the sky is limitless and thus lends itself to be the scenery for the unstoppable ascent in mania. The ocean feels bottomless; one can lose one's sense of direction, and movement is more sluggish and cumbersome in water.

Perfection's SME spoke more abstractly about her experiences. A textual analysis of her transcripts didn't foster fruitful leads to a bigger, implied structural metaphor. In retrospect, it would have been a great idea to try to leverage the medium the SME was most comfortable with—dance—to identify a metaphor. Body movement has great symbolic potential and could have served as our access point to the SME's abstract thoughts, making them concrete through physical enactment. Instead, the designer suggested a core metaphor based on her understanding of the SME's reported experiences. The SME was then invited to give her input to the designer's suggestion. Initial ideas revolved around a science laboratory metaphor as a representation of the SME's inner world. The lab was messy, and a computer voice (representing the ED voice) would instruct the player that the goal was to make the lab sterile/perfect (= devoid of emotions). However, the process of sterilization exerted a lot of energy. The lab would shut down once all energy was depleted, and the game would be lost. The goal was to keep the lab in an ideal state for as long as possible before running out of energy (dying). Press a red button in the center of the lab to restore energy (= eating). Unfortunately, pressing the button would also open the lab's door and let in all sorts of gross things (= emotions) that would contaminate the lab again. We ran this by our SME who loved it and responded with a request to also model strategies of recovery. Her email from Sept. 11, 2013, is as follows:

> I was also hoping to clarify that restoring energy (eating) doesn't just bring the emotions, but is a necessary part of recovery. Restoring weight and eating is a good/healthy thing. Is there a way that we can portray that or do you think that that is already underlying it... or maybe it can be in the instructions? Can we also portray that the healthy way of living is in regulation and balance of total mess vs. perfection? A big part of leaving the ED!

This made us rethink the lab metaphor because it is hard to make a case for a *contaminated but healthy lab*. Sterility is such a strong, established value for a laboratory that it doesn't leave room for doubt or ambiguity. Ambiguity around the declared goal, however, is necessary if we want players to figure out that their behavior is destructive and they need to adopt a different strategy. Hence, we changed the metaphor to the body as a garden. It makes sense to want a perfect garden without slugs and weeds, but it also makes sense that you need to tolerate some amount of that for the garden to be healthy. Changing the metaphor after the SME's input allowed us to honor her request to include the process of recovery into our design.*

Working with reflective, self-aware, and extraordinarily creative SMEs (even if they had never applied their creativity to games) facilitated PD. While we had to find different strategies to work with each SME, we arrived at each game's core metaphor in a truly collaborative manner. It deserves to be noted, though, that the process of identifying *Perfection's* core metaphor is probably the least desirable. While the metaphor is perfectly coherent and relates dimension for dimension to the aspects of the ED experience reported by the SME, it is somehow less authentic than the other core metaphors. It wasn't born from *feeling*, an image that arose naturally from the SME exploring and making sense of her inner world; it was artificially constructed by the designer. *Perfection* is thus the most intellectually informed of the four *FtR* games, which might be the reason it is also the least relatable (at least without explanation), as indicated by playtests.

Lesson learned: metaphors offered by SMEs or identified through a process of textual analysis of the SME's expressions (be they verbal, visual, or physical) are more authentic and thus have better chances of being relatable to other people (even without mental illness) than metaphors artificially constructed by the designer. The metaphors constructed by the designer might be clever and coherent and fit the SME's reported experience dimension for dimension, but they might not ring true. They aren't born from feeling but

---

*As a general note, it is often not possible, nor desirable, to try to capture the subjective experience of a concept, as well as its objective mechanisms, in a deep game. Portraying what something *feels like* means subjective perception informs the rules, not how things really work. From the outside, no mental illness makes sense. If we remain on the outside, we can't foster understanding. If we adopt an inside view, we better commit to it. If you want to convey that something feels hopeless, it's hard to also show that it really isn't. Subjective beliefs inform the rule system. If you undermine the rule system by questioning those beliefs and show them as just that—beliefs—you undermine the experience. Trying to model the problem, as well as its inherent solution (e.g., how to overcome OCD or an ED), to some extent, muddles up the message. It alleviates the severity of the disorder and how inevitable and insurmountable it can feel. It has to be carefully considered where it makes sense and whether/how it is possible to show both sides: the subjective, as well as the objective, *truth*.

from *intellect*, and metaphors that help us make sense of our experiences should be born from feeling. The designer's job is to make sure the metaphors that are introduced by SMEs actually work in the context of a game. Similar to identifying the communicative goal, it is worth experimenting with creative arts approaches to prompt the SME's access to his or her inner world and to facilitate the emergence of authentic metaphors. *Clean Language*, as introduced in Chapter 3, to explore the SME's inner landscape in conversation, is another technique that deserves a shot. By using *clean language*, the designer stimulates an exploration of the inner landscape without contaminating it with his or her ideas about what the core metaphor should be.

7.3.2.3 SMEs versus Playtesters—Pitfalls of Making Design Decisions in PD There is not one, single game element in any of the four *FtR* games that doesn't have meaning in regard to the mental disorder that is being portrayed. Every rule, every game object, and even every audiovisual representation has been carefully and purposefully designed to capture yet another aspect of the issue. With layer upon layer of meaning, these games can truly be called *deep*. Not all of their depth and cleverness, however, has been conducive to their communicative goal. The following is an exploration of the pitfalls of making decisions in participatory deep game design. It relates back to the question of stakeholders from the beginning and how to balance the values that are at play in the PD process: in our case, the values of *authenticity, compelling design,* and *game comprehension.*

We put our emphasis on authenticity, meaning that we privileged SME's input over concerns of compelling game design or game comprehension. Almost all game aspects were either derived directly from the SME's descriptions of their experiences or from their concrete design suggestions. For example, the ED SME explained,

> Restricting makes me lose focus and shrinks my ability to concentrate and be present—a large reason for me to get out of the ED—but somehow blurring vision or lack of focus, shaking, cognitively overriding physical sensations of hunger, ignoring the body could be a part of the game…

This translated into *Perfection's* art style becoming more and more abstract to capture the dissociation from self/the body the more encompassing the disorder gets.

The intro party sequence in *FLUCTuation*—where your avatar's jumping (= dancing) is first mimicked by the crowd that surrounds him before he takes off through the roof and into the sky—was informed by the SME's description of being the heart of the party in mania and wondering why friends *can't keep up*. Even parts of the game's sound design are owed to the SME's input as this excerpt from a feedback session in the Fall 2013 shows:

> I like the fractal visualization ... the "architecting a divine plan" is a terrific addition, and I can't think of a better way to represent it visually. I wonder if there's a way to create a soundscape with audio coming into unison/harmony as a way to capture the multisensory perception of shit coming together as if planned by god—like erratic, cacophonous sounds shaping themselves into a symphony that sounds something like the "THX: The Audience is Listening" thing at the beginning of movies in the cinema.

Working with our SMEs was eye opening, insightful, and rewarding. There was a lot of mutual respect, and we learned so much about a broader range of the human experience. I also believe we created unique projects that can contribute to the players' understanding of what it's like to live with the portrayed disorders, especially in the bigger context of the *FtR* interactive documentary. We also found that all four games can truly stimulate powerful aha moments, but they all (and particularly *Perfection* and *FLUCTuation*) benefit from external explanations and reflective prompting that helps to clarify their various elements and to create the connection between the emotional experiences evoked by the game and how they relate to the modeled disorders. In other words, we were only somewhat successful in achieving the games' declared goal of increasing the understanding about mental illness. The most relevant reason in regard to a PD approach was that we prioritized our SMEs' input over playtesting data.

We playtested every game from the start approximately every two weeks with a wide range of players from different disciplinary backgrounds and with varying game/tech knowledge. This shed light on a lot of usability issues with various game controls. We addressed them as well as we could within the given time frame. We found that *Perfection's* original art style was confusing, that people didn't understand what was happening in the game, and that no one seemed to read the quotes in between stages. Hence, we extended this project's life for another six months, completely revised the art, and added a voice-over to the quotes.

What we did not address as radically were issues with game elements our SMEs had declared their love for, such as *FLUCTuation's* unreliable depth meter or the people in the down phase that sent lights toward the avatar.

Players were consistently confused by these features. While we tried to make them clearer (e.g., we revised the depth meter to at first indicate progress toward the surface before we *broke* it), we didn't have the heart to take them out or redesign them completely because our SME had praised them so highly: "I love, love, love the unreliable depth meter. Fucking brilliant." And "I really, really like the floating flashlights. Shit, that's good."

Lesson learned: it is hard to kill your own darlings, but it is even harder to kill somebody else's, especially if your goal is to give that person a voice. Also—and this aspect shouldn't be underestimated—if you, as a designer, manage to capture an element of somebody else's experience that makes that person feel truly understood, it creates a special kind of connection. Changing the design feels like betraying that connection. Whatever the reason, though, if your goal is to make a game that effectively communicates a message to players, the SMEs' input has to be carefully weighed against playtesting results. The SMEs' approval (or disapproval!) has to be put into perspective, especially if they are not game designers. There needs to be a division of responsibilities: it is the designer's job to look out for the game and to make sure it fulfills its purpose (if it has one). The SME's job is to look out for the authenticity of the modeled experience (in the sense that the SME helps to identify the vision and what is most essential about the experience that should be communicated). If both sides do their jobs with an open mind, a deep, mutual respect and understanding of the other's perspective, and the intent of creating the best game possible in regard to the communicative goal, they can make productive design decisions that successfully balance the values at stake. If the designer feels like the ideas brought up or praised by SMEs are untouchable, they are neglecting their duties toward the medium and the prospective players. Vice versa, if SMEs start worrying about the game aspect, they might lose sight of what is most essential about the experience that should be modeled. For successful collaboration, each side needs to play to their strengths.

7.3.3 Final Thoughts about Participatory Deep Game Design

While complex and complicated in many ways, PD has an amazing potential to open our minds as designers, to learn about others, to develop a deeper understanding for the spectrum of human experiences, and to make games about themes that would otherwise be inaccessible to us. For SMEs, it is an opportunity to reflect on their experiences and share them with a receptive audience. In some cases, this can promote emotional hygiene and have a therapeutic potential (more about that in Chapter 8).

The case study in Section 7.3 described a project that intended to educate players about various mental illnesses. We were lucky to be working with highly reflective, enthusiastic, and creative SMEs. Our main challenges revolved around negotiating the authenticity of the modeled experience, the SME's approval of the design, and players' game comprehension. Different communicative goals/purposes and different SMEs will come with different challenges and the need to balance different values in the PD and the design decision-making process. Nevertheless, the reflection on the *FtR* project produced some takeaways of general applicability and usefulness:

- Preproduction is more important than ever; it pays to schedule plenty of time for SMEs and the game development team to get to know each other, build trust, and explore the topic before even thinking about game design.
- Finding the key message/voice for a project needs to take priority over any design considerations for the sake of authenticity and the clarity of vision that will guide the design process.
- Giving SMEs the opportunity to express their thoughts and experiences through a medium they are familiar and comfortable with before worrying about the application to game design helps to crystallize key messages and to find a clear voice for the project.
- SMEs and designers agree on the vision for the project (including the key message/experience, purpose, and audience) before moving toward design.
- Agree on divided responsibilities, particularly when working with SMEs who are not game designers: SMEs focus on communicating their experiences as authentically and vividly as possible. Game designers focus on creating a game that does the SME's experiences justice but under consideration of the affordances of the medium and player feedback.

References

Danielsson, K. & Wiberg, C. 2006. Participatory design of learning media: Designing educational computer games with and for teenagers. *Interactive Technology and Smart Education*, Vol. 3, Iss. 4 (pp. 275–291).

Harris, B., Rusch, D., Shattell, M., & Zefeldt, M.J. 2015. Barriers to learning about mental illness through empathy games—Results of a user study on "perfection." In Jacobs, S. & Fay, I. (Eds.), *Well Played Video Games, Value and Meaning*. Vol. 4, No. 2. (pp. 56–75). Pittsburgh, PA: ETC Press.

Isbister, K., Flanagan, M., & Hash, C. 2010. Designing games for learning: Insights from conversations with designers. In proceedings of the *28th International Conference on Human Factors in Computing Systems, CHI'10* (pp. 2041–2044). New York: ACM.

Jones, N. & Shattell, M. 2013. Engaging with voices: Rethinking the clinical treatment of psychosis. *Issues in Mental Health Nursing*, Vol. 34, Iss. 7 (pp. 562–563).

Jones, N., Shattell, M., Harris, B., Sonido, C., Kaliski-Martinez, N., Mull, A., & Gomez, A. 2014. Multi-level stakeholder engagement: Community-based work on psychosis and voices. Midwestern Psychological Association, Chicago, May [Data-based symposium].

Khaled, R. & Vasalou, A. 2014. Bridging serious games and participatory design. In *International Journal of Child–Computer Interaction*, Vol. 2, Iss. 2 (pp. 93–100). Elsevier B.V.

Lange-Nielsen, F., Lafont, X.V., Cassar, B., & Khaled, R. 2012. Involving players earlier in the game design process using cultural probes. In proceedings of the *4th International Conference on Fun and Games, FnG'12* (pp. 45–54). New York: ACM.

Mazzone, E., Read, J.C., & Beale, R. 2008. Design with and for disaffected teenagers. In proceedings of the 5th *Nordic Conference on Human–Computer Interaction: Building Bridges, NordiCHI'08* (pp. 290–297). New York: ACM.

Sanders, E.B. & Stappers, P.J. 2008. Co-creation and the new landscapes of design. *CoDesign: International Journal of CoCreation in Design and Arts*, Vol. 4. Iss. 1 (pp. 5–18).

Schrader, S., Jones, N., & Shattell, M. 2013. Mad pride: Reflections on sociopolitical identity and mental diversity in the context of culturally competent psychiatric care. *Issues in Mental Health Nursing*, Vol. 34, Iss. 1 (pp. 62–64).

Schuler, D. & Namioka, A. 1993. *Participatory Design: Principles and Practices*. Hillsdale, NJ: Lawrence Erlbaum Asscociates.

Shattell, M. 2014. Guest Editorial—Critical, participatory, ecological, and user-led: Nursing scholarship and knowledge development of the future. *Advances in Nursing Science*, Vol. 37, Iss. 1 (pp. 3–4).

Sotamaa, O., Ermi, L., Jäppinen, A., Laukkanen, T., Mäyrä, F., & Nummela, J. 2005. The role of players in game design: A methodological perspective. In proceedings of *DAC—Digital Experience: Design, Aesthetics, Practice*, Vol. 6 (pp. 34–42). Copenhagen, DK.

Tan, J.L., Goh, D.H.-L, Ang, R.P., & Huan, V.S. 2011. Child-centered interaction in the design of a game for social skills intervention. *Computers in Entertainment (CIE)—Theoretical and Practical Computer Applications in Entertainment*, Vol. 9, Iss. 1, Article No. 2, New York: ACM.

Vasalou, A., Ingram, G., & Khaled, R. 2012. User-centered research in the early stages of a learning game. In proceedings of the *Designing Interactive Systems Conference, DIS'12* (pp. 116–125). New York: ACM.

8

The Same New Kid in Yet Another Hood—Deep Game Design as Creative Arts Therapy?

Coauthored with Susan Imus

Wherein we explore the potential of game design as a process for creative arts therapy. This includes the following:

- *An overview of the basic concepts and criteria of creative arts therapies, as well as*
- *The fundamental mechanisms, such as safety, risk taking, various approaches, intentional goals, symbolic and metaphoric explorations, etc.*
- *A comparative case study of a dance-and-movement therapy session with an exploratory game design therapy-like session to illustrate the similarities and differences of game design as a creative arts therapy modality:*
  - *The game design session includes a detailed description of the setup, the design process, and the interactions between the designer and the volunteer "patient"*
  - *A detailed discussion of the process by witnessing creative arts therapists*
  - *A clear relation of the fundamental mechanisms of creative arts therapies to this exemplary game design therapy-like session*
  - *A debriefing report of the volunteer patient who reflects on her experiences with the exploratory therapy-like game design session*

8.1 Introduction

This chapter might be unexpected. What are musings about creative arts therapy doing in a book about game design? On second thought, however, it brings us full circle: the whole notion of deep games was born out of personal crisis. Design was a tool to work through issues, gain distance and clarity, and regain a sense of agency. Speaking with game design colleagues all over the world made it clear that they, too, used game design to make sense of what was going on in their lives. It was the beginning of a parallel-path journey. One path has been sketched out in the previous chapters: how can we make games for players that increase their understanding of the human condition? The other path that accompanied this inquiry was how can game *design* increase our understanding of *ourselves*? The purpose of this chapter is to explore the latter and to make an argument for including game design into the canon of creative arts used for therapy.

This is breaking new ground, and, as such, this chapter is tentative and exploratory and intended to start a dialogue between designers, players/ patients, and the mental health care community rather than presenting a final word on the matter. It is coauthored with Susan Imus, chair of the creative arts therapies department at Columbia College Chicago, who provided the theoretical background to this chapter and facilitated an experience in which we applied theory to practice in an exemplary *game design as an arts therapy-like session*. This session serves as our case study to illustrate our argument later in the chapter and to open it up for future dialogue with designers, players, and mental health care practitioners.

8.2 An Introduction to Basic Concepts and Criteria of Creative Arts Therapies

Creative arts therapies are an interdisciplinary human services profession combining science and the arts (Goodill 2005). The National Coalition for Creative Arts Therapies (NCCATA n.d.) states that

> Creative Arts Therapists are human service professionals who use arts modalities and creative processes for the purpose of ameliorating disability and illness and optimizing health and wellness. There are more than 15,000 Creative Arts Therapists practicing in the U.S. and around

the world. CAT organizations have been active in this country for over 50 years. The CATs include Art Therapy, Dance/Movement Therapy, Drama Therapy, Music Therapy, Poetry Therapy, and Psychodrama. Each CAT discipline has its own set of professional standards and requisite qualifications, and are, as a group, highly skilled, credentialed professionals having completed extensive course work and clinical training. (http://www.nccata.org)

Creative arts therapists are employed in schools, correctional facilities, nursing homes, residential centers, group homes, day care centers, community centers, mental health centers, rehabilitation facilities, inpatient hospitals, outpatient clinics, private practices, etc. They work with people across the life span. The terms *client, patient, student, inmate*, and *member* are all used depending on the context. Patient will be the term used in this chapter.

The amelioration of disability, the treatment of illness, and the promotion of health/wellness are the purposes of all of the creative arts therapies. Because each creative discipline within the creative arts therapies intentionally addresses illness and disability and creates health objectives, they are considered therapy. Therapy has numerous definitions and forms. The basic requirement for therapy is that there is a helping relationship between a professional and the person seeking help from the professional for an improved health outcome (Bruscia 1998). According to Bruscia, therapy is a process that requires interventions by a therapist:

> The interventions must meet three criteria: the client must need outside help to accomplish a health objective; there must be a purposeful intervention, regardless of outcome; and the intervention must be carried out within the context of a therapist-client relationship. (p. 20)

It is important to note that some artists are mistaken as therapists because they use their work for therapeutic purposes. Therapeutic purpose is not the same as therapy. Therapeutic does not assume the creative process is employed. It means that the activity may be art related and is healthy for your body, mind, and spirit. It can be measured as having physiological benefits. It does not take into consideration the interpersonal relationship, nor are the outcomes specific to the individual. In the case of game design as arts therapy, an individual outcome-oriented session would mean the patient models a game about a personal issue with the guidance of a designer-therapist in order to gain clarity about this issue and resolve it. The creative process is always engaged.

Who seeks the assistance of a creative arts therapist? Anyone with a health goal may seek a creative arts therapist. Someone, for example, may seek art therapy for treating anxiety, music therapy for children with a cognitive intellectual disability, dance/movement therapy for treating eating disorders, drama therapy for treating chronic pain, poetry therapy for someone with bipolar disorder, and psychodrama for treating addictions. The choice of arts modality is often dependent on the patient's illness, the availability of qualified personnel, the patient's perceptual preferences and medium, and the use of creative arts therapies as primary or ancillary treatment. Who might seek game design as the art modality of choice? With a whole generation of digital natives, many of them growing up playing video games, there might be an increased demand for game design as the medium of choice due to the patient's perceptual and cultural preferences. People with an affinity toward games might be more willing to engage in therapy that uses game design methods than any other creative arts approach. That doesn't mean game design therapy is only for gamers. Its benefits definitely translate to people who have no experience or interest in playing games. Games are systems, and, as such, their playing and designing foster system literacy—seeing the connections between elements and how they relate and are dependent on each other. Being able to apply this kind of thinking to personal problems can be highly beneficial. It can open one's perspective to the bigger picture rather than focusing on an issue in isolation. A systemic view can contribute to the experience of psychological agency because there are several *points of attack* and multiple ways to impact the system, adjust the goal, add or subtract elements, and tweak its variables. Any issue can be modified in different ways; there is more than one solution to *fixing a system*, and this systemic playfulness can help patients get unstuck. It also implies that game design is rather cerebral. It favors a cognitive over a *feeling* approach. Systematically and methodically exploring the conflict, the goal, and the elements at play is the main means of psychological inquiry in the envisioned game design therapy. In this process, the designer-therapist asks guiding questions, and the patient provides potential solutions and ideas for system modification and is able to try them out and see their effects play out.

8.2.1 Criteria for Consumer Safety and Optimal Health Outcomes in Creative Arts Therapies

8.2.1.1 Education of Creative Arts Therapists   The following general criteria are required for consumer safety and optimal health results in the creative arts therapies: a qualified creative arts therapist, purposeful interventions, and an ethical reciprocal patient–therapist relationship that effectively utilizes the creative process. Each criterion will be examined and followed by an explanation of the fundamental mechanisms to achieve a desired health outcome.

Creative arts therapists are all required to meet the educational standards, codes of ethics, and standards of practice in their specific discipline. All educational standards, at minimum, require education in normal and abnormal psychology, including appraisal and treatment planning, group dynamics, development across the life span, research and ethics, and clinical practice in the field. Theories and techniques in counseling or the therapeutic relationship are also required. Anatomy, kinesiology, and neurobiology are further required in music and dance/movement therapy. All creative arts therapists need a master's degree to practice, except music therapists. If someone is using arts-based approaches in counseling under the American Counseling Association's Creativity in Counseling Division, counselors must pass a state licensure exam to practice in their field. There are no further qualifications required to implement the use of the arts into counseling practice through the American Counseling Association. Counselors self-select their use of creative media with or without artistic familiarity. Many creative arts therapy–approved programs have incorporated their state's counseling licensing standards into their educational programs, so creative arts therapists and expressive arts therapists can apply for jobs that allow them to practice as counselors at the state level and board-certified art, dance/movement, drama, music, psychodramatist, or poetry therapists at the national level.

For acceptance into the creative arts therapy field, candidates must be skilled in their specific art discipline and demonstrate a continued course of study and practice for a specified length of time determined by each certification board. Many artists entering the creative arts therapies have performed and exhibited professionally. The creative arts therapist is an artist proficient in predominately one art modality and uses this primary art form to systematically assess, treat, and evaluate patients or clients in their practice. To establish game design as an arts therapy modality, it might be desirable to emphasize a practice of deep game design. There is a big difference between being an accomplished designer of casual puzzle games and creating games about aspects of the human experience. Being able to use game design to model complex abstract concepts, externalize inner worlds, and systemically portray aspects of the human experience takes practice and its own course of study. It also privileges systems design over level design.

8.2.1.2 Purposeful Interventions   The second general criterion of the creative arts therapies is the therapists' use of purposeful interventions based on clinical assessment. It is difficult to make an intervention if there is no assessment. This is a distinct difference in artists working in a health care environment or counselors attempting to use arts in their verbal counseling practice. Creative arts therapists are trained to assess their client's artistic expression and behavior for various reasons, including, but not limited to, diagnosing, evaluating, interpreting, describing, and prescribing treatment (Bruscia 1998). Interpreting as a form of assessment is one crucial avenue for connecting artistic expression to psychological paradigms. Evaluating allows you to create a measurement at the beginning of treatment, a baseline, as a way to measure progress over time. Describing as assessment is unique to the individual and is not comparative. The appraisal tools in each creative discipline are unique to the art form and often require intense study, particularly those that are diagnostic. Appraisal tools may be standardized by the specific arts therapies discipline. The knowledge obtained through assessment is required to make informed decisions in using the arts as therapy and/or the arts in therapy. Many creative arts therapists differentiate between the use of their art *in* therapy from the use of their art *as* therapy. In art as therapy, art is used as the primary intervention for change and falls under the therapeutic category. It appears on the *continuum of approaches*, on the far left of the arrow (Figure 8.1). This promotes therapeutic benefits that are inherent in the art form and confuses the understanding by the consumers of artists as therapists. Art in therapy includes the inherent value of the art and the intentional use of the creative process in the enhancement of the patient–therapist relationship. Deep game design resembles art in therapy. The designer–therapist relationship is crucial to the creation process.

The choice of intervention in therapy is dependent on a thorough understanding of many arts-based approaches including the therapeutic, aesthetic, recreational, educational, rehabilitative, and psychotherapeutic. In other words, the therapist may choose to focus and act on the following:

- The therapeutic approach includes engaging in the art-making activity and experiencing the biological benefits such as the increase of cytokine Interleukin 6 ("Art Does Heal" 2015). It can facilitate the relaxation response (Benson 2000), the flow response (Csikszentmihalyi 2008), and/or mindfulness (Kabat-Zinn 2007). It may or may not include engagement in the creative process.

- An aesthetic approach always incorporates the creative process and orients the patient to the styles, design, and techniques in art-making expression and communication, including performance and exhibition.
- A recreational approach develops arts structures and rituals for increasing enjoyment and enhancing socialization.
- A rehabilitative approach facilitates identifying, adapting to, and practicing new patterns of behavior through the arts medium.
- A psychotherapeutic approach uses the arts in relationship and facilitates identifying and integrating one's biopsychosocial, spiritual, and cultural aspects of self and others to make meaning and create change (Figure 8.1).

The creative arts therapist understands and can direct the interventions along this continuum (see Figure 8.1) to intentionally assist patients in achieving their health outcome. Interventions are typically a combination of approaches within one session. The patient's health goal, the length of treatment, and context directly influence the approach to an intervention, as does the patient's willingness to enter into the creative process and develop the therapeutic relationship. Resistance by the patient may be encountered depending on numerous factors, including, but not limited to, age, cognition, personality, disease, attachment issues, and comfort using expressive media. As of now, deep games as therapy might speak most strongly to a

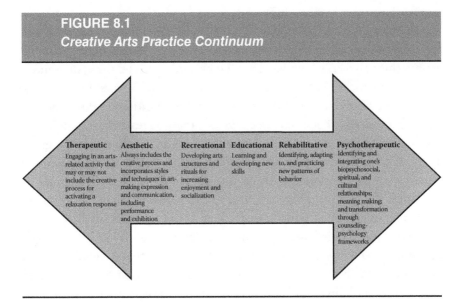

FIGURE 8.1
Creative Arts Practice Continuum

Therapeutic	Aesthetic	Recreational	Educational	Rehabilitative	Psychotherapeutic
Engaging in an arts-related activity that may or may not include the creative process for activating a relaxation response	Always includes the creative process and incorporates styles and techniques in art-making expression and communication, including performance and exhibition	Developing arts structures and rituals for increasing enjoyment and socialization	Learning and developing new skills	Identifying, adapting to, and practicing new patterns of behavior	Identifying and integrating one's biopsychosocial, spiritual, and cultural relationships; meaning making; and transformation through counseling-psychology frameworks

younger audience—adolescents and young adults—and could be a way to overcome potential resistance to therapy through the use of a medium this audience is more familiar and comfortable with than other expressive forms. Its potential benefits are by no means limited to this audience, though.

8.2.1.3 Therapeutic Relationship The therapeutic relationship in the creative arts therapies is an interesting one in contrast to other helping practices. There is always a third and fourth relationship at work: the art making and the art product, in addition to the patient with themselves (intrapersonal), and the patient with the therapist and/or other patients if it is a group (interpersonal). There is a valuable, reflective process leading to insight in all four relationships, and each must be treated with equal respect; for instance, the patient makes a painting and is asked to reflect on the art making and describe their art product: how is this painting a projection of the patient's life experience, and what is the symbolic meaning? (Exchange *painting* for *game* here, just to try it on for size, and it still works!) They may be asked about the interpersonal dynamic: what was it like to be actively witnessed by the therapist and/or other members of the group when making and showing work? They may also be asked what they noticed about themselves after this process has occurred: what insight has occurred? Has there been a change in their experience of their presenting problem or health objective? Transformation is defined as the ways the patient changes from their treatment. The patient–therapist relationship is one of the two crucial methods for transformation (Jones 2007).

The therapist guides the patient to transfer their understanding of the present transformational moment into his or her real-life experience. In game design, this connection can be very tangible and concrete: the system modeled by the patient, with the help of the therapist, represents, in some way and to some degree, a real-life source system. Modifications to the game system to achieve a goal or a desirable *win state* must be realistic in some sense. The use of *magic* is not allowed. Transformation and healing through game design rest on the condition that the path from a broken to a functioning system is actually feasible and can be translated into real life. For example, if you think you perform poorly at work and can't hold a job because you are overly anxious, the way to fix this problem is not by artificially decreasing your game protagonist's *anxiety score* or equipping him or her with a magic potion that makes the problem go away. The conflicts that are modeled need to be anchored in reality (Note: a metaphorical approach is still anchored in reality as its source) and how the problem presents either externally or internally. (Sometimes, it is easier to start with the external factors as a way to discuss and modify internal factors.)

The interpersonal relationship between the patient and the therapist is also dependent on how well the therapist knows himself or herself and his or her aesthetic preferences. In order to ensure that the therapist is not meeting his or her own needs, a process of personal self-discovery is necessary to becoming and practicing as a therapist. It is also essential for the therapist to understand his or her own aesthetic preferences, which affects the choices he or she makes in the creative art-making process. A personal insight of the therapist reduces bias. The creative process is the final general criterion and is another way transformation may occur. It is an extensive topic that extends far beyond the scope of this chapter; however, creative arts therapists of all disciplines utilize the creative process in similar ways. First, in creative arts therapies, the creative process is intentional. The process is focused on coping with or resolving an identified problem or creating a positive health outcome. Creative arts therapists have to fully understand all the creative media, and the tools of their art form(s), including the clients' illness, to assist the client in making changes.

8.2.1.4 Creative Process The creative process described in the creative arts therapies takes into consideration the client's presenting problem and its accompanying issues. The process includes the content, the *what is existing and available*; as Arieti (1976) asserted, "Whereas theologians and religious people in general believe that God's creation comes *ex nihilo* from spatial and temporal nothingness, human creativity uses what is existing and available and changes it in unpredictable ways" (p. 4) to bring about an enlargement of existence. The creative arts therapist takes what is existing and available, such as the client's presenting problem, different art materials, or medium, and works with the client to make changes in unpredictable ways to improve or transform his or her health. This creative process is typically dynamic and mutual, incorporating both the therapist and the client in the decision-making process. In game design, this starts with the identification of the conflict, the goal, the source system, and the mechanics (= actions available to navigate and interact with the modeled scenario) as a collaborative process between the designer-therapist and the patient.

There is always a story, the symbolic content in the art form that surfaces through the patient's art making. The story now lives outside of the patient in a concrete form and provides emotional distancing. The patient feels in charge; the locus of control shifts from the symptom controlling the patient to the patient controlling the symptom (or, in game design, the patient controlling the system!). The patient can identify that he or she created his or her art product, whether it is a poem, a drawing, a dramatic enactment, a song, a dance, or a game. The patient creates it, controls it, and has the option to transform it. Each and every identified problem has the potential for a new possibility. In game design, this would mean adding or subtracting game elements, changing their

TABLE 8.1
Overview of the Fundamental Mechanisms of Creative Arts Therapies

Safety	A trusting relationship that promotes comfort and openness, allowing the patient to experience being vulnerable.
Mutuality and reciprocity	Shared leadership, cocreation, and the practice of exchange.
Dynamism	Lively, action oriented, filled with vitality.
Risk taking	Courage to create something new.
Witnessing and reflection	Attunement, awareness, insight, understanding, and empathy.
Meaning making, transferability, and generalizability	Pattern identification and its application from the here and now to everyday life. From the specific to the generalizable and its reverse.
Empowerment	Self-efficacy is achieved, reducing helplessness and promoting self-control and confidence.
Varied approaches	Along the continuum (see Figure 8.1).
Knowledgeable and informed decision making	Systematic rationale, empirically based taxonomies, and theories in science and the arts to appraise, formulate the treatment, and evaluate the biopsychosocial–spiritual domains of a patient. Decisions are made with knowledge from both science and art, including clinical experience.
Intentional goals	Purposeful, patient centered.
Coherence and integration	Congruence between verbal and nonverbal representation. Integration of sensing, moving, imaging, feeling, and thinking to create understanding.
Symbolic and metaphoric	A representation of experience or an implied comparison of experience from the past to a new *event*. Assists in the identification of new possibilities. Works in bringing the subconscious into conscious awareness.
Improvisation and play	A spontaneous expression of imagination with and without planning. Includes trying on new behavior.
Relational	Identifying and understanding qualitative elements within the art making, art observing, and intrapersonal and interpersonal dynamics.
Concretization and distancing	Bringing concrete form and containment to sensations, movements, images, feelings, and thoughts to gain objectivity in viewing one's own creation and forming a new perspective (Siegel and Bryson 2012).

Source: Imus, S., Home (in) on the range: The practice continuum in the creative arts therapies and allied fields. Keynote address presented at Sharing space creatively: Interdisciplinary collaboration with creative arts therapies, presentation at the 1st Integrated Creative Arts Therapy Conference, Evanston, IL: Institute for Therapy through the Arts, March, 2016.

variables, redefining how elements are connected with each other, and taking different perspectives (e.g., stepping into the shoes of a different protagonist and exploring the system from that vantage point, e.g., the person one is having a conflict with, an uninvolved bystander who witnesses what is going on). This perspective taking and system tweaking promotes a much-needed playfulness to get unstuck and find new solutions to intricate problems (something that is already a benefit of playing games, but even more so of creating them).

8.2.2 Fundamental Mechanisms

In addition to the aforementioned general criteria in Sections 8.2.1.1 through 8.2.1.4, the following fundamental characteristics/mechanisms are used across the creative arts therapies (Table 8.1).

These fundamental mechanisms assist in the transformative process and are utilized by the creative arts therapist to assist patients in achieving their desired health outcome. To illustrate the role game design could play in this process, we will compare two case studies: one of them focused on the use of an established creative arts therapy modality (dance) and the other on an explorative game design as a creative arts therapy-like session.

8.3 Comparative Case Studies

8.3.1 Dance and Movement Therapy Case Study

A woman with Parkinson's disease (PD) fell while participating in an out-patient dance/movement therapy group with 18 participants (ADTA 2015). Her loss of balance and subsequent fall became a positive opportunity for her to face her fear of falling and to find strength and support by moving in a different way. The patient's balance stabilized while scooting across the floor on her bottom, and she was able to access incredible strength and mobility in her upper body. She used that strength to partner with the dance/movement therapist in a movement improvisation on and across the floor. The duet included weight sharing that is characteristic of contact improvisation, a particular style of dance improvisation started by American choreographer Steve Paxton in 1972 ("About Contact Improvisation" n.d.). The patient physically lifted her therapist off of the floor, which is common in contact improvisation but a surprise to all the participants witnessing the interaction and a surprise for the patient herself. What had started as an embarrassing fall, a characteristic of balance instability with those suffering from PD, became an empowering moment for this patient. She ended up physically supporting the therapist.

The dance/movement therapist was familiar with the symptoms and issues of Parkinson's patients. She knew that balance, motor control, the lack of strength, the fear of falling, and the loss of self-esteem (the biopsychosocial profile of a person with PD) are a part of the content that needed to be addressed to meet the patient's intended health goals. When the patient demonstrated all of these symptoms within the group, the dance/movement therapist needed to use her own creative process to provide opportunities for growth and change. She chose to work with the patient on the floor. She chose to encourage and support mobilization through the lower body. She spontaneously played with movement interchanges and shifts of weight with the patient. The exchange was dynamic and mutual. The therapist did not lead the movement. It was a reciprocal evolution. The patient, as previously mentioned in this section, was surprised by and joyous through her dance. Surprise is the indicator that change had occurred. Joy was an emotion that would shift her biochemistry ("Art Does Heal" 2015). A predictable pattern from the fall had been interrupted. This can lead to new wiring and firing in the brain (van der Kolk 2014). The patient did not feel despair, embarrassment, and a decreased motivation to accomplish her motor task. She moved across the room, as was her original intent. She accomplished mobility on a different level in space, the floor, while dancing with her therapist. She discovered new opportunities for strength and stability that she felt she had lost. The dance/movement therapist was able to support and trust the movement improvisation due to her personal understanding and artistic experience in and of the dance expression, communication, and contact improvisational form. Following the new dance, the patient was able to verbally communicate about what had just occurred, relate it to her fears and sense of loss, and have a discussion with the other members of the group who could relate to the same issues. The patient was asked to title her dance following the improvisation.

8.3.1.1 Creative Process and the Patient–Therapist Relationship: Essential Criteria for Change What occurred during the creative process in this example? The creative process was entered into by both the therapist and the client. It was mutually dynamic. The creativity of the therapist facilitated the creativity of the client (Pruyser 1983) and vice versa. The more creative the dance/movement therapist was through her aesthetic choices, the more it influenced the patient to deepen her creative responsiveness and choices. The patient felt free to risk moving in a way that was unfamiliar to her while being observed by the group. It was clearly a reciprocal relationship and was essential for the creative process of the patient to unfold. Without the relational support of the dance/movement therapist, the patient would not have continued her pursuit toward her goal to mobilize across the floor. The dance/movement therapist provided the permission for improvisation, free dance (Laban 1963), to occur. If it was a dance class, the opportunity for spontaneity would have been minimized, and the patient's feelings of embarrassment and fear of falling would have remained unaddressed. A more structured approach is typical of artists working in health care. The spontaneity and dynamism of the mutually shared moment during the creative arts therapy session incites the cocreation necessary for change. Decision making was also informed from a humanistic, person-centered approach to psychotherapy and included an ongoing descriptive and evaluative appraisal from Laban Movement Analysis, a standardized tool in dance/movement therapy. The emphasis from this psychological paradigm is on the unconditional regard for the creation. The focus is relational: between the therapist and the patient, the patient with her dance, and the patient with the support of her group participants. The creative arts' purpose is to develop empathy and promote self-efficacy. The patient is empowered to mutually create, and the therapist's role is to consistently physically, mentally, and emotionally attune to the patient, which is a technique used for both assessment and intervention. In dance/movement therapy, the therapist attunes to the dance/movement of the patient by moving her body in ways similar to, without mimicking, the patient. Attunement may be to the body parts being moved; the shape of the body's posture; the effort dynamics of weight, space, time, and flow; and the spatial pathways the movement travels.

The dance/movement therapist empathically reflects through their body the patient's dance/movement experience in the moment. This provides the therapist with further descriptive knowledge of the patient through the lens of the Laban system and then allows the patient to see them self-reflected through the therapists' movement. The dance was titled like any work of art may be. Although the title was lost to the therapist at the time of this reporting, its purpose was to create a symbol, a representation of the experience (to provide further safety through containment), to concretize the experience into the level of cognition, and to provide distance from which to reflect and see oneself more objectively in the experience. The title or symbol would be evaluated by the arts therapist to ensure that its meaning is congruent with the nonverbal arts-making product and process. This congruence is highlighted as a method of integrating the symbol as image, with moving, sensing, thinking, and feeling. Symbols and metaphor making are common in the creative arts therapies and are used to understand the psychic content of the patient.

8.3.2 Game Design Therapy Case Study

Game design, so goes our argument, can have comparable benefits for patients as other creative arts therapies, as exemplified by the case study in Section 8.3.1. As with other creative arts therapy modalities, the medium is used to explore personal issues and identify opportunities for growth and transformation. The patient–therapist relationship is just as important an ingredient as it is in dance and movement therapy or other expressive art forms used for healing. It is one thing to make a theoretical case for game design to become accepted into the canon of creative arts therapies. It is quite another thing, however, to illustrate its potentials through practice. Thus, we conducted a case study of an exemplary game design arts therapy-like session at Columbia College Chicago. We brought together a young woman who volunteered as the *patient*,* five faculty members (including Susan Imus) from Columbia's creative arts therapies department, all practicing creative arts therapists, and me as the game designer. When game design becomes an established part of the creative arts therapies, the game designer, who will have been trained in both her creative practice and counseling/psychology, will take the role of the therapist.

The session took 2 hours. It started with brief introductions of everyone present, a brief summary of my previous work with deep games, a statement of the session goal—to explore the potentials of game design as a new expressive art form to be included in the canon of creative arts therapies—and a statement of what I expected of the therapists in the room: to make sure I didn't cause emotional harm to our model patient and to observe the process closely and critically so that they could offer their expert opinions on the potentials and pitfalls of game design as arts therapy. The session concluded with a debriefing in which the patient reflected on her experiences of our interaction, and the therapists shared their thoughts and observations. For the ease of future analysis, we video-recorded the session; the patient wrote a debriefing report on her experiences and how they evolved over the hours

---

*Note: we are using the term *patient* here only to clarify the role the participant took for the sake of creating the experience. Since this was not a real therapy session, our patient cannot be understood as a real patient. Also, there was no formal recruitment process in place to identify the patient, but the participant volunteered in the moment at the beginning of the experience.

following the interaction; and we solicited the various notes that had been taken by the faculty members/therapists of their observations. The following is structured in three parts: part 1 offers a description of the session itself, focusing on applying game design tools to the exploration of a personal issue, as well as the interaction between the patient and the game designer. Part 2 presents an analysis of the session in regard to the general criteria and fundamental mechanisms of arts therapy presented in Sections 8.2.1 and 8.2.2 to situate game design within the canon of established modalities. Part 3 concludes the experiment with debriefing notes from the model patient and offers an outlook and next steps.

8.3.2.1 Part 1: "Social Value, I am Worth Talking To"—An Exemplary Game Design Therapy-Like Session   Paula (name changed for privacy reasons) is the young woman volunteering a personal issue to be explored in the game design therapy-like session. The setting is a classroom at Columbia College. Tables are arranged in a large square with a patient and a designer sitting next to each other where two sides of the square intersect. A Columbia staff person operates the camera, and the present therapists sit on either sides of the square, observing.

The tools at hand are paper-prototyping materials including a large piece of grid paper, legos, small colorful cubes, differently colored animal paper clips, sharpies, and some other small objects that have been chosen for convenience's sake, such as a plastic snail and a wooden stamp. The materials only serve to represent game elements and they can be anything. Allowing the patient to choose which materials to use as game elements and stand-ins for real-life objects and concepts can be revealing and worthy of discussion so it might be nice to provide a variety of different colors, textures, and objects that signify differences in *value* (e.g., some objects suggest they are more "precious" than others or have other attributes that can shed insight on the patient's perceptions). Paper-prototyping tools are preferable to digital tools due to their tactile nature and ease of access. Both the therapist *and* the patient should be able to build the game with their own hands. In a paper prototype, technical insecurities can't interfere with the work, and manipulating a system built of tangible objects is faster and more direct than changing code. It reinforces the idea of the patient's control and agency not just over the modeled experience but also over their own issues.

The segue from the designer's introduction to the therapy-like sessions starts with the designer explaining to the patient that the game that is about to be created is not for anybody else's use but her own, and that the goal is not to create an awesome project but rather to use game design tools to explore a personal problem. Imus notes that this is very similar to other creative arts therapy approaches, where the patient is assured that they don't need to know how to dance or paint, etc., and that whatever they make is not judged by its artistic quality. The designer then goes on to state that she is not a therapist but rather a designer, and is going to work with Paula in this capacity but with a focus on using game design tools as a means of self-exploration and problem-solving.

The designer and the patient then discuss what Paula would like to work on. Paula explains that she "gets freaked out at parties," particularly when interacting with strangers. She defines her goal as wanting to feel more comfortable in these social situations and engage more with other people. The designer takes notes on the grid paper on which they will build the game so they both can refer back to them in the design process. Notes are loosely organized into categories such as *goal, conflict,* and *resources.*

The emphasis in this first phase of the session is on understanding the issue better, to determine a desired outcome (which can change depending on how the design evolves), and building trust and a relationship with the patient. The designer listens actively, summarizes what she is hearing to make sure she got it right, and is affirmative toward the patient. Exploring the problem is crucial to getting a better understanding of the *conflict* and to be able to start modeling it as a game with the patient. The patient describes the conflict as perceiving herself to be boring, not being a good storyteller and not having a great memory, so people stop paying attention when she is talking to them and don't enjoy having a conversation with her. The focus is all on her and her shortcomings—*she* and her perceived lack of storytelling and entertainment skills are the problem.

Paula goes on to elaborate the conflict and adds the *fear of rejection* as a relevant aspect. This points toward a *risk-versus-reward* situation: Paula might risk herself in a social interaction without a guarantee that it will be successful, e.g., that she would be favorably received and "make a friend." The designer asks what's at stake when Paula is being rejected. Why is rejection a problem? This is a general characteristic of deep game design: to always ask "the second question," to not let a preliminary answer be good enough, and dig deeper. The point is not to do this endlessly, but until some sort of *aha moment* occurs or at least a more nuanced understanding of the issue. Challenging why something so obviously negative as *being rejected* as part of the conflict is important to get a better sense of what is going on underneath the surface. Paula pauses before answering this question and then speaks of having had painful experiences in the past where she thought someone was her friend and then turned out not to be. This relates back to her perceptions of herself and doubting that they are accurate: she might think someone likes her but then doesn't, but it is also possible that she thinks someone doesn't like her but actually does. In that case, this would prohibit her from "offering herself" (Paula's words) in a social situation out of fear of getting her feelings hurt. The phrase *offering herself* is interpreted in game design terms as a *resource*, something the patient has and can bring into play to sway the system outcome (= outcome of a social interaction) in one direction or another. At this point in the design process, the function of this potential resource isn't sufficiently understood, yet. The designer goes back to challenging the declared goal some more: "Why is it desirable to engage more with people at a party?" Questioning goals can reveal the values behind them. A goal always sounds so absolute, as if it were all or nothing—achieve it or fail. But there is more than one way to live according to one's values and maybe that's more important than that one goal seen in isolation. Thus, exploring values can help increase agency while focusing on one specific goal can keep one stuck. The patient explains that interacting with others is desirable because one has a better time—it's more fun to engage than to not engage and be "a wallflower" (patient's words). The preliminary exploration of the issue takes about 15 minutes and then segues into the active game design part of the session.

The design process starts with identifying a concrete situation or setting; in this case, patient and the designer focus on modeling a party scenario. This approach helps to ground the conversation in something tangible and increases the *presence* of the issues at play. In order to derive essential game elements from the patient's lived experience, the designer asks, "What are the things at a party that are most important to you?" Patient responds, "Food, that's usually where I start." Both the designer and the patient laugh about this, and the designer presents patient with a jar of plastic objects from which she chooses some to represent tables and food and puts them on the grid paper. The designer asks, "Where do you come in?" Patient asks for other objects to find a representation for herself and picks a small figurine that happens to be a *glow-in-the dark zombie* with arms outstretched. The designer points that out, and they both share a laugh. Patient jokes that she's a zombie at parties, makes a zombie gesture and says, "Here I'm reaching out, no response." The humor in this helps to lighten the mood and create a bit of distance to the personal and painful issue at hand, yet it also points toward the previously uttered fear of rejection. The choice of representational objects can become its own avenue of exploration in the patient–designer dialogue. Investigating random objects and how they might fit into a scene can also help to materialize deeper conflicts. For example, among the designer's prototyping tools are plastic Halloween eyeballs. The patient chooses to use one of them to represent her *self-judgment, looking at herself* at the party. The eyeball is initially positioned at a safe distance from the table with food on the board. The designer keeps pulling objects out of her prototyping jar and putting them on the board. A small plastic snail catches the patient's eye and she picks it to represent her *slow speaking*. Again, this is accompanied by laughter. Patient brings in the idea of a *speed bar* to measure talking speed. According to the patient, the snail would move up and down to indicate talking speed, much like a health bar indicates how much health one has left in a game. The designer and patient explore the idea of deliberately raising talking speed and whether that would make social interactions more successful. This approach doesn't seem convincing and the snail's meaning is explored further, including a speculation that it could represent other speech modalities such as volume. There is a strong focus on the insecurity around *speaking* without a clear understanding what impact it really has on the success of social interactions or the patient's well-being at a party. This needs to be investigated further and the way to do so is to keep modeling the scene to identify other elements and their interrelationships. The emphasis thus shifts from *self* (= representation of food as safe starting point for the patient, the eyeball as self-judgment, and the snail as a representation for *speech*) to other people.

Paula picks a handful of small, square blocks that are identical except for their different colors: "This works well because, to me, they are all strangers and I don't know much about them except for how they look." She places the people blocks on the board, set apart from her position at the chips and dips table, and then reaches for one of the animal-shaped paper clips and puts it on the board, too: "If there is a cat, I will also be with the cat." The next step is to explore what happens when an interaction with a stranger occurs. The designer pushes one of the *block people* toward Paula's in-game representation. Paula immediately moves the self-judgment eye (that is held in place by a large clip) closer to scrutinize her game piece as it is about to engage with this new person. The following enacted conversation goes well, the *non-player character* Paula is having a conversation which displays interest and the self-judgment eye moves further away again. This raises the question about the game's goal again, which can now be explored in the concrete context of the situation, rather than abstractly. Designer: "You made a friend. Is the goal to make ten friends in this game? What is the goal?" Patient thinks. "I don't know about friends; I just want to feel good about the conversations and not come away from them feeling worse about myself." The designer aims to concretize the goal again: "So let's say our play-through time for this game is 'enter party to taxi'—at the end of the night, what's the win condition? How do you know you've won?" Paula: "When I've made one significant connection and I feel better about myself than before—I feel social value." Introducing the idea of *social value* suddenly changes the whole conversation. The designer recognizes that social value is the ultimate resource in this game. Since it determines the win condition, it is at the center of the game's system—every other element and interaction needs to affect it somehow. Whatever Paula does at the party will affect her social value. The designer draws a *social value meter* on the board, saying, "Social value, OK, great, that's our resource—that's the thing that goes up and down." The designer and patient now collaborate to assign numbers to the social value bar in order to make Paula's in-game actions quantifiable in regards to how they affect social value. They define the end points of the bar as 0 (no social value) to 100 (maximum social value). Patient says she'd start out with 50 points on the scale at the beginning of a party, because having been invited already boosts social value. The bar can still go down from there, though, depending on how the party unfolds. With the social value as the ultimate resource in place, the win condition stated as *one significant connection* can be revisited. How does it impact the social value meter? Patient says it would be an immediate *win*, worth 50 points. That is consistent with the earlier-stated win condition of making one significant connection. Does that mean after that one significant connection is made, social value is set in stone forever, the 100 points remain fixed? This challenges the assumption that there is only one way to win or lose. Patient and the designer now explore different social party situations—interactions that go well or not so well—and how they impact social value. Every interaction gets a point value based on the patient's perception of how much it would affect their social value. The snail that previously represented the patient's *speech* has been redefined as an index for social value and as patient and the designer play through several scenarios, the snail moves up and down, drawing attention to the fact that social value is always in flux. It further produces the insight that social value is also dependent on the patient's standards. Not every interaction counts the same for Paula. Some are more valuable than others and their success or failure affect Paula's social value meter more or less. This shows that the patient has agency over which interactions she seeks out and how she interprets them. She is not purely a victim of social interactions, but has control over which groups she tries to join, who she attempts to talk to. This becomes obvious when Paula assigns concrete numbers to how interactions impact the social value meter. See Table 8.2 for how specific social interactions impact the social value meter.

To summarize, by exploring the concept of perceived social value as a system of interconnected elements, the *all-or-nothing* approach to party success could be opened up to consider different ways to win. Assigning points to risks, rewards, and various types of social scenarios allowed a success strategy to emerge: engaging in many low-risk social interactions provides the most flexibility to the social value meter. Recovery from failures is easier (less points lost), and there is more to be gained by trying than by doing nothing. Even trying and failing are better than passivity, since the points lost due to an unsuccessful attempt are compensated for by *self-appreciation* points for taking the risk.

By seeing her own standards at play in the system—how her personal interest in a subject or person affects the stakes—control is regained. It is clear that social value is not purely determined by outside factors—how much Paula is liked or accepted by others—but also by internal factors: how much she cares about an interaction and how willing she is to put herself out there. Her courage is recognized as a positive element in the social value system.

At this point, the session, which took 45–50 minutes, is being wrapped up, and the conversation segues into the debriefing phase. The present therapists ask Paula how she's doing. Then, the loose ends are addressed, such as what should happen with the self-judgment eye? Paula says she'd like to ignore it more in the future. She takes the plastic eyeball, removes it from the scene, puts it in a flip chart paper clip, and traps it there, facing inwards. As a last symbolic act, Paula names her game "*Social Value*, I Am Worth Talking To."

8.3.2.2 Part 2 The following observations about the exemplary game design therapy session are derived from the debriefing with the present creative arts therapists. It was stated that the designer provided a safe environment necessary for her participant to become vulnerable and take risks through the creative process. The grid paper or the *gaming play space* was reminiscent of an art therapy session where the art making physically takes place on a table between the therapist and the patient, and symbols are created by the player and reflected back and deepened by the game designer. The concern was raised that, depending on the patient's problem, game design might be too time consuming to use effectively in one session. Therapists agreed that it was best suited for a series of interventions, possibly spanning five sessions. This would correspond well with other solution-oriented, short-term therapies. Each session could focus on another aspect of the issue, thus exploring it in more depth and from different angles (e.g., were Paula to continue treatment, a new game design could focus more on her perception of being boring, or the nature of her self-judgment). The patient could possibly be asked to create designs at home and bring them to the session for discussion, analysis, and modification. This would require a certain level of game design literacy, which is something a new generation of patients who are growing up playing games can be expected to gain quickly. The cerebral nature of the approach was emphasized in the debriefing, linking it to other cognitive behavioral therapies. The process felt similar to drama therapy and psychodrama where a scene is created and enacted. Parallels were also found to play therapy and sandplay. Movement dynamics were illustrated through orientation to time, space, and strength concepts, linking it also to dance/movement therapy. The uniqueness of game design as creative arts therapy was located in the question of a win state, the focus on identifying system rules (how does it work?), and assigning specific numbers/values to game elements/interactions. There was consensus that the session just witnessed was indeed therapy and that game design could bring something new to the table, effectively complementing existing creative arts therapies modalities.

See Table 8.3 for an overview of how our exemplary therapy-like game design session reflects the fundamental mechanisms used in creative arts therapies.

8.3.2.3 Part 3: Paula's Response and Outlook   In the end, the main measure of a therapy's success is the patient's transformation. Obviously, one individual session cannot be expected to completely resolve a psychological problem. Paula's debriefing report, however, written the day following our experiment, points toward the potential of game design as a vehicle for change. It addresses her experiences during the session, the insights won about her issue, and how they could be translated to and impact real life:

> Co-designing a game to explore the personal issue of social anxiety at a party was fun and rewarding. I enjoyed choosing game pieces to represent people, concepts, and objects; arranging the pieces in space; and role-playing briefly through the pieces. Enough options were presented to allow for spontaneity and creativity without it being too open ended or overwhelming. I was relieved that I did not have to create everything "*from scratch*" (as I might have to do in making art, acting out a skit, or choreographing a dance). Creativity came through the power to choose what pieces to use, where they would go, what they would represent, how they might behave, etc. This ultimately led me to conclude that the control I had in the game could translate to real life: I could be more active in changing my circumstances.
>
> Designing the game was a pleasant, collaborative process through question and answer, during which I felt supported. The empathetic responses and structure provided by the facilitator helped me to engage

TABLE 8.3

Overview of How Exemplary Therapy-Like Game Design Session Reflects the Fundamental Mechanisms Used in Creative Arts Therapies

Fundamental Mechanisms Used in Creative Arts Therapies	How the Deep Game Design Case Study Incorporated Creative Arts Therapies' Fundamental Mechanisms
Safety	The game designer facilitated safety and set her boundaries. Imus was included in the therapeutic relationship, as she is a licensed clinical professional counselor and a board-certified dance/movement therapist.
Mutuality and reciprocity	The game designer and Paula clearly created the system together, and there was a give-and-take in the system development.
Dynamism	It was active, vibrant, and energizing as evidenced by smiling, laughter, and parodies.
Risk taking	Paula allowed herself to become vulnerable and took a lot of risks in front of many people. Everyone told her after the session how courageous she was.
Reflection and mindfulness	The game designer frequently asked questions and encouraged Paula to enter into the moment.
Meaning making, transferability, and generalizability	Paula was constantly asked questions that encouraged her to make decisions and place value on the decisions. She was encouraged to make a system from the onset that was representational of a recent experience. She was asked to transfer the decisions that she made within the game to her daily life. She fluctuated between generalizing her past behavior and relating to a specific memory.
Empowerment	Paula demonstrated self-efficacy. It was clear that she was in control of her choices and would easily disagree with the designer to clarify and assign meaning. Anxiety was not evident.
Varied approaches	It was evident that the designer utilized all of the approaches with emphasis on the recreational, educational, and psychotherapeutic.
Knowledgeable and informed decision making	Systems theory is evident, as was solution-focused brief therapy. The principles of game design at an advanced level were necessary for the designer to guide the modeling of the patient's conflict and work out potential solutions.
Intentional goals	Paula chose to focus on her social comfort and self-worth. The goal was to increase comfort in social situations and perceived social value. Ways of winning the game were identified.
Coherence and integration	The game designer was frequently reality-orienting Paula. She particularly encouraged Paula to integrate her real-life images, thoughts, and behaviors into the process of designing the game.
Symbolic and metaphoric	The entire game board and its miniature objects were all representational of Paula's conscious and subconscious experience.

(Continued)

TABLE 8.3 (CONTINUED) Overview of How Exemplary Therapy-Like Game Design Session Reflects the Fundamental Mechanisms Used in Creative Arts Therapies	
Fundamental Mechanisms Used in Creative Arts Therapies	*How the Deep Game Design Case Study Incorporated Creative Arts Therapies' Fundamental Mechanisms*
Improvisation and play	The game designer herself would frequently enact some of the miniature objects through dramatic characterization. She would bring meaning into the symbols through dialogue and movement throughout the game space. This provided humor and an atmosphere of play.
Relational	Strong relationships were created to the game system in general and its discrete objects. The whole to the parts was clear. Less emphasis was placed on the relationship of Paula to the game-making process, her relationship to the game designer, and all of the Columbia College Chicago Creative Arts Therapies (CCC CAT) observers.
Concretization and distancing	This occurred through the forms and symbols that Paula made from the questions the game designer asked. It allowed her to see her social behavior from a new and distant perspective, as evidenced by Paula's session response.

in the process and become more comfortable. The facilitator was warm and attentive and, in a sense, embodied the type of person I would want to encounter at a party. When she pretended to be excited characters at a party and improvised conversations, we shared laughter that helped release tension and reduce my self-judgment around answering questions. I was at a loss for answers at times—ironically the same problem I encountered when trying to talk with strangers in a party. Her role playing helped me to see that it was in the realm of possibility that people I will interact with could be very enthusiastic and friendly, like the facilitator, or perhaps that I could take on that role in future conversations to make other people feel the happiness I felt when the facilitator was eager to talk with me.

Assigning points while constructing the game was valuable. First, it made me reconsider the severity of problems. By itself, a failed social interaction can feel debilitating and horrifying. However, when I compare the moment to a scale of 100, or what other situations might make me lose or gain points, the moment is put into perspective. Maybe that situation is not as bad compared to other scenarios or is negated by positive scenarios. Second, I realized that a person can have a positive outcome (or "win") in a number of ways. This may help me to quell disappointment because there are other ways to win, and it also helps me to strive for many small victories. Overall, this activity planted a seed of hope and optimism.

Paula's response also points toward the power of the approach to stir up uncomfortable emotions.

> After my hands-on experience with game design, I can confirm that this tool is powerful and could be incorporated into the creative arts therapies. However, I would caution game designers to do this without any outside influence from trained therapists. When I arrived home that night, I ended up weeping in my partner's arms. Emotions that arose during the session became raw and loomed over me, waiting to be processed. This seems to confirm that game design for this purpose should include follow up sessions, ideally under the supervision of a therapist, or should be facilitated by a game designer with mental health credentials.

This draws attention to the responsibility of the facilitator and the importance of uniting game design skills with psychological training. It reinforces our argument that game design deserves a place within the canon of creative arts therapies. It further emphasizes that we need to establish new creative arts therapy programs that offer game design as a practice domain alongside existing arts modalities (e.g., dance, theater, performance, poetry, painting). Game design needs to be recognized as valid, artistic expertise so that game designers can be accepted into such programs and be properly trained as creative arts therapists.

References

About contact improvisation (CI). n.d. *Contact Quarterly: Dance & Improvisation Journal*. Available at http://www.contactquarterly.com/contact-improvisation /about/. Accessed December 21, 2015.

American Dance Therapy Association (ADTA). 2014. The difference between "therapeutic" dance and dance/movement therapy [Video file], November 6. Available at https://www.youtube.com/watch?v=UCFRcDhfKDI. Accessed December 20, 2015.

Arieti, S. 1976. *Creativity: The Magic Synthesis*. New York: Basic Books.

Art does heal: Scientists say appreciating creative works can fight off disease. 2015. *The Telegraph*, February 10. Available at http://www.telegraph.co.uk/news/health /news/11403404/Art-does-heal-scientists-say-appreciating-creative-works-can -fight-off—disease.html?utm_source=facebook&utm_medium=social&utm _content=11-22&utm_campaign=telegraph-art-heals. Accessed December 18, 2015.

Benson, H. 2000. *The Relaxation Response* (Rev. ed.). New York: HarperTorch.

Bruscia, K. 1998. *Defining Music Therapy* (2nd ed.). Gilsum, NH: Barcelona Publishers.

Csikszentmihalyi, M. 2008. *Flow: The Psychology of Optimal Experience* (Harper Perennial Modern Classics ed.). New York: Harper Collins.

Goodill, S. 2005. *An Introduction to Medical Dance/Movement Therapy: Healthcare in Motion*. London: Jessica Kingsley Publishers.

Imus, S. (2016, March). *Home (in) on the range: The practice continuum in the creative arts therapies and allied fields*. Keynote address presented at Sharing space creatively: Interdisciplinary collaboration with creative arts therapies. Presentation at the 1st integrated creative arts therapy conference. Evanston, IL: Institute for Therapy through the Arts.

Jones, P. 2007. *Drama Therapy Volume 1: Theory, Practice, and Research*. New York: Routledge.

Kabat-Zinn, J. 2007. *Arriving at Your Own Door*. New York: Hyperion.

Laban, R. 1963. *Modern Educational Dance* (2nd ed.). London: MacDonald & Evans.

National Coalition of Creative Arts Therapies Associations. n.d. *NCCATA*. Available at http://www.nccata.org/. Accessed December 11, 2015.

Pruyser, P. 1983. *The Play of the Imagination: Toward a Psychoanalysis of Culture*. New York: International Universities Press.

Siegel, D. and Bryson, T.P. 2012. *The Whole-Brain Child*. New York: Bantam Books.

van der Kolk, B. 2014. *The Body Keeps the Score: Brain, Mind, and Body in the Healing of Trauma*. New York: Viking Penguin.

Index